Do More Than Give

DO MORE THAN GIVE

The Six Practices of Donors Who Change the World

Leslie R. Crutchfield

John V. Kania

and Mark R. Kramer

JOSSEY-BASS
A Wiley Imprint
www.josseybass.com

Published by Jossey-Bass

A Wiley Imprint
989 Market Street, San Francisco, CA 94103-1741—www.josseybass.com

Jossey-Bass books and products are available through most bookstores. To contact Jossey-Bass directly call our Customer Care Department within the U.S. at 800-956-7739, outside the U.S. at 317-572-3986, or fax 317-572-4002.

Jossey-Bass also publishes its books in a variety of electronic formats. Some content that appears in print may not be available in electronic books.

Library of Congress Cataloging-in-Publication Data

Crutchfield, Leslie R., 1968–
  Do more than give : the six practices of donors who change the world / Leslie R. Crutchfield, John V. Kania, and Mark R. Kramer.
      p. cm.— (J-b us non-franchise leadership ; 390)
  Includes bibliographical references and index.
  ISBN 978-0-470-89144-5 (hardback)
  1. Charities. 2. Charitable uses, trusts, and foundations. 3. Endowments. 4. Fund raising. 5. Social change. I. Kania, John V. II. Kramer, Mark R. III. Title.
  HV40.C78 2011
  361.7—dc22

                                                                              2010053644

Printed in the United States of America
FIRST EDITION
HB Printing 10 9 8 7 6 5 4 3 2 1

Contents

Preface   vii

Acknowledgments   xi

The Authors   xv

1   Catalytic Philanthropy   1

2   Commit to Your Cause   19

3   Practice 1: Advocate for Change   37

4   Practice 2: Blend Profit with Purpose   63

5   Practice 3: Forge Nonprofit Peer Networks   87

6   Practice 4: Empower the People   119

7   Practice 5: Lead Adaptively   143

8   Practice 6: Learn in Order to Change   165

9   Toward a More Catalytic Future   185

Appendix A: Research Methodology   191

Appendix B: Peer Survey Questions   199

Appendix C: Research Advisors   203

Appendix D: Review of the Six Practices of
             High-Impact Nonprofits
             in *Forces for Good*   205

Appendix E: Getting Started with Catalytic
             Philanthropy   211

Notes   227

Index   239

For Caleigh and Quinn
For Nate, Lucy, and Mia
For Toby, Elizabeth, and Benjamin

PREFACE

When the three of us joined together to coauthor this book, we each brought different life experiences and professional training to the project. What has united us is our urgency to find ways to make faster progress toward solving the pressing social and environmental problems that persist in the world and our shared belief that philanthropy has much to contribute to those solutions. Although countless books have been written about the difference donors and nonprofits have made in causes both local and global—advancements in understanding that we applaud and from which we have learned—we believe that donors can do even more.

For Mark, growing up in a family with a small private foundation awakened him to the idea that philanthropy could do more. He saw how isolated most family foundations were. He observed that much money could be given to hard-working nonprofits year after year with the very best of intentions but without changing much of anything. He often saw foundations that were convinced of their uniqueness and unable to learn from others' experiences. He observed family foundations that were determined to avoid overhead expense and as a result were perpetually short staffed. And he saw foundations that struggled to meet their 5 percent payout requirement—in an era when real-world needs were growing and problems were crying out for answers.

This irony—that in the face of such vast need some foundations could barely find ways to make the minimum contribution required to maintain their tax-exempt status—persuaded Mark that the system just wasn't working. These experiences formed the basis for his lifelong commitment to understanding how philanthropy's performance could be improved. In 1999, he and his friend Michael Porter established the Center for Effective Philanthropy to help define and advance foundation effectiveness, and at the same time they cofounded the consulting firm Foundation Strategy Group (FSG) to work in depth with leaders of foundations to develop and pursue effective strategies for social change. (At its founding in 1999, the consulting firm was called "Foundation Strategy Group [FSG]." The firm later officially changed its name to "FSG," so later in the book, we refer to it as FSG.) In 2009, Mark crystallized many of the lessons he had learned from his decade of work at FSG in "Catalytic Philanthropy," an article published in the *Stanford Social Innovation Review* (*SSIR*).[1]

When that edition of *SSIR* landed in her mailbox, Leslie was preparing to write her next book. Her first book, *Forces for Good: The Six Practices of High-Impact Nonprofits*, coauthored with Heather McLeod Grant, had been released in 2007. During the subsequent three years Leslie had been traveling across the United States and Canada, speaking to groups of nonprofit and philanthropic leaders about how they could achieve better outcomes if they focused on advancing larger causes and leveraging change through each sector of society—government, business, nonprofit organizations, and individuals—rather than just shoring up their own institutions. She also was advising family foundations on how to increase the impact of their giving. The more Leslie interacted with foundation leaders, the more intrigued she became with the role that philanthropy plays in creating—and sometimes holding back—social change. So she decided to write a book about applying the practices in *Forces for Good* to philanthropy.

At first, Leslie thought the best advice she could give donors was to use the six practices of high-impact nonprofits as a screen to guide their giving. If foundations channeled more of their funds to nonprofits that employed cross-sector approaches such as advocating for policy change or partnering with private enterprise to advance social objectives, she reasoned, they could get more bang for their charitable dollar. But she soon realized that just picking great grantees wasn't enough. She knew that donors could do more. They could fund groups that advocate, but donors were also uniquely qualified to *engage in advocacy* and to raise their voices on behalf of causes. Donors could support nonprofits that partner with business, but they could also *leverage their business connections and know-how* to advance causes.

Initially, Leslie didn't know of many good examples of this kind of giving. Then she read Mark's article on catalytic philanthropy. "This is it!" Leslie thought, "this is what high-impact philanthropy looks like." Catalytic donors do the same things that the social entrepreneurs in *Forces for Good* do, they just start with a concentration of wealth rather than raising funds from scratch. So she asked Mark and also FSG managing director John Kania if they would like to team up and collaborate on this book.

John brought a final critical perspective to round out the premises in this book. He had worked for two decades in the private sector consulting to businesses. But helping companies compete for more market share wasn't fulfilling John's desire to make a meaningful difference. So shortly after the terrorist attacks on the United States on September 11, 2001, he had joined FSG to apply his strategy and organizational development background to solving social sector problems. John quickly learned just how hard it was to effect change in the social sector. Executives in business typically have much more control over the outcomes they seek to achieve than leaders in the social sector do. Making change happen in the private sector is about developing the right strategy and lining up the people *inside* the company to make it happen. Whereas in the social sector, change requires not only lining up the people inside an organization but also influencing the mind-set and behavior of a whole set of stakeholders *outside* the organization's four walls. Achieving success in the social sector requires a special type of leadership.

Recalling a divinity school course on spirituality and leadership in which he had learned about Ron Heifetz's notion of *adaptive leadership*, John realized that Heifetz's framework was especially applicable to addressing social and environmental challenges because social sector problems typically require adaptive rather than technical solutions. This requires leaders who can mount responses that take an organic view and that focus on system change. John coauthored (with Ron Heifetz and Mark Kramer) an article titled "Leading Boldly" that discussed how adaptive leadership ideas apply to social change,[2] and he has continued to emphasize the need for this type of leadership in FSG's work with clients.

Eventually we found that the theme of leading adaptively was the common thread that bound together all of the best practices we write about in *Do More Than Give*. Being a catalytic donor is, at the end of the day, an act of leadership—but not the linear, command-and-control variety that most funders are used to. The best nonprofit leaders understand this, and donors who want to be equally effective agents of change embrace it as well.

This book, then, is the culmination of our attempt to codify what each of us has learned through a decade of advising donors and researching, thinking about, and experiencing philanthropy as a vehicle for social change. As you will see in the pages to come, we focus on the six highly leveraged practices that catalytic philanthropists employ to achieve systems-level change. Although we acknowledge that the concept of catalytic philanthropy itself is not new—social entrepreneurs and high-impact donors alike have been achieving wide-scale societal change for centuries—we also know that catalytic philanthropy is rare. We hope that as a result of reading this book, you will make it less so.

January 2011

Leslie Crutchfield
Washington, D.C.
John Kania
Boston, Massachusetts
Mark Kramer
Boston, Massachusetts

ACKNOWLEDGMENTS

This book is stronger because of the combined contributions of our esteemed colleagues, trusted advisors, close friends, and family members who supported us at each step and encouraged us to complete this work.

If we were to name a fourth author to this book, that writer would not be one individual but dozens of FSG team members based around the world—from San Francisco to Seattle and from Boston to New York to Geneva—who contributed in significant ways. FSG managing directors Rebecca Graves, Fay Hanleybrown, Laura Herman, Greg Hills, Jeff Kutash, Kyle Peterson, and Marc Pfitzer were critical thought partners in the concepts, cases, and frameworks included throughout this book, and FSG executive director of strategic learning and evaluation Hallie Preskill contributed significantly to the development of our ideas on how learning happens in the social sector. We recognize FSG director of strategic communications Dana Yonchak and communications assistant Stephanie Cubell who helped disseminate our Peer Survey. And we especially thank FSG consultant Amber Johnson, whose critical insights, literate writing, and project management prowess played a significant role in every phase of our work. We also thank FSG's many clients over the past decade, whose thoughtful innovations have taught us many of the lessons that are captured in this book. It has been our great privilege to partner with and learn from such inspiring philanthropic leaders.

We extend our deep respect and gratitude to Heather McLeod Grant, who coauthored *Forces for Good* with Leslie. Without Heather's contributions to the development of the original six practices framework that makes up the basis for *Do More Than Give*, this book would not exist. Soon after the publication of *Forces for Good*, Heather joined Monitor Institute, where she is a senior consultant. We also extend our deep appreciation to Heather and Leslie's research partners at Duke University's Center for the Advancement of Social Entrepreneurship (C.A.S.E.) at the Fuqua School of Business, J. Gregory Dees and Beth Anderson (Beth has since moved on to work with Teach for America). And we extend our sincere thanks to Jenny Shilling Stein of the Draper Richards Foundation and to Jane Wales and Alan Abramson of the Aspen Institute.

We owe a special debt of gratitude to Paula Ellis and Alberto Ibargüen for the financial support that the Knight Foundation provided to make possible the research for *Do More Than Give*. And we recognize Paula for her intellectual camaraderie in codeveloping the ideas that frame this book: a former journalist and newspaper publisher, Paula brings to philanthropy a lifetime of experience in perceiving and interpreting news events as they unfold. So it is not surprising that she sees social problems as emergent, constantly changing phenomena that can't necessarily be solved through linear processes. She recommended *Getting to Maybe* to us—a book that expertly applies complexity theory to social innovation and that became a key influence on our thinking. We recognize our trusted thought partners whose funding also made possible this research: Paul Brest and Jacob Harold of the Hewlett Foundation; Phil Cutter, Rita Berkson, and Ben Goldhirsh of the Goldhirsh Foundation; and Sonia McCormick and Craig Pascal of PNC Bank (Craig has since moved on to another firm). We hold great admiration for the poetic and compelling insights of the authors of *Getting to Maybe*, Frances Westley, Brenda Zimmerman, and Michael Quinn Patton. Their research was underwritten by the J.W. McConnell Family Foundation, and we applaud that institution's bold commitment to catalyzing change nationally in Canada.

We owe very special thanks to our research advisors, who included national and global philanthropy experts who collectively devoted hundreds of hours to reviewing our online peer survey results, advising us on which examples might best illustrate catalytic approaches, and reading and commenting on manuscript drafts. These advisors were Kathy Calvin, Paula Ellis, Peter Goldmark, Jacob Harold, Darin McKeever, Tom Reis, Edward Skloot, and Diana Wells, as well as Brian Byrnes, Jack

Hopkins, Dori Kreiger, Laura McKnight, and Susan Price. The ideas and the cases in this book are stronger because of each of their contributions, and we are honored to have them as our thought partners in this work.

And Leslie expresses heartfelt personal thanks to her D.C. Philanthropy Brain Trust: Katherine Bradley, Kristin Ehrhood, Ann Friedman, and Courtney Clark Pastrick. Each took the time to read and make copious comments on draft chapters, sharing her personal perspective. And to Katherine a special note of recognition is in order, for it was while consulting with CityBridge Foundation that Leslie got a first-hand glimpse of how a truly catalytic family foundation operates.

More thanks go to our friends and colleagues who gave us new ways to think about philanthropy and about framing this book—and who, as the project progressed, sympathized with our complaints and helped us devise solutions as we worked through both the creative and administrative challenges entailed in this intensive research project: Victoria Vrana, Raj Vinnakota, Trabian Shorters, Eric Kessler, Lowell Weiss, Deborah Fugenschuh, and members of Incito. Our great appreciation goes out as well to FSGers who spent countless hours working to improve and complete our manuscript: Mike Stamp, Valerie Bockstette, Tracy Foster, Matthew Rehrig, Roxann Stafford, Sadie Peckens, Mary Pietrusko, and Cathy Severance.

To our editors at Jossey-Bass/Wiley, Allison Brunner and Kathe Sweeney, and to our literary agent, Rafe Sagalyn, we extend our sincere thanks. Allison and Rafe advocated for this book from the start and supported us each step of the way. And when Allison departed Wiley, Kathe expertly carried it over the finish line. Thanks also to Wiley editors Alan Venable and Alan Shrader, who helped us sharpen our prose and streamline our thinking. And to Eric Nee and Regina Ridley of the *Stanford Social Innovation Review* (*SSIR*): We appreciate your extending to each of us opportunities to contribute to *SSIR* over the years and allowing us to adapt portions of these pieces for publication in this book. We are also indebted to Ron Heifetz for introducing the ground-breaking concepts of adaptive leadership to the field, and for his partnership with FSG in applying those concepts to social sector challenges.

On a personal note, we express our appreciation for and love of our spouses, Holly Kania and Anthony Macintyre, and for our extended families for giving us moral support and the scheduling flexibility to get this book done. We recognize that precious vacation days, sabbatical time, and more than one travel adventure were sacrificed in order to complete this work, and we are grateful to our loved ones for their patience with us. (They will not soon let us forget that Leslie awakened before dawn to write on her family's beach vacation, John e-mailed comments between jeep rides in Malawi, and Mark filed chapters from a sick bed in India.)

Finally, we have dedicated this book to our children: to Nate, Lucy, and Mia and to Caleigh and Quinn in the hope that they will be so fortunate as to one day be in a position to *do more than give*, and to Toby, Elizabeth, and Benjamin in recognition of their having already demonstrated the commitment and ability to do so.

The Authors

Leslie R. Crutchfield is an author, speaker, philanthropic and nonprofit advisor, and leading authority on scaling social innovation and high-impact philanthropy. She is a senior advisor with FSG, and coauthor with Heather McLeod Grant of the critically acclaimed book, *Forces for Good: The Six Practices of High-Impact Nonprofits*, recognized by the *Economist* on its best business books of 2007 list. Leslie guides nonprofit and philanthropic organizations in the United States and abroad on how to increase their impact. She has served as managing director and director at Ashoka, and she cofounded and ran a nonprofit social enterprise that published a national magazine for social entrepreneurs and growing nonprofits. Leslie is frequently invited to lecture at domestic and international events and to conduct workshops and private training sessions for nonprofit and philanthropic leaders. She is an active media contributor whose work has been featured in the *Washington Post, Fast Company,* the *Chronicle of Philanthropy,* and the *Stanford Social Innovation Review,* and she has appeared on such networks as ABC, NPR (National Public Radio), and PBS. She serves on the boards of the SEED Foundation and Kiva, and she has volunteered with Crossroads Africa. Leslie holds MBA and BA degrees from Harvard University.

John V. Kania is a managing director at FSG and brings twenty-five years' experience in advising senior management on issues of strategy, leadership, organization development, and change management. At FSG, John leads strategic planning and evaluation efforts for foundations, nonprofits, and corporate philanthropy, on issues ranging from international health, U.S. health care, and U.S. education to the environment, community development, and nonprofit capacity building. He has developed numerous applications of FSG's strategy and problem-solving tools for the social sector. Prior to joining FSG, John was a partner at both Mercer Management Consulting and Corporate Decisions, Inc. He has been published in the *Stanford Social Innovation Review*, the *Wall Street Journal*, and the *Journal of Business Strategy* and is a featured author of *Learning from the Future*. John speaks frequently on improving the impact of philanthropy and corporate social responsibility. He has an MBA degree from Northwestern University's Kellogg Graduate School of Management and a BA degree from Dartmouth College.

Mark R. Kramer is cofounder and a managing director at FSG and a Senior Fellow in the Corporate Social Responsibility Initiative at the Mossavar-Rahmani Center for Business in Government at Harvard University's Kennedy School of Government. Together with Harvard Business School Professor Michael Porter, he cofounded the Center for Effective Philanthropy and served as the center's initial board chair from 2000 to 2004. Mark has spoken and published extensively on topics in catalytic philanthropy, corporate social responsibility, evaluation, social entrepreneurship, venture philanthropy, and impact investing. He is the coauthor, with Michael Porter, of several influential *Harvard Business Review* articles, and has published extensively in the *Stanford Social Innovation Review* and in the *Chronicle of Philanthropy* and has been quoted by the *Financial Times*, the *Economist*, and NPR. Prior to founding FSG, Mark served for twelve years as president of Kramer Capital Management, a venture capital firm, and before that he was an associate at the law firm of Ropes & Gray in Boston. He received a BA degree from Brandeis University, an MBA degree from The Wharton School, and a JD degree from the University of Pennsylvania Law School.

About FSG. FSG is a nonprofit social impact consulting firm founded by Harvard Business School Professor Michael Porter and Mark Kramer specializing in research, strategy, and evaluation, originally founded in 2000 as Foundation Strategy Group. Today FSG works across sectors in every region of the globe—partnering with foundations, corporations, nonprofits, and governments—to develop more effective solutions to the world's most challenging issues. The FSG team is passionate about finding better ways to solve social problems by leveraging the power of philanthropy, government, and private enterprise to build a more effective social sector. With offices in Boston, Geneva, San Francisco, Seattle, and Washington, D.C., FSG has completed more than 400 consulting engagements, published articles in the *Harvard Business Review* and the *Stanford Social Innovation Review*, and produced dozens of research reports designed to advance social sector thinking and practice. Its work has been featured in the *New York Times*, the *Wall Street Journal*, the *Economist*, and the *Financial Times* and on NPR, among other media. Learn more about FSG at www.fsg.org.

Do More Than Give

CHAPTER ONE

CATALYTIC PHILANTHROPY

"What business are you in?"

Peter Drucker, the renowned author and management expert, regularly posed this naive-sounding question to corporate executives whom he advised. How a donor answers this query can reveal a lot about his or her approach to philanthropy too.

Most foundation leaders and individual donors might answer that they are in the business of "giving away money." These funders define their philanthropic purpose as making grants to worthy charities. Many do so with great thought and care. Some are exceptionally strategic in their approach, guiding their grantmaking with highly refined theories of change.

That's not what this book is about. The donors profiled here cast their role in a different light. They see themselves as active participants in the business of solving social and environmental problems—or at least, making a significant dent in an issue. They define their purpose as achieving as much impact as possible. Indeed, their aim is no less than to change the world. So even though donating money to nonprofits is one means of achieving that goal, it's often just a starting point. It's not the endgame.

As a result this book doesn't talk much about how to give away money. Instead, we focus on what donors can do to become more proactive players in solving problems and advancing the causes they care about. The donors we profile don't just write checks or make grants. Instead, they catalyze action across each sector of society. They speak out to ask government leaders to change ineffective laws or create new ones. They use their clout and influence to steer businesses to become engines of social progress. They collaborate with their foundation and nonprofit peers, rather than operating at arm's length. And they empower the very individuals that they seek to help, treating them as partners in progress rather than as recipients of charity. Their impact isn't driven by the amount of money given away but by the six key practices they use to catalyze change, as we describe later in this chapter and throughout the book. They *do more than give*.

This book contains stories that can be inspirational and useful to all kinds of donors; however, you may not recognize many of the individuals and foundations profiled here. Most would not make it onto a media list of the wealthiest donors, although a few do—Bill Gates, for example. The donors we write about have all given away large sums of money—hundreds of thousands, millions, even billions of dollars—yet the principles we describe can be used by donors with charitable-giving budgets of any size. In every case it is the knowledge and leadership of the funders—and their adeptness at employing the tools of catalytic philanthropy—rather than the size of their giving budgets that has earned them a place in this book.

You'll meet philanthropists like Emily Tow Jackson, executive director of her parents' foundation and a mother raising three school-age children in a small, bucolic Connecticut town. For the first seven years, The Tow Foundation did not employ any staff and funded mostly "meds and eds"—gifts to medical research to cure a disease that afflicts a family member and professorships at family members' various alma maters. After Tow Jackson became its full-time leader, The Tow Foundation grew more committed to solving social problems and soon emerged as a leading advocate for reforming the state's broken juvenile justice system. Tow Jackson had never before worked with court-involved or incarcerated youth, nor was she trained as a lawyer. But through the foundation's funding and advocacy, Tow Jackson's efforts contributed to dramatic decreases in Connecticut's rates of incarceration and to major legislative changes that moved sixteen- and seventeen-year-olds from the adult criminal justice system back to the juvenile justice system, among other reforms.

Large private foundations may also do more than give, as the Shell Foundation in the United Kingdom does. The impetus for creating this independent philanthropy, endowed with a US$250 million start-up gift in 2000 by Royal Dutch Shell plc, was largely environmentalists' and antiglobalization activists' outrage over the Anglo-Dutch company's plan in the 1990s to dump a defunct oil rig in the North Sea off Brent Spar, among other infractions.[1] But instead of launching a traditional corporate foundation designed primarily to placate nonprofits with grants or provide public relations cover, Shell Foundation did something entirely different: it decided to apply its business know-how to solving global problems like poverty, and it has since been financing and assisting entrepreneurs to launch and grow small and medium-sized businesses in some of the most underdeveloped regions of the world. Of course Shell benefits from helping communities where it operates. But what's unique is that the Shell Foundation leverages the power of private enterprise to solve social problems, rather than taking the path of the more traditional corporations that sprinkle gifts across a range of local issues in towns where their employees happen to live and work.

In this book you will also meet individual donors who go beyond giving money to find ways to leverage their time, talents, and connections to advance the causes they care about, whether they give through their community foundations, donor-advised funds, or directly to nonprofits. They may advocate as shareholders at annual company meetings. They may sign petitions to change government policy. They may join coalitions to collectively push for other reforms. However they act, these donors *do more than give*.

We call these foundations and individuals *catalytic*. It's popular these days for donors, particularly those who fund start-ups or help existing nonprofits to grow, to refer to themselves as catalysts; however, we mean something more specific by the term *catalytic*. In chemistry the addition of a small amount of catalyst causes or accelerates a much larger chemical reaction, although the catalyst is not itself a part of that reaction. In philanthropy, donors who define the act of giving more broadly than as simply donating money to nonprofits, and who focus their time or the time of a foundation's trustees, staff, and board on highly leveraged, cross-sector activities, produce an effect that is much *greater than the sum of its parts*. This is what enables small donors to have more impact than some billionaires who rank above them in sheer giving. These catalytic donors *punch above their weight*.

Origins of Catalytic Philanthropy

The idea behind catalytic philanthropy starts with two main premises. Our first premise is this:

> **Donors have something valuable to contribute beyond their money**. The clout, connections, business know-how, and political savvy that foundation leaders, business executives, and many individual donors possess are key resources in advancing causes—resources that nonprofits often lack.

We believe that the most valuable contribution donors can make to advance significant change in the world is to extend their practice of philanthropy beyond financial gifts and volunteered time. To achieve the highest possible level of impact with their philanthropic resources—to create real results—catalytic donors cast themselves in a different role. They shift their stance from that of passive grantmaker to that of proactive problem solver. In addition to funding nonprofits and serving on boards, they *act* as catalysts for change by leveraging the power of each of society's sectors—public, private, nonprofit, and individual.

Our second premise is this:

> **We all inhabit an increasingly complex and globally interdependent world that is changing with unprecedented speed**. Although social and environmental problems have been with us throughout human history, today's challenges are of a whole new order.

Today's problems and the solutions they require are no longer confined within a community or a country or even a continent. Witness global climate change, propelled not only by gas-guzzling luxury cars in the United States and factories spewing carbon across Europe but also by the unrelenting construction of coal-fired power plants in China, deforestation in Latin America, and the dung-fueled cooking fires of impoverished families in Africa. The world is, indeed, flat. It's also complex. This applies as much to the social and environmental problems that societies face as it does to the interwoven economic systems that are financially tethering the world together. And it is with this realm of complex systems that donors must deal if they want to make a bigger difference. Whether across a continent, inside a country, or within a neighborhood, the social and environmental problems people face exist within complicated ecosystems of individual actors and institutions representing government, corporate, and nonprofit sectors. Working through one sector alone, such as by funding only nonprofit organizations, is no longer sufficient to achieve lasting change.

"We must move from seeing the world as simple, or even merely complicated. To understand social innovation, we must see the world in all its complexity," write the authors of *Getting to Maybe*, a thoughtful book about how social innovation happens. They explain how traditional methods of seeing the world compare its workings to a machine—people say, "things are working like clockwork," or everything is "shipshape." Whereas by looking at the natural world, complexity theorists see life as it is: unpredictable, emergent, evolving, and adaptable—not the least bit mechanical.[2]

Emergent, evolving, and complex societal problems call for equally dynamic and adaptive responses. Today's challenges and their solutions are not so well defined that they can be wedged into a grant request. Answers are often not known in advance but require innovation and learning among many different actors before progress can be made. Even when a solution is discovered, no single entity has the authority to impose it on others. The stakeholders themselves often must create and put the solution into effect. Donors who want to solve pressing problems must take into account the systemic nature of the issues and acknowledge the complex ecosystem of actors that influence them. And so catalytic philanthropy, at the end of the day, is an act of *adaptive leadership*.[3]

TODAY'S GOLDEN AGE

Despite these challenges we believe that more donors can—and should—aim to change the world. And perhaps now, more than ever before, they are able to.

The philanthropic funds available today, and the wealth that supplies them, are growing at a staggering rate; the number of billionaires worldwide has more than *tripled* in the last decade, up to 1,011 in 2010 from 306 ten years prior.[4] Nearly half of the 75,000 private foundations in the United States alone were created *in the previous decade*, as were a majority of community foundations,[5] and the rate of growth among both private and community foundations has been even faster in Europe, Asia, and Latin America. Matthew Bishop, a writer for the *Economist*, has called today's era of giving the "second Golden Age" of modern philanthropy (the first golden age of philanthropy in modern times having come a century ago when industrialists such as John D. Rockefeller and Andrew Carnegie were establishing their private foundations in the United States).[6]

This growth in giving volume is being matched by advancements in new philanthropic tools and approaches—starting with the changing role of private enterprise, which is becoming a stronger force for solving societal and environmental problems. Major corporations are taking far more active roles in addressing social and environmental issues, and new types of corporate entities are being created that blend profit making with social purpose. At the same time, foundations are pouring hundreds of millions of dollars into innovative financial investments that deliver social as well as economic impact.

The role of government has shifted as well, creating new opportunities for philanthropists to make common cause with the state. The spread of democracy and vast new private wealth in Asia, Eastern Europe, and Latin America over the last thirty years has opened to donors doors that were once bolted. Meanwhile, in Western Europe the idea of the state as the sole guarantor of social progress has started to soften, a process spurred by the recognition that philanthropy can do things government cannot and also that the needs of a growing aging population cannot be supported by tax-funded programs alone.

The implications of these changing state roles are profound. Philanthropists who want to make a difference in today's socio-politico-economic climate must proactively *leverage* government resources to advance the causes they believe in, rather than keeping their private philanthropic pursuits separate from public affairs.

In the context of these global trends, the dozens of specific examples throughout this book demonstrate our point: donors *can* make lasting and systemic change in today's complex social sector ecosystem, and they are most successful when they *do more than give*. When donors play this catalytic role, they leverage their philanthropic resources to the highest extent possible. We believe that if philanthropy is going to rise to the complex interdependent challenges the world faces at the beginning of the twenty-first century—if philanthropy is going to solve even a fraction of the problems in the world—then the way it is commonly practiced today must change. More donors must move from traditional giving practices to embrace catalytic philanthropy.

WHAT'S DIFFERENT ABOUT THE CATALYTIC APPROACH?

Donors often see their primary task as deciding which organizations to fund. This follows from the commonly held belief that donors are in the business of giving away money. Many donors subscribe to a linear process that typically begins with a funding proposal, proceeds to a grant or donation, and ends with a final report that describes what the gift accomplished. Even sophisticated funders—those who develop theories of change and map out logic models for how to accomplish results—often seem to approach issues as if their grants will set in motion a predictable series of events that leads directly to the intended result. They act as if their money might buy a ready-made solution from a nonprofit organization. And because most donors receive so many promising appeals from nonprofits year in and year out—each group making a compelling case about how the donor's gift will make all the difference—funders typically repeat this linear process time and again, scattering their gifts across dozens of issues and sometimes hundreds of grantees in response to the myriad requests.

The problem is that most nonprofit organizations today aren't equipped to provide the kind of solutions this complex world requires—no more than any other single actor, such as a business, government agency, or even a dedicated group of volunteers, is able to. "Social change is complex, and causal chains are often murky," write Paul Brest and Hal Harvey in *Money Well Spent*, an authoritative guide to strategic philanthropy that encourages donors to go beyond grantmaking. "It often takes more than one tool to solve a problem."[7] Today's challenges require cross-sector solutions, and so focusing on nonprofits in isolation from society's other sectors is often not the most effective means of approach.

Catalytic donors see the world differently from the average donor. Rather than only fund nonprofits to address society's problems, these donors catalyze change by influencing the behavior of others, working across sectors, and leveraging nonfinancial resources to create systems-level change. To achieve the highest possible level of impact—to create lasting results—catalytic donors shift their stance from that of passive grantmaker to that of proactive problem solver.

Figure 1.1 illustrates the difference between common and catalytic philanthropy. As we have discussed, catalytic funders

FIGURE 1.1. COMMON VERSUS CATALYTIC DONOR MIND-SET.

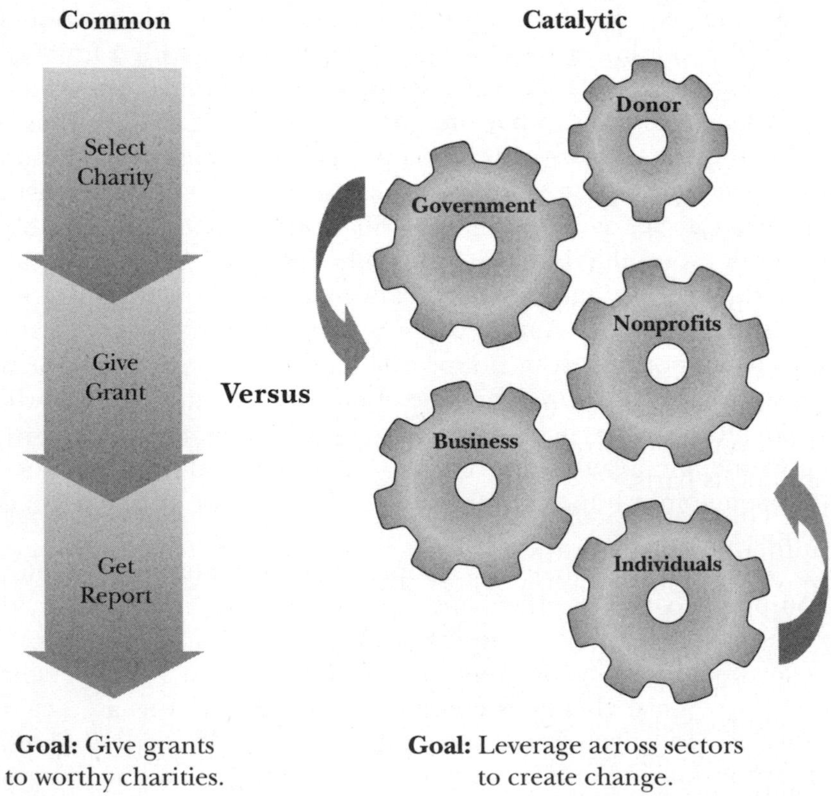

Common

Select Charity

Give Grant

Get Report

Versus

Catalytic

Donor

Government

Nonprofits

Business

Individuals

Goal: Give grants to worthy charities.

Goal: Leverage across sectors to create change.

don't operate according to a linear mind-set that starts with a grant proposal and concludes with a year-end report. Instead, they seek points of leverage in each sector of society—government, business, nonprofit, and individual—and use those levers to achieve greater levels of impact than they could if they simply focused on writing checks. Although we illustrate the concept of systems change here (and in other places in this book) as a series of interlocking gears, we will also draw on metaphors from complexity science and ecosystems research to illustrate the notion that a systems view is required if donors are to achieve significant change. None of these metaphors is perfect—the interaction among society's sectors is not as formulaic as that of interlocking cogs nor as intricately symbiotic as that of the components of a natural ecosystem. But the intention of these frameworks is to help donors see beyond their individual grantees to perceive the larger systems in which nonprofits exist and operate.

Catalytic donors are no different from systems-changing social entrepreneurs—their counterparts on the grantee side of the funding equation. Donors just advance a cause from a place that begins with a concentration of wealth, rather than having to raise resources from scratch. One might call catalytic funders *philanthropreneurs*, the foundation equivalents of social entrepreneurs, who, according to Ashoka founder Bill Drayton, "are not content to merely give a man a fish, or even teach him to fish; these entrepreneurs won't stop until they've revolutionized the entire fishing industry."[8] Whatever their moniker, they embrace a proactive, results-oriented, transformative mode of philanthropy. They use leverage to produce an effect that is much greater than the sum of its parts.

This leads catalytic donors to create coalitions and work in authentic collaboration with other foundation leaders and the grantees that they fund—their nonprofit peers. Catalytic donors also work across other sectors, reaching out to business and government and seeking ways to harness market forces and to create policy change so their impact spans issues on a regional, national, or global scale. And to push for policy change and advocate for causes, they engage directly with individuals at neighborhood and community levels, listening to them and mobilizing them in the campaign to advance their cause. They don't treat individuals with needs just as *recipients of charity*. They see these individuals as *part of the solution*, as people who have meaningful perspectives and, most important, are powerful actors.

In short, catalytic philanthropists *use all of the tools*, working across sectors to create wide-scale system change. As Gwen Ruta, director of corporate alliances for the Environmental Defense Fund, said when she was interviewed for Leslie Crutchfield and Heather McLeod Grant's 2008 book, *Forces for Good*, "We're all about results. It doesn't matter whom we work with if we can get credible results. And we'll use whatever tool it takes to make progress: we will sue people, we will partner with business, we will lobby on ... [Capitol] Hill or educate the public. Every one of these tools is in our tool kit, and we deploy the one most likely to get us to our goal."[9] For donors to do this well, they must exercise a unique type of leadership that is highly adaptive, and they must maintain a relentless focus on learning, to gain the knowledge to guide them as they act. These characteristics make up the essence of the six practices of catalytic philanthropy.

THE SIX PRACTICES OF DONORS WHO CHANGE THE WORLD

As you will see in the chapters to come, the catalytic practices in *Do More Than Give* correspond to the six practices of high-impact nonprofits articulated in *Forces for Good*. Our research for *Do More Than Give* began with the premise that the six practices of high-impact nonprofits apply to donors and that they can be applied by these philanthropists to achieve systems-level change. As described in *Forces for Good*, Leslie Crutchfield and Heather McLeod Grant ascertained the original six practices through four years of research on high-impact nonprofits, conducted with the Center for the Advancement of Social Entrepreneurship at Duke University. (Appendix D of this book presents a brief overview of the original six practices for donors who would like to either refresh or begin to acquire their knowledge of these practices.)

While the practices of both high-impact nonprofits and donors who change the world are similar, we discovered in writing *Do More Than Give* that donors and nonprofits apply these practices in different ways. This led us to new insights about how social change happens and about the evolving and unique role that donors play—discoveries that are summarized here and described in detail in the ensuing chapters.

Catalytic philanthropy begins with a bold initial step: before funders can employ the six practices of donors who change the world, they must first *commit to their cause*.

FIRST, COMMIT TO YOUR CAUSE

The world faces so many urgent needs that funders often find it impossible to choose a specific issue. But we have found that donors who do pick a strategic focus are able to achieve more than donors who scatter their funding and attention across many disparate causes. Once they have made a firm commitment, they can then go on to act in catalytic ways and focus the majority of their efforts (although not always all of their funds) on advancing that cause. They channel their personal time and the time of key trustees, board members, and staff. They bring to bear know-how and subject-matter expertise. They leverage their political, business, social, and familial connections. And although they also may reserve funds to support familial or local community concerns, they carve out a significant portion of resources to catalyze change. Then they use all of the tools—the six practices in this book—to tackle the problem. *This is the essence of strategy*: by getting clear on what they aim to achieve, donors are suddenly able to see what they need to do—as well what they need to *stop* doing.

In Chapter Two, "Commit to Your Cause," we outline a strategic-thinking process that donors can use to position them-selves to leverage change. Then the ensuing six chapters address the practices that define catalytic philanthropy. If you have already chosen an area of strategic focus and are fully committed to advancing one or a few issues, you may wish to skip Chapter Two and dive right into the third chapter: "Practice 1: Advocate for Change."

PRACTICE 1: ADVOCATE FOR CHANGE

Advocacy is an uncomfortable concept to many donors, and it is restricted in numerous ways by governments around the world.

Traditional notions of charity are linked to giving aid or supporting direct service programs, and the results are appealingly tangible—it's heartening for donors to know that their gift helped feed a hungry family or clean up a polluted stream. *But systemwide change is rarely achieved without a range of advocacy efforts*, including raising awareness and educating the public on the issues, as well as direct lobbying. As you will discover, advocacy is what enabled The Tow Foundation to help alter the ways in which the Connecticut criminal justice system treated juvenile offenders and the New Hampshire Charitable Foundation protected 100,000 acres of conservation land. Donors who eschew these tactics miss an important opportunity to advance their cause.

PRACTICE 2: BLEND PROFIT WITH PURPOSE

Why is a major corporation like General Electric staking its growth on solving medical problems in developing countries in Africa, Asia, and Latin America, or a large private funder like the Shell Foundation investing in entrepreneurs who start profit-making businesses? Until recently, large companies, private foundations, and wealthy individuals typically avoided mixing business with charity, while the recipients of charity saw philanthropy as their only source of potential revenue. But some of the world's leading corporations are finding that they can do more good through their core business activities than through their philanthropy or corporate social responsibility programs. And social entrepreneurs are finding that business models that blend profit with purpose can scale up to address social problems more rapidly and sustainably than traditional nonprofits. Foundations are even finding ways to invest their endowments in enterprises that further their social objectives while yielding market-rate returns. Across both the nonprofit and for-profit sectors, catalytic philanthropists are learning to *tap into the power of business* as an engine for advancing the greater good.

PRACTICE 3: FORGE NONPROFIT PEER NETWORKS

In Cincinnati, Ohio, high school graduation rates are increasing. So are fourth-grade math scores, and thousands of children are entering kindergarten better prepared. But don't ask which new educational program or savvy policy proposal has made the difference. The changes have come from the Strive Partnership, a network made up of hundreds of groups—nonprofits, corporations, foundations, school boards—working together across the entire educational spectrum from cradle to career in order to achieve a collective impact that no single organization could ever deliver alone. Instead of focusing on a few grantees, donors are in a unique position to see needs across entire fields, build alliances, and foster collaboration between nonprofits that would otherwise be locked in a competitive cycle pursuing independent strategies as they vie for scarce resources. It's popular today for funders to say they "partner" with their grantees, and almost every donor participates in some form of information sharing and cooperative behavior. But what these congenial convenings lack is the force of mutual accountability that comes when funders and nonprofits alike hold themselves and each other responsible for larger outcomes they seek to achieve, and funders *give power away* by sublimating their own ideas to the goals of the larger network. Catalytic donors understand the power of collective impact: they see the forest despite the trees.

PRACTICE 4: EMPOWER THE PEOPLE

Imagine if, instead of reviewing dozens of grant requests, you asked 100,000 Oregonians how to fix their own educational system. Or if instead of funding social service agencies in a low-income urban neighborhood in California, you gave neighborhood residents what they really wanted—a nearby major grocery store and bank. Listening to stakeholders turns out to be a powerful vehicle for change—not only because of the ideas that emerge but also because it helps people figure out answers for themselves. Catalytic donors don't treat individual community members just as recipients of charity. Instead, they view individuals as *essential participants* in the process of solving problems for themselves. These donors solicit individuals for ideas and involve them in campaigns to build political will, organizing them on the ground to create change at the block, neighborhood, regional, national, or even global level.

PRACTICE 5: LEAD ADAPTIVELY

How can a community foundation seeking to create greater economic opportunity in its region convince local employers to hire more low-income people and provide them with prospects for advancement? The foundation has no authority over local companies and cannot even make grants to them. Instead it must use the tools of adaptive leadership in order to create and sustain the conditions that motivate other leaders to advance the foundation's agenda. To work effectively across all sectors of society—government, business, nonprofit, and individual—catalytic donors must learn a rare, critical leadership skill: the ability to perceive changes and opportunities in their environments and to orchestrate—subtly but persistently—the activities of key players to advance their causes. The key to success is rooted neither in donor personalities nor in the fact that donors hold the purse strings. Catalytic donors are inordinately influential—not because they hold the formal authority afforded to elected officials or the CEOs of foundations and corporations—but because they are *adaptive* leaders.[10]

PRACTICE 6: LEARN IN ORDER TO CHANGE

The Bill & Melinda Gates Foundation carefully evaluated its work to provide housing for homeless families in the Pacific Northwest region of the United States, and every one of its grantees achieved the objectives set for it. The foundation could easily claim its program was a success except that, over the same period of time, family homelessness actually increased. Instead of announcing either success or failure, the foundation staff used the information to better understand the issue, revise its strategy, and adopt a more systemic approach. Catalytic donors like Bill and Melinda Gates are obsessed with measuring and evaluating their own performance as well as the effectiveness of their grantees. This sets them apart from most donors, who rarely bother to invest in evaluations, or even read the year-end reports their grantees submit. But catalytic donors don't conduct *evaluations* in the conventional sense of the term. They are less interested in receiving reports on past progress and more interested in building systems that enable them and their grantees to learn about what's working and what needs to be fixed in real time in order to advance a cause. As a result, they build *learning organizations*.[11]

FROM THEORY TO PRACTICE

To illustrate how these practices apply in action, we draw from examples of more than two dozen catalytic donors. The philanthropists who appear in this book were selected to represent a wide range of giving institutions—from relatively modest family foundations and locally focused community foundations, to some of the world's largest private and corporate foundations. The cases are intentionally diverse along other dimensions as well, such as geographical location and scope, and the range of issues or causes funded. These donors came to our attention for further study in two ways: either because they were recommended by their peers as leading examples of catalytic philanthropy through a large-scale survey FSG conducted in 2010, or because we knew of their work through our own research and consulting practices. (For a detailed description of our research methodology, including the online peer survey nominations process, please see Appendix A.)

Although every donor profiled here employs some of these best practices, only a handful effectively employ all six. Several are still developing their catalytic approach, as they layer in more practices over time. As a result, this book is not meant to be a set of profiles of the world's "best" donors. Instead, these cases constitute a diverse sample of funders who effectively exemplify a few or all of our six catalytic practices.

To help you scale up your own learning curve, at the end of this book Appendix E offers a series of checklists that contain next steps organized by two levels of difficulty—beginner and experienced. This way, readers can immediately begin to apply these practices in their own work or heighten their commitment if they're already using some of them. We also include advice for donors who may not want to dive into these practices right away but simply to augment their current strategy by applying the concepts of catalytic philanthropy to their grantmaking. You don't need to become a world changer overnight, but we hope that you will take at least a few steps in that direction.

EMBRACING THE FUTURE

When Bill Gates was asked at a World Economic Forum meeting at Davos, Switzerland, whether it was easier to make money or give it away, he paused for a moment, then said "They are surprisingly similar."[12]

We agree—catalyzing large-scale change *is* every bit as challenging as building a business—and in many ways, harder. One would think it must be so much easier for donors than for the nonprofits they fund. After all, donors have a leg up because they don't need to raise the money to keep the lights on and the staff paid. But as will become clear in the following chapters, money alone rarely solves any of the major problems society faces. Catalytic philanthropists must do the same hard work as their grantees and apply creative, adaptive skills to advance their causes.

Change is hard—whether at the global level, on one city block, or for one individual. Forces conspire to resist change. Change entails movement, and movement involves friction. Lance Lindblom, president and CEO of the Nathan Cummings Foundation, said it well: "When you try to create any kind of major change, more than 75 percent of the time there is an 'interest' with an 'interest' in defending [the status quo]."[13]

And yet, as hard as it is, we want to stress that *making change is possible*. In the stories to come, you'll encounter a wide range of donors—some who give hundreds of thousands of dollars annually and others who donate billions—who all became more catalytic.

The last point we'd like to emphasize is that the practices of catalytic philanthropy are not new. In various forms the six practices explored here have been used by social change leaders for millennia—whether these leaders have resided on the donor or the grantee side of the funding equation. There are prime past examples of major foundations taking a catalytic approach. For one, take the Rockefeller Foundation's role in the powerful Green Revolution that has fed billions of people who might otherwise have gone hungry. The foundation not only funded research by hiring staff scientists to solve a problem, but then proactively went into the developing world and devised ways to distribute and implement effective programs. Similarly, the Ford Foundation's key role as a brave and early funder of the civil rights movement is another prime example, cited by respondents to our peer survey and by thought leaders many times.

Although catalytic philanthropy is not new it is rare, and that is something we want to change. We're calling for a shift in the way donors participate in solving the world's most pressing social and environmental problems. Today's philanthropists have an opportunity to engage in more proactive, highly leveraged forms of philanthropy than at any other time in history—at a time when adaptive, systemic solutions are needed more than ever before. Business as usual is no longer acceptable.

"Although the amount of money given away each year continues to rise, there are lingering doubts about what the billions of dollars backed by good intentions have ultimately produced," writes Peter Frumkin, author of *Strategic Giving*, a definitive work on the subject.[14] No one should pretend that philanthropy as it is commonly practiced today will change the status quo.

It is in this context that we urge donors to *do more than give*. They should aspire to create real change in the world, utilizing every new tool available in this second modern golden age of giving. And catalytic philanthropy is the best route we know to accomplishing that. Which leads to the central thesis of this book:

We believe that if more donors adopt a catalytic approach, philanthropy can make a greater impact on the challenges facing the world. Every donor—no matter the level of wealth—has opportunities to go beyond straightforward grantmaking, and become a catalyst that effects systemwide change.

Our passionate hope is that catalytic philanthropy will stop being the exception and will grow to become a more common mode in this twenty-first century golden age of giving. The need for catalytic philanthropy has never been higher. And the opportunity for donors to become more active catalysts for change has also never been greater. Now more than ever, donors must *do more than give*.

CHAPTER TWO

COMMIT TO YOUR CAUSE

What do you get when a family foundation's board includes a conservative *Fortune* 500 company founder and his three liberal daughters—one a practicing social worker and another a licensed psychotherapist?

A huge argument, for starters.

This certainly was the case for the Jacobs Family Foundation of San Diego, California. The foundation was created in 1988 by the late Joseph "Joe" Jacobs Jr. and his wife, Vi, at the time that Joe's company, Jacobs Engineering Group, went public in the early 1970s; Joe Jacobs had grown the company from a one-man consultancy into what is today an $11 billion corporation with approximately 35,000 employees. Joe and Vi invited to serve on the foundation's board their three daughters—Meg, Linda, and Valerie—whom they lovingly called "screaming liberals." Joe Jacobs was a self-described "compassionate conservative."[1]

So it shouldn't have surprised Joe Jacobs when one of the first grants he proposed—a gift to the conservative think tank Institute for Contemporary Studies—was shot down. At first he got angry, saying, "It's my money, I can do what I want with it," recalls his youngest daughter, Valerie. "Yes, it is, and you can," she replied. "But you told us we all had equal votes. If that's not the case, then you and Mom can give it away yourselves. But if you want us involved, we all have to agree."[2]

Jacobs eventually softened his stance, reasoning that it was his daughters' money too, as they would have inherited it. So the trustees "agreed to agree." But then they confronted the next heated subject: what could they actually agree on?

The first cause that had universal appeal was microfinance, a practice that involves lending small amounts of money to circles of people (typically women) in developing regions to help them start or build up small businesses. "This approach satisfied both the liberals and the conservatives on our board in helping poor people with a 'hand up, not a hand out' approach," explains Valerie Jacobs. And because Joe Jacobs was of Lebanese descent—born and raised in Brooklyn by immigrant parents—it also honored the Jacobs family's cultural heritage. The foundation's first unanimous grant was made to FINCA, and it soon also gave to Trickle Up and to other international organizations that support women in poverty in developing regions. It also supported ACCION New Mexico. Then, when the Los Angeles riots occurred in 1992, the Jacobs's interests turned closer to home, and they started supporting grassroots organizations in southern California serving low-income and minority communities.

This strategic focus helped, but as they continued to make grants, Jacobs Family Foundation board members became increasingly dissatisfied with their arm's-length approach. They also began to realize that if they wanted to help people in poverty in a more permanent way, they would need to alter the systems that work against these individuals on a daily basis. Helping a microentrepreneur in a developing region or providing jobs in the United States can increase individuals' income, "but you also have to address lack of access to health care, quality housing, transportation, and child care and so much more," Valerie Jacobs explains. This realization caused the board members to recast their entire approach to philanthropy.

At this moment—just a few years into the foundation's early history—the Jacobs family quit the business of traditional grant-making and entered the realm of catalytic philanthropy. They decided to shift all their foundation giving into a narrowly conscribed area, the Diamond Neighborhoods of southeastern San Diego (named after the area's diamond-shaped business district). These ten contiguous neighborhoods were once closely connected, thriving urban communities but had been since carved up by freeways. Mostly poor and working-poor residents remained as middle-income families moved to the suburbs and businesses closed or moved elsewhere. At the heart of the region was a twenty-acre property with a dry creek bed running through it and an abandoned aerospace factory decaying in the middle of an ecologically devastated brownfield.

The Jacobs Family Foundation purchased the property for $2.1 million in 1997, and over the next eight years worked hand in hand with local residents, business leaders, and public officials to develop the site. The foundation ultimately leveraged its portfolio to attract a total of $23.5 million to build what has grown to become Market Creek Plaza, a thriving and architecturally noted commercial and cultural center that has created hundreds of jobs for local residents, attracted dozens of profitable businesses—including major national chains and homegrown enterprises—and contributed to the economic and cultural revitalization of a community for thousands of residents. What was once an eyesore of urban blight and neglect had become a vibrant, self-sustaining community, brimming with hope and possibility.

We'll return to the Jacobs family's story later in this chapter to explore how this foundation, working together with residents of the Diamond Neighborhoods, was able to achieve these impressive results. But first, let's examine more closely how the foundation overcame one of the foremost hurdles preventing donors from becoming more catalytic—committing to a cause—and how other donors can do the same.

GETTING COMMITTED

Given the extreme political differences among the Jacobs Family Foundation board members, it's remarkable that they compromised and found a common cause to support in the first place—let alone went on to galvanize major change in an impoverished community. This is a problem for all kinds of foundations—community, corporate, and large private ones as well as family ones—but funders rarely achieve as much as the Jacobs family.

For example, for community and other place-based foundations, choosing a single issue of focus can prove particularly challenging. Community foundations are accountable to a wide spectrum of stakeholders, including large boards, hundreds or thousands of donors, and entire communities whose residents possess myriad concerns about the region. For community foundation leaders, it might seem impossible—or at least politically infeasible—to pick just one cause.

The same goes for corporate foundations, which typically orient their giving programs to the geographical areas where their employees live and to issues that concern those areas. It's more popular to give numerous modest charitable gifts that touch as many community members and issues as possible than it is to focus all of a foundation's resources on advancing one cause or another. For large private foundations—those with hundreds of millions or even billions in assets—it might seem illogical to pick only a few areas when they have so much money to give away.

For relatively smaller private foundations, like the Jacobs Family Foundation, committing to a particular focus area can be equally vexing. Family boards are governed by parents, spouses, siblings, children, and grandchildren, among others—all of whom can represent vastly different political and generational perspectives. And the larger a family grows, the more likely its members are to scatter and live in disparate places. Not only might each individual support a smattering of pet causes, but individuals' interests might range from arts to the environment to medical research. So family foundation boards often find it difficult to agree.

This dilemma applies even to everyday donors—people who may give away a few hundred or a thousand dollars a year as private citizens. Anyone looking through his or her mail at home today is likely to find several compelling donation requests: malnourished children in an overcrowded slum; the local food bank; a campaign against carbon emissions; the orchestra in the next town; an animal shelter; the capital campaign for an alma mater; cancer research; an emergency appeal for victims of another major natural disaster. Each appeal is carefully crafted to elicit empathy and promises that the contributions received will make an important difference.

So how does a donor choose? Is it more important to help a destitute earthquake victim in Haiti or a hungry family through a local food bank? The orchestra or the hospital? No moral calculus can dictate which is most important. Usually, donors are drawn to the causes they know well or have personally witnessed. Perhaps a family member has had cancer or the donor has just watched a documentary about climate change or she is passionate about the arts. Even so, dozens of compelling solicitations remain and most donors end up giving to many different causes.

This problem only compounds for philanthropists and foundation staff workers who scan grant requests at the office. As a result, each year most foundations make hundreds of grants across a wide range of issues. That's why most philanthropy today is practiced in the scattered, unfocused mode that we described in the previous chapter.

Then you pick up this book—or almost any book on strategic philanthropy—and read that above all else, you must focus on a single cause or issue in order to have greater impact. "Don't they understand," you may wonder, "how many compelling grant requests I receive and how many other people are involved in my foundation's decisions?"

Moreover, on top of that we advise that even picking a strategic focus is itself no longer enough—that whatever the chosen cause, donors should go well beyond writing checks and volunteering if they want to make the biggest difference.

Feeling daunted?

Don't worry. The stories in *Do More Than Give* show that many donors started out—perhaps like you—first by defining their role primarily as a check writer and donating to many disparate causes. They then went on to develop strategic focus areas, and from there to act as catalytic agents of change, leveraging their nonfinancial resources to advance major causes.

They were able to do this because, first, they opted to take a *portfolio approach* to their giving—an approach that enabled them to clear the air, meet different needs for important personal and community reasons, and then focus the balance of their time and energy on advancing their cause.

The Portfolio Approach

Fortunately, catalytic philanthropy is not an all-or-nothing pursuit. Just as most donors maintain a diversified portfolio of for-profit investments, they can also take a portfolio approach to their philanthropic contributions.[3] They do this because individual donors and foundations have many different motivations for their giving. Of course the primary objective of most philanthropists is to make a positive difference. But the reality is, all funders are also asked to support a range of causes because a family member, business associate, or friend has asked them to or because they want to give back in multiple ways to the community where they live. These are entirely legitimate reasons for giving. The trick for those donors who want to become more catalytic is learning to allocate their resources in a more systematic way across these various categories of giving so that they can place the majority of their focus (if not always the majority of their funds) on advancing the cause.

MOTIVATIONS FOR GIVING

Through FSG's work with hundreds of donors—including individuals; corporations; and family, community, and institutional foundations—and through our personal experiences, we've learned that charitable contributions most often fall into one of three motivational categories. Donors generally give because they possess:

- A sense of obligation to the different communities with which they identify
- A commitment to honoring personal and professional relationships
- A desire to make meaningful change in the world

Clearing the way to take a catalytic role in making change on an issue often requires setting aside a portion of the annual giving budget to satisfy the first two motivational categories. (Exhibit 2.1 illustrates these categories.)

EXHIBIT 2.1. THE PORTFOLIO OF MOTIVATIONS FOR GIVING.

Community or Geography

- Giving to support schools, religious or arts groups, and neighborhood or regional affiliations

- Giving to respond to natural disasters

Relationships

- Giving that reinforces personal or professional bonds

Impact

- Giving in order to make a meaningful change in the world

Fulfilling Obligations to Different Communities

Each of us is a member of multiple communities—the towns or cities where we grew up or currently live, the religious or ethnic communities we belong to, and the schools and universities we and our children attend. We are part of other communities too, such as the arts organizations that enrich our lives, the religious institutions that guide us, the places where our jobs may be located, and the medical institutions that heal us. Each of these communities needs philanthropic support, and as members of the community with resources to donate, we feel an obligation to respond. We have benefitted by our association with these communities, and our sense of gratitude and responsibility encourages us to contribute to help support their ongoing vitality.

In times of crisis we may also feel part of a global community—when an earthquake or tsunami devastates a population far away, we may feel a sense of obligation to respond to the urgent need, as a member of the larger human community.

Supporting our communities and responding to crises are important and noble acts of philanthropy, but in most cases these are not places where we seek to make a catalytic change. More often, we are primarily helping an institution—whether a place of worship, university, hospital, or even a disaster relief organization—stay on its current course or perhaps do what it already does a bit better. We contribute in each case because we are confident in the organization's leadership and ability to execute its given tasks, and it is enough for us to take out the checkbook and do our part. We may want to investigate to be sure the organization is as well run as it appears to be, or to review the use of funds to be sure they are being well spent, but our investigations are really just routine due diligence to be sure we have picked a sound organization to carry out our sense of communal responsibility.

Reinforcing Personal and Professional Relationships

The second motivational category relates to contributions we make because of the person who asked us, rather than because we were personally moved by the cause. These requests may come from family members, close friends, or important business acquaintances—whatever the nature of our connection, when these people ask us to contribute to causes that matter to them, we respond. These contributions are also entirely legitimate. Giving to a charity for the sake of a friend or colleague honors that relationship and strengthens that bond. And those bonds make a difference: Much of what we can accomplish comes from the strength of our associations with friends and business acquaintances. As we support their causes, we know that we can call upon them to support ours.

Making Meaningful Change in the World

In all likelihood, most philanthropic dollars go to the first two categories—communal and relationship-based giving—and our world would be much diminished if the many institutions that depend on this support were to disappear. In most cases, however, it would be hard to describe these contributions as catalysts for social progress.

So the catalytic philanthropist adds a third category of giving that is targeted toward achieving progress in specific social or environmental objectives. This type of giving is not about any personal relationship to the institution that receives the funds or the person that requests them. Instead, the donor is determined to make change on an important social or environmental issue that matters deeply to him or her.

The tools and advice in this book are primarily oriented toward this third category of impact-seeking philanthropy. This is not because the first two motivational categories are inferior but because they don't require special expertise. After all, contributing to an alma mater's capital campaign does not require the same kind of effort that would be necessary to fund and work in collaboration with a network of education reform groups to increase graduation rates at an inner-city high school.

Donors who apply the portfolio approach to their giving simply set aside a portion of their annual giving budget to meet their communal and relationship obligations. Then they can go on to focus on the third category—achieving a measurable social impact—to which this book is addressed.

CHOOSING YOUR CAUSE

Like a would-be professional athlete who must choose and focus on the one sport she is best suited for physically and mentally, a philanthropist seeking social change must choose among many different worthy causes and focus on the area where he or she can do the greatest good. The question to ask is not what the most important issue is but rather where can the individual donor or foundation accomplish the most.

Catalytic donors who want to make the greatest possible impact with the resources at their disposal will pick an issue on which they have the most leverage. And how much leverage a donor brings depends both on factors internal to the foundation or individual giver and on external circumstances. Once donors find an overlap between their internal capabilities and external opportunities, they can home in on their catalytic focus (see Figure 2.1.)

FIGURE 2.1. CHOOSING A FOCUS.

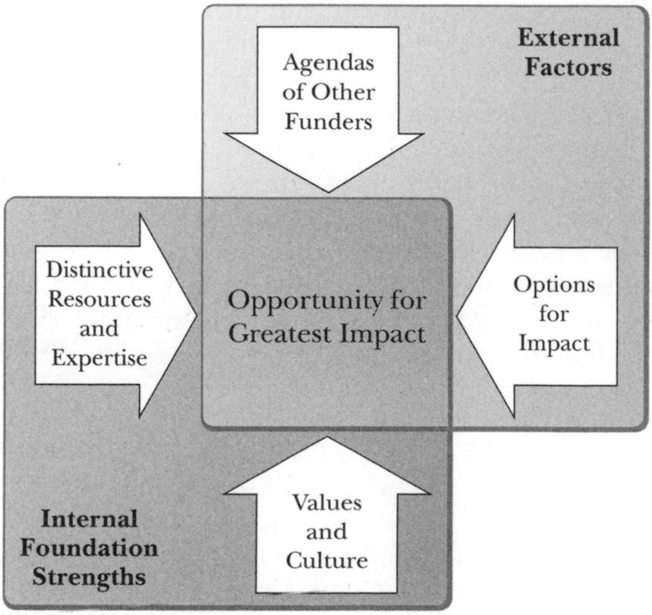

INTERNAL CAPABILITIES

Every donor brings a unique combination of capabilities to the issues he or she addresses. No two donors have the same scale of resources, geographical presence, personal or institutional values, funding history, relationships, motivations, and areas of expertise. This is true of individuals and corporate funders as well as family, community, and institutional foundations. It takes some effort to draw up a list of these internal assets, but once you do, you begin to see how you are positioned to make better progress on some issues than on others.

First and foremost, find an issue that really matters. It might not be an issue that you have personal experience with, but as you gain awareness and understanding of its importance, its significance and meaning grows. This was the case for Emily Tow Jackson and her family foundation. She had no prior experience with court-involved youth or the state's criminal and juvenile justice systems. Yet, as The Tow Foundation gained exposure to the young people in these systems and built relationships with public officials and advocates involved with the systems, Tow Jackson and other members of the board began to see opportunities where the foundation could make a critical difference. (Tow Jackson's experience is described more fully in the next chapter.)

For other donors the issue that really matters might stem from a personal life experience, such as dealing with a particular disease, like cancer or Alzheimer's. For a corporate donor the issue might be a particular social need that deeply affects the business's supply chain, operations, or products. For a community foundation the issue might stem from a careful analysis of local residents' needs. For a family foundation the issue might be anchored in the founder's original intent or the family's history and values. Whatever the type of funder, its leaders should pick an issue that is truly important to them if they are to have the energy, determination, and stick-to-itiveness to create catalytic change.

A second factor to consider when picking a focus is the relevant capabilities you bring to bear. These affect your chances for meaningful impact. Do you (or does your board) already know a lot about the issue? That can help. Do you live nearby? That makes it easier. Do you have a long history and network of relationships in that field? Good. Do you bring particular skills and nonmonetary resources that can affect the issue? Even better. The more relevant assets you have, the more leverage you can exert to achieve catalytic change.

EXTERNAL OPPORTUNITIES

Apart from determining the interests and capabilities of the funder, there is an entirely separate set of questions to be asked about the external environment. Consider for example whether the issue being considered is ripe for change. Funders need to be savvy about their timing. Not all causes are equally ripe for change at any given moment in time. If you really want to have impact, you'll need to figure out which issues offer the greatest opportunity for change, and also be prepared to put in the length of time that will realistically be required to solve the problem. For example, consider questions such as these:

- Have promising nonprofits recently emerged that seem to be achieving real progress in the area of interest?
- Is the issue well enough understood that there is a consensus on how to approach it? Have any recent developments accelerated or dampened the momentum for change?
- Are other funders interested? If not, is it because the issue has been overlooked, or do other funders believe that it is unwinnable?
- Is there a favorable political climate for adopting government policies that could improve progress on the issue?
- Are there current financial trends or incentives that might prompt businesses to get involved?
- Are there promising sources of new funds that might be tapped, whether from public or private entities?

These questions about external factors are all about facts, not opinions. They require serious research to collect the data on which to base a decision. But the key point is this: a decision about where to focus the foundation's efforts can be made on which all participants agree precisely because that decision will be anchored in objective facts like these, not merely a subjective debate about which issue is the most important. Once decision makers agree to focus on an issue where they have the greatest leverage, they can use the data about external factors to make a reasoned identification of the issue that offers that leverage. They don't have to argue, like the Jacobs Family initially did, over whose issue should take precedence.

How the Jacobs Family Foundation Got Committed to Its Cause

Let's return to the Jacobs Family Foundation described at the outset of this chapter. When we left off, foundation board members had agreed that they wanted to take a more catalytic approach to their philanthropy; they wanted to go beyond writing checks and tackle the systemic issues that confront people living in poverty in a more holistic way.

Two defining experiences sparked this radical change in the foundation's' course.[4]

One was a trip that family members took in 1995 to the Middle East and Northern Africa with the foundation's executive director, Jennifer Vanica. While visiting villages in Cairo, Egypt, they witnessed the remains of large-scale United States Agency for International Development (USAID) projects that had been abandoned. When Jacobs family members asked the villagers why this had happened, the residents said that they hadn't wanted the projects in the first place. "They'd been given a manufacturing plant, when what they really needed was something more in their frame of reference. They needed things like more goats or beehives, not some big industrial facility they had no means of or interest in maintaining," explains Vanica. The villagers had received someone else's vision of what economic success should look like, rather than more practical tools.

The second defining moment for the Jacobs family struck with the Los Angeles riots of 1992. Joe Jacobs was deeply disturbed by the sight of the residents burning down businesses. He interpreted these acts as their reaction to a system from which they felt excluded. According to Valerie Jacobs, he was quoted in the *Los Angeles Times* as saying, "People don't burn businesses they own." The Jacobs foundation phones rang constantly after that piece ran, as callers advocated for Jacobs to "put his money where his mouth is." So the family foundation started looking for opportunities to fund economic development programs serving low-income and minority communities in the foundation's home state of California.

Around that same time the middle Jacobs daughter, Linda, had been working in the Middle East and had gained knowledge about the practice of community building, and the importance of taking a holistic approach to helping people in poverty rather than funding one social service or advocacy group at a time. (These ideas were similar to the asset-building approach beginning to emerge in the United States.) The members of the Jacobs Family Foundation board collectively made a decision that what they wanted to do was focus on a specifically defined geographical area and help the community and economy to develop in a holistic way. At the invitation of a grantee, they zeroed in on the Diamond Neighborhoods in southeastern San Diego, a once-thriving community that suffered from economic disinvestment and decline.

One of their first moves was to move, literally. The Jacobs Family Foundation relocated its offices to the center of the Diamond Neighborhoods. The board members concluded that if the foundation was concerned about convincing businesses to relocate there, why wouldn't it lead the way? As Vanica put it, "Instead of trying to get 'buy-in' from the community, we realized that we needed to 'buy in' to the community ourselves."

During a meeting with the CEO of one of the foundation's grantees, Joe Jacobs looked across the street and saw an abandoned factory surrounded by barbed wire. This twenty-acre eyesore was once the bustling economic hub of the community; now it was a brownfield. The grantee explained that it was a very dangerous place—gang violence and drug deals regularly occurred there. And a dry creek bed ran through the center of it, which had caused developers to declare the site undevelopable.

Despite these challenges, the foundation purchased the site for $2.1 million and over the next eight years invested or attracted more than $20 million more from partners, such as Clearinghouse CDFI, and private funders, such as the F. B. Heron Foundation and Annie E. Casey Foundation, to develop it. Foundation board members and staff also invested their time, their social connections, political chits, and sweat equity to turn that blighted spot into one of the most remarkable examples of effective community and economic development in the urban United States. They essentially put everything they had into this cause.

"We quickly realized that we were making both a financial commitment to this neighborhood as well as a long-term time commitment.... [We] were committing to putting all of our assets into this one grand experiment," explains Valerie Jacobs.[5]

Tour the brownfield today, and instead of a vacated factory with windows of broken glass, you can walk through Market Creek Plaza—a colorful shopping, dining, and public area that is unlike any mall most people have ever encountered. The plaza's skyline is studded with unusually shaped building tops with odd angles, such as pyramid-capped towers. The facade has smooth adobe archways, with each architectural feature saturated in vibrant colors—deep violet, adobe red, yellow-gold, turquoise blue. It feels like a cross between a Native American village, an ancient Mayan metropolis, and Disney World (for grown-ups).

The Jacobs Family Foundation board members credit their success to taking the time to reach out and ask local community residents what they wanted. They didn't treat residents of these low-income neighborhoods as charity recipients, nor did they continue to fund the type of social service or job counseling programs typical of other community development efforts. Instead, they *asked* the residents what they needed—a process that we explain further in Chapter Six. They also experimented with ways to transfer ownership to the people living in the local community, inventing and ultimately launching an innovative community development initial public offering (IPO). During this first-ever IPO in the community, more than 400 local residents—many of them low-income people and some who had never before purchased stock in a public company—became part owners of the enterprise.

These activities have not been easy. As we'll see in Chapter Six, the Jacobs Family Foundation received criticism as well as accolades for its work. Some residents did not trust or perhaps didn't fully understand the foundation's motivations for pursuing commercial development in an area that had suffered from disinvestment and neglect for so long. And as is often the case when a group of white, wealthy donors enters into a community that is underinvested and extremely culturally diverse, divisions of race and class can create setbacks.

These challenges have not yet deterred the Jacobs family. The foundation is now gearing up to develop as commercial and residential space the forty-five acres surrounding and including the plaza. It will all be planned, designed, built, and managed by mostly local residents—and ultimately owned by them as well, as the Jacobs Family Foundation plans to spend down its assets (or sunset) by 2030. By then it intends to transfer to the community residents financial ownership of everything the foundation and the residents built together.

THE ULTIMATE CATALYTIC COMMITMENT

The Jacobs Family Foundation was successful because, when it decided to invest everything in the Diamond Neighborhoods, it chose an issue to which it brought many significant resources. Yes, it offered money. But perhaps more important for catalytic donors, it brought know-how, proximity to the community, and an all-in attitude and perseverance in the face of obstacles.

The know-how started with Joe Jacobs, an engineering and construction expert who had made billions in that industry and who brought extensive leadership skills as well as financial management prowess. The family's know-how also included the daughters' combined social change and community development knowledge, which helped the family members in creatively devising ways to fuse Joe Jacobs's compassionately conservative "hand up" philosophy with approaches that made sense in underserved communities. And most important, it included the wise philosophy of *asking* local residents what they wanted, rather than *imposing* on residents a preformed solution.

CHOOSING *YOUR* CAUSE

All types of donors can become more catalytic, although not every funder need take the all-in approach as the Jacobs family did. Many foundations create a philanthropic portfolio—allocating a portion of resources to each of three giving categories: meeting communal obligations, recognizing relationships, and seeking social impact. This approach allows donors to address multiple motivations for giving—which almost all donors in our experience have—while freeing them up to focus on achieving impact with the resources they put behind their results-driven philanthropy.

In the chapters to come, we will show you in greater detail how to employ each of the six practices of donors who change the world—using examples from a wide range of foundations that include community, corporate, and institutional foundations as well as family foundations.

For instance, we will see how some foundations choose *not one but a few* carefully selected causes. This was the case for the New Hampshire Charitable Foundation, a community foundation based in Concord, the capital of New Hampshire. Its then-president, Lew Feldstein, aware that community foundations are charged with responding to a range of regional causes, selected one issue to focus on at first but also recognized that catalytic change could occur across a series of issues over longer periods of time.

"There could be twenty or thirty issues that are important," explains Feldstein. "Just pick one to start and pick one that will work—[one that you know will have] good partners, a history of concern, some momentum around the issue."[6] Feldstein first chose environmental preservation, and once the foundation helped the community to attain traction in that area, the foundation went on to tackle other problems vexing the community, such as teen pregnancy, prison reform, and drug abuse.

The need for focus applies to corporate foundations as well. When Jim Rohr became chairman and CEO of PNC Financial Services Group, he wanted to focus the firm's philanthropic efforts in a concentrated way that differed from past approaches. Historically, PNC operated like other large, multistate corporations, with regional presidents handling community affairs and giving grants at the local level. Rohr was sensitive to the philanthropic interests of the many leaders across the corporation and knew that they would not easily accept any cutback or sudden shift in their charitable giving at the community level. So he kept local giving programs intact, and created a new $100 million initiative to improve early educational opportunities for low-income children through a program called Grow Up Great.

PNC's program included classic types of contributions such as grants and volunteered employee time in classrooms and out-of-school programs. But another, less traditional component involved committing to train and dispatch the firm's powerful cadre of regional presidents to work in state-based advocacy campaigns to change educational opportunities at the systemic level. Like other catalytic donors, PNC not only made a strategic choice to commit to a cause, it defined its role as much broader than simply check writer and direct service volunteer.

For large private foundations with catalytic aspirations the challenge of picking one or a few areas of focus and making all-in commitments is harder but still essential. This was the case for the Bill & Melinda Gates Foundation, now famous for its focus on two main issues—global health and public education reform in the United States. Other large private philanthropies, such as the AVINA Foundation, have narrowed their focus as well. AVINA employs about 100 staff based in countries across Latin America, and gives millions of dollars annually in funding and in-kind assistance as its representatives seed collaborations and foster networks among local leaders to drive change. With so many networks and a vast array of programs underway in more than a dozen different countries, AVINA leaders recently engaged in an intensive strategic planning process that led them to focus on five key issues to which the foundation believes it can contribute on the pancontinental level.

Finally, conversion and operating foundations, as well as other types of funding institutions (such as intermediaries), can also choose and commit to advancing causes in one area. The venture philanthropy movement has taken this challenge in a creative direction, setting its *cause* as building the capacity of and scaling up promising nonprofit solutions. Groups like Venture Philanthropy Partners and Social Venture Partners have shown this strategy can make a difference when a donor employs catalytic approaches and a business mind-set to investing in nonprofits at the local level; meanwhile NewSchools Venture Fund concentrates nationally on the issue of educating at-risk youth. And intermediaries such as Ashoka, the Draper Richards Foundation, and New Profit Inc. have chosen social entrepreneurship as their primary cause, channeling funds and nonfinancial resources to help emerging social entrepreneurs create systemic change at national and global levels.

Donors will differ in how intensely they focus. Full-time philanthropists, whether program officers at large foundations or family foundation trustees who have chosen to commit most of their time to their philanthropy, can do a great deal that others who are still consumed by building a business or raising a family may not be able to do. Throughout this book we offer suggestions for both beginning and more advanced donors. Often the differences in these two categories depend less on how long people have been active in philanthropy and more on how much time they can commit to their giving.

Conclusion

> A pig and a chicken were walking down the road. As they passed a church, they noticed that a potluck charity breakfast was under way. Caught up in the spirit, the pig suggested to the chicken that they each make a contribution.
>
> "Great idea!" the chicken cried. "Let's offer them ham and eggs!"
>
> "Not so fast," said the pig. "For you, that's just a contribution, but for me, it's a total commitment."

The theme of total commitment lies just beneath the surface of every story in this book, and it is a necessary precursor to the six catalytic practices that follow in subsequent chapters. The funders we describe, who each became a stronger force for good in the world, took personal risks to accomplish their goals. Fortunately, it didn't involve the same degree of self-sacrifice as faced by the pig in the parable, but catalytic philanthropists, by definition, do much more than just make a contribution.

As you read the following chapters, ask yourself these two questions. Which issue among the ones I care about may be ripe for change? What cause can I advance by employing the six practices of catalytic philanthropy? Give great weight to the emotional pull you feel about an issue, but take a hard look at the facts as well. Catalyzing social change is not easy, so pick the issue that gives you the greatest chance of success as well as one that you are most willing to stick with. With that as your assignment, let's begin.

CHAPTER THREE

PRACTICE 1
Advocate for Change

Advocacy is an uncomfortable concept for many donors, and for many kinds of foundations direct lobbying is illegal. But advocacy and policy work are powerful tools for change, so catalytic philanthropists find innovative ways to influence government action.

The philanthropist Emily Tow Jackson might seem an unlikely prison system reformer. She runs her parents' family foundation, based in affluent New Canaan, Connecticut. Historically, the Tows had funded mainly medical research and professorships at their alma maters. But when Tow Jackson and her siblings joined the foundation board, they pushed for a focus on vulnerable youth and families. While they were exploring funding opportunities, the local case of a young girl who dropped out of middle school and needed special care, but instead got locked up in a juvenile detention center, launched Tow Jackson into the unfamiliar role of policy provocateur.

A TALE OF TWO EMILYS

"Emily J.," the child of a homeless, single mother, was thirteen years old when she was arrested in Connecticut in 1993. After her arrest she was incarcerated for truancy at the Bridgeport Juvenile Detention Center. She had been absent from school for two years.

At that time Emily J. had no permanent place to live; her mother was living on the streets and her father was missing. So she was detained in Bridgeport until the court could determine what to do with her next.[1]

At the detention center Emily J. was confined to a small cell with two other girls sometimes for more than twenty-one hours a day. Ventilation was poor and breathing difficult. The cell had no toilet, so Emily J. urinated on the floor. When she did this, she was punished and placed in separate confinement. Locked away alone for up to three days at a time, she was left to eat in her cell and received no educational services. When finally released from her cell, she spent much of her time in a crowded dayroom that also served as an education and recreation area. Other than playing cards, there was little to do.

Emily J.'s case was not unique that summer. Hundreds of other boys and girls, teens and tweens, languished in Connecticut's three hot, overcrowded, underventilated detention centers. Sexual and other assaults were prevalent. Medical and mental health services were inadequate at best. Adolescents locked in one facility spent the entire summer seldom breathing fresh air. Some children, including Emily J., cried themselves to sleep at night.

Nearly every adolescent in these centers came from a low-income family.[2] Some of the young people jailed in these abject facilities had committed serious offenses, such as robbery or assault. But the majority of the detainees had not committed any crime. Like Emily J., they were charged with *status offenses*—skipping school, writing graffiti, running away from home or a shelter.

These conditions came to light in the summer of 1993 when Attorney Martha Stone of the Center for Children's Advocacy at the University of Connecticut School of Law filed a class action lawsuit on Emily J.'s behalf: *Emily J.* v. *Weicker*. The suit set off an extensive, complex series of court and legislative battles joined by litigators, advocates, and nonprofit leaders. Collectively they lobbied Connecticut officials to change the way adolescents were treated in the juvenile justice system. What disturbed the advocates was not just the wretched facilities. As the *Hartford Courant* reported, "It's the missed opportunity to bombard this captive audience of 8-to-16-year-olds with schooling, counseling, and other treatment services to prevent them from becoming the prison population of tomorrow."[3]

ENTER EMILY TOW JACKSON AND THE TOW FOUNDATION

In 1994, soon after the *Emily J.* lawsuit was filed, Emily Tow Jackson was named executive director of The Tow Foundation, created by her parents, Claire and Leonard Tow. Tow Jackson was inspired over the next few years to work with her foundation's board to direct more of their philanthropy toward solving social problems. Although unsure of quite where to begin, she says, "I had my eyes open to the fact that some foundations were doing very intentional work, not just check-writing."[4] Shocked by the facts revealed in the *Emily J.* case and by other juvenile justice statistics, Tow Jackson hosted in 1999 a series of educational roundtables for her foundation's trustees. The speakers included youth service providers, child advocates, court administrators, and state officials involved in all aspects of the juvenile justice system. One presenter was lawyer Martha Stone of the Center for Children's Advocacy, who had mounted the lawsuit.

Tow trustees were deeply disturbed by what they learned as they absorbed detailed accounts about the mistreatment of young people like Emily J. They also came to see evidence that the state's dysfunctional juvenile justice system played a critical role in Connecticut's rising adult imprisonment rates and the growing number of youth with bleak future prospects. The Tow family's home state of Connecticut incarcerated more youth under age eighteen in its adult criminal system than any other state in the United States and had the worst rate of any state of minority overrepresentation in its justice system.[5]

It wasn't that Connecticut youth just happened to be more violent or criminally minded than youth elsewhere. The problem centered on an ill-designed and punitive system that helped to escalate the state's out-of-control crime and incarceration rates. And too often, mere status offenders, like Emily J., were mixed up in that system designed to punish criminals as adults rather than help adolescents who sorely needed treatment in order to escape the destructive spiral that too often leads to further detention and eventually adult imprisonment.

The Tow Foundation board members decided to commit to juvenile justice reform. They realized that although grants to direct-service organizations had an impact on a subset of court-involved youth, the juvenile system itself would need to be reformed if they wanted to have the greatest impact. And this meant the foundation would need to support advocacy. So, in 2001, The Tow Foundation teamed up with Martha Stone and the Center for Children's Advocacy and with two other groups—Connecticut Voices for Children and the Regional Youth/Adult Social Action Partnership (RYASAP)—to form the Connecticut Juvenile Justice Alliance, which The Tow Foundation funded with a start-up grant of $25,000.

One big challenge for advocates for juvenile justice reform in Connecticut was to change the perceptions of state administrators and judicial branch leaders about the problems in their system. At this time, young, urban criminals were depicted in the media as "super-predators," and images of the very worst offenders represented all youth in the juvenile justice system to the public's eye. So any reform proposal that appeared to be "soft on crime" or to "coddle" incarcerated youth would not receive a warm reception. Therefore it would be difficult to argue for changing the system to address the requirements of youth like Emily J., who needed therapeutic, educational and psychological help, without first persuading legislative officials and justice system leaders with facts about what kind of youth really made up the detained and incarcerated juvenile population and the long-term benefits of a more rehabilitative approach.

Breakthrough Sessions

To meet this challenge The Tow Foundation first funded a series of research studies, one of which unveiled some surprising statistics about the youth detained in the state's largest city, Bridgeport—most important was the fact that the vast majority of detainees were merely status offenders (like Emily J.), rather than violent criminals, and therefore in need not of a high-security prison facility but of counseling, a safe and stable home, and other basics. This laid the groundwork for other activities undertaken by the Connecticut Juvenile Justice Alliance.

A key breakthrough came when the alliance hosted annual educational forums at the state capitol for state legislative, judicial and agency leaders. The speakers constituted a national who's who of experts, advocates, and practitioners who had helped to develop more effective practices and systems in other states. One session that was particularly influential featured professor Abigail Baird, a leading researcher on the adolescent brain, a member of the Vassar College faculty at the time, and a recognized national expert on her topic. One of her many influential stories went like this. "Imagine you have a shark tank, and a bunch of adolescents and adults are sitting next to it. You ask both groups, would you jump in? The adults say 'no' in a millisecond. But the kids ask questions: Have the sharks eaten recently? Could I take a friend? It takes young people *almost 10 times* as long to make that decision. Most opt not to take the risk, but a few of them will say they'd actually jump in."[6]

What Baird conveyed to the state officials was that the adolescent brain is clinically different from a fully mature adult mind. Young people make judgments differently from adults and they are far more prone to take risks. So treating these kids as if they were adults and punishing them for minor offenses without providing treatment or helping them learn new habits was nonsensical.

Connecticut officials began to see detained kids in a new light and to see the need for treatment rather than punishment, for juvenile offenders. The Tow Foundation and other alliance members were soon invited to participate and sometimes lead statewide committees addressing juvenile justice matters. One committee was charged with developing a statewide juvenile justice strategic plan; others with proposing changes to state policies to better address the needs of status offenders and girls. Meanwhile, Tow Jackson and other alliance members called on media contacts to encourage publication of hard-hitting articles and opinion pieces that advanced the alliance's agenda.

Within a decade alliance members, working collectively, had won a series of policy changes. One, in 2007, was a new state mandate that all children who were truants, runaways, or otherwise status offenders were to receive services in the community and be handled outside the juvenile delinquency process. This new law meant that young people like Emily J. would no longer be locked up in punitive jail cells and instead would receive alternative treatments and services. Another law raised the age of juvenile court jurisdiction from sixteen to eighteen, so that more young people would be treated in alternative settings with age-appropriate services.

As a result, by 2009, Connecticut had invested $39 million in community and family-based services for court-involved youth—an enormous increase over the $300,000 the state had been spending in 2000 on these types of services. During the same period, referrals to juvenile court dropped by more than one-third (from more than 20,000 to approximately 13,000), and the number of youth convicted and removed from their communities dropped by almost two-thirds. And now Connecticut is recognized nationally as an innovative leader in handling juvenile cases, rather than as a leading incarcerator of minors.[7]

WHERE CREDIT IS DUE

No one would give sole credit to The Tow Foundation for these advancements in Connecticut's juvenile justice system. And today, even though The Tow Foundation gives about $1.5 million annually to juvenile justice nonprofits—a field that most donors still avoid—a majority of its funds, nearly $7 million, go to support other causes such as medical research and the family's alma maters. In so doing, The Tow Foundation maintains a portfolio approach to its giving (a concept we explored in Chapter Two). But its greatest impact comes from nonfinancial contributions: the sweat equity, knowledge of best practices, national and local networks, relationships, and decade of near full-time perseverance that Tow Jackson and her staff have contributed to reform the state's juvenile justice system.

What can be fully credited to Tow Jackson is the help she gave to her board in order to *transform* this family foundation from a traditional grantmaker into a powerful force for policy change. Without becoming a lawyer and with minimal knowledge about court-involved youth, Tow Jackson became a leading player in legislative and policy reform. She did this because she recognized that if her foundation wanted to help a young person like Emily J., the system would need to change. And to change the system, as Tow Jackson recognized, The Tow Foundation needed to advocate to change the rules that governed it.

EMBRACING ADVOCACY

High-impact donors like Emily Tow Jackson eventually embrace advocacy, but many other individual funders and foundations eschew it. "Spines stiffen when you talk about advocacy and public policy . . . even among friends," says one community foundation CEO.[8] Some funders confuse advocacy with policy lobbying and avoid it because they mistakenly believe that lobbying is illegal for nonprofits.

Others perceive lobbying to be distasteful or "unclean."[9] And for many, advocacy conjures images of protestors gone wild—hooded "black bloc" activists outside World Trade Organization meetings; Earth Firsters chaining themselves to trees; family values campaigners staging protests outside the Argentinian Senate to persuade senators to vote down a new gay marriage law; Tea Party activists boiling anti-Obama campaigns.

Whether due to fundamental ideological differences, hyperbolized myth, or simple misunderstandings about the legalities of lobbying, funders often shy away from mixing advocacy and philanthropy. For understandable reasons, most funders are more comfortable simply writing checks to direct-service organizations and feeling good that their money produced tangible results like clothing and sheltering a homeless person or building a community theater.

But *catalytic donors*—such as the ones we mentioned in Chapter One and exemplified by Emily Tow Jackson—are different from average givers. It's not that they don't want to feel good—they do. But they feel better when they try to leverage their philanthropic resources to the highest possible levels of impact. This often leads them into advocacy. In addition to The Tow Foundation's work, consider these other, more celebrated examples of donor advocacy. Particularly renowned are conservative funders such as the Olin, Bradley, and Scaife Foundations, who systematically have seeded and nurtured a new crop of right-wing policy thinkers and established think tanks, including the influential Heritage Foundation, to house them. Their efforts bore fruit with the election of President Reagan to two terms and the election to the presidency of both George H. Bush and George W. Bush, and built the foundation for the "Republican revolution" of 1994 under House Speaker Newt Gingrich. More recently, the Koch brothers have poured tens of millions of dollars into funding the Tea Party movement that has altered the political climate for the 2010 U.S. congressional elections. Over toward the political left, philanthropies like the Moriah and Needmor Funds and the Gill Foundation are recognized for advancing progressive policy reform agendas and social justice advocacy—protecting reproductive rights, fighting poverty, and advancing lesbian, gay, bisexual, and transgender issues, among others.[10]

Yet it's hard to point to many family foundations deeply involved in advocacy. Indeed, whether private, community, or corporate, most foundations avoid it for similar reasons: fear, misunderstanding, and basic distaste for anything that smacks of activism or the "L" word—lobbying. Much of this is fueled by misperceptions about what advocacy is and how much of it is allowed. So before sharing other examples of the ways in which different types of foundations embrace it, let's first define advocacy.

WHAT IS ADVOCACY?

In its broadest sense, the term *advocacy* refers to activism around an issue, such as climate change or free trade or youth justice. It involves a spectrum of activities that range from educating and mobilizing voters to pitching media stories and raising public awareness to directly influencing elected officials. Sometimes the goal is to change laws and influence other public acts; at other times it is to change public behavior. *Policy advocacy*, also known as *lobbying*, refers to specific efforts to change public policy or obtain government funding for a social program. Much of the confusion among funders lies in the difference between *lobbying*, which in the United States is a prohibited activity for most types of foundations, and *advocacy*, which is an all-encompassing term for a whole range of activities, one of which is lobbying[11] (see Table 3.1).

TABLE 3.1. LOBBYING IN THE UNITED STATES.

This Is Lobbying	This Is Not Lobbying
• Direct lobbying: communication with a legislator (federal, state, or local) or legislative staff member that refers to specific legislation and takes a position on that legislation • Grassroots lobbying: communication with the public that refers to specific legislation, reflects a view of that legislation, and contains a call to action	• Convening nonprofits and decision makers to discuss social, economic, and other issues not tied to specific legislation • Educating legislators about broad issues • Conducting public education campaigns that do not include calls to action or mention specific legislation • Building relationships with legislators; helping grantees build and sustain relationships • Influencing officials in the executive branch of federal, state, or local government—such as U.S. mayors, governors, or the president; cabinet members; and administrative agency leaders—to adopt specific policies • Nonpartisan analysis, study, or research • Litigation, such as signing on to amicus briefs or filing lawsuits • Training grantees how to lobby • Regulatory efforts • Self-defense lobbying, such as advocating for changes to legislation that directly affect the philanthropy industry

Source: Alliance for Justice, *Investing in Change: A Funder's Guide to Supporting Advocacy* (Washington D.C.: Alliance for Justice, 2004), pp. 5–10.

Outside the United States other patterns are found. Lobbying is unlikely to be welcome in totalitarian societies. But in democratic countries other than the United States it is typically lightly regulated, if at all. For example, at the time of writing, there were no binding legal restrictions on lobbying the European Commission at all, though lobbyists were subject to voluntary registration. Providing a comprehensive global assessment of legal frameworks for advocacy is beyond the scope of this book. In the remainder of this chapter we focus on U.S. legislation, which is both well documented and relatively restrictive. Whether based in the United States or other countries, donors engaged in advocacy should seek legal counsel to understand the specific parameters that apply to their situation.

Figure 3.1 depicts examples of the range of activities entailed in advocacy.

Most donors can conduct nearly all the advocacy activities depicted in Figure 3.1 as long as they follow prescribed legal parameters. The main exception is that private foundations, which include most family foundations, are *not* allowed to either fund or engage in direct lobbying, but they can make general operating grants to nonprofits that directly lobby. Conversely, public foundations such as most community foundations are allowed both to

FIGURE 3.1. ADVOCACY HAS MANY DIMENSIONS.

engage in lobbying themselves *and* to fund nonprofits that lobby. For a summary of the ways that The Tow Foundation engaged in many of the advocacy activities depicted in Figure 3.1, see the sidebar "How The Tow Foundation Advocated."

How The Tow Foundation Advocated

The Tow Foundation story shows how one family foundation participated in a broad range of activities that could be described generally as *advocacy*. The only action the foundation explicitly avoided was direct lobbying (which is prohibited for private foundations chartered in the United States). The Tow Foundation advocated in the following ways:

- **Funding and participating in collaborations**. Much of The Tow Foundation's advocacy was tied to its annual funding of and active involvement in the Connecticut Juvenile Justice Alliance. Through the alliance The Tow Foundation could give general funds to an organization that directly lobbied for policy change without lobbying itself, and Tow Jackson could also engage personally in general advocacy, such as educating legislative and system leaders, serving on state task forces, meeting with elected officials and taking other actions.

- **Educating legislators and justice system leaders**. Members of the Connecticut Juvenile Justice Alliance had determined that many of the state's elected officials were not highly knowledgeable about young offenders and how they were being ill-treated in the detention system. Because Tow Jackson was involved in national juvenile justice reform networks and was constantly reviewing other states' strategies to glean and bring home best practices, she and her staff were able to convince many experts to come to Connecticut to brief state leaders on the issues and share leading national reform strategies.

- **Participating on local and state government committees**. Tow Foundation staff were invited by the State of Connecticut to participate and take leadership positions on committees addressing juvenile justice matters. Through this committee work The Tow Foundation actively promoted and contributed to the development of a statewide juvenile justice strategic plan and supported advocates to lay the groundwork that led to legislative change that raised the age of juvenile court jurisdiction from sixteen to eighteen.

- **Raising public awareness through media**. The Tow Foundation and the alliance cultivated media coverage of juvenile justice issues in Connecticut. They drafted and pitched editorials that appeared in media like the *Hartford Courant* and the *New York Times*, among others. The foundation also sponsored trainings for its grantees to learn how to better tell their stories and advocate on behalf of their clients.

- **Giving general operating support to nonprofits**. The Tow Foundation funded an array of juvenile justice groups, including direct-service providers—agencies that previously had relied primarily on government support—and advocacy groups. Many grants were for general operating support, so grantees could use them to reduce the need to fundraise specifically for advocacy—and The Tow Foundation actively encouraged its grantees to advocate and lobby to the full extent laws would permit to advance the cause of youth like Emily J.

So What Holds Most Donors Back?

Although The Tow Foundation's story is inspiring, advocacy is unfortunately rare among private family foundations—just as it is among other types of foundations, including corporate and community philanthropies. Their resistance isn't due only to misperceptions about lobbying or fear of activism. Other reasons for the holdup are connected to the internal makeup of the different kinds of foundations and how they are governed and funded.

Corporate foundations, for instance, exist through the generosity of the companies that host them. They are understandably concerned with protecting and enhancing their company's brand and reputation. So risky projects, those with even a hint of radicalism on either side of the ideological aisle, will be unpalatable to most corporate philanthropists. The same goes for community foundations, which are public charities created with the funding of numerous local donors who have other choices of where to place their funds. As a result, many community foundations fund many disparate causes to satisfy the preferences of each of their donors and address the myriad causes in their regions—and at the same time shy away from supporting direct lobbying.

As for family foundations, they are chartered as private foundations and governed primarily by family members. Because most of them are modest in size and employ few or no program staff, the time and mind-share that advocacy requires present a high hurdle. Moreover, it's often difficult for family foundation board members to rally around a single cause. As discussed in the Jacobs Family Foundation example in Chapter Two, trustees who represent different generations and political views can bring conflicting agendas to their board service. This can lead to disagreements over pet projects and sibling spats and can prevent the board members from coming to agreement on, and committing to, advancing a central cause.

Despite these internal barriers, foundations representing every type of legal incorporation have overcome the advocacy aversion we have just described. In the next sections we explore examples of these corporate, community, and large private foundations that have advocated for change.

CORPORATE LOBBYING—THE GOOD KIND

When Jim Rohr became chairman and CEO of PNC Financial Services Group in 2000, he found himself unexpectedly facing a host of problems, including bad debt and some questionable accounting procedures that had attracted the negative attention of the U.S. Securities and Exchange Commission. According to a Harvard Business School case,[12] Rohr set out to overhaul the PNC's performance through reorganized business operations, more robust risk management, and targeted public relations. It might not seem like the best time to have introduced a potentially risky, new community affairs program that would put PNC's leadership into the unfamiliar role of advocacy for outside causes, but Rohr did it anyway.

It started with his vision for uniting PNC's many disparate giving initiatives. "Wouldn't it be amazing if we could focus the power of PNC behind one cause?" said Rohr to the director of community affairs and chair of the PNC Foundation, Eva Tansky Blum. Until that point, Blum explains, the firm had conducted its philanthropy "like most large, multi-state companies," with the PNC executives in each market essentially running the company's local giving programs and scattering grants across issues ranging from arts to health, education, and civic affairs. Rohr tasked Blum with consulting with employees and other key stakeholders to come up with a cause that all could rally around, and then devising a program leveraging each of the company's assets to advance that cause.

The result was Grow Up Great, a $100 million, ten-year initiative in early childhood education launched in 2003. The campaign consisted of a range of offerings including executive-level state and national advocacy forays as well as traditional grantmaking and volunteered employee time. To inform its understanding of the issue and shape the advocacy agenda, PNC assembled an interdisciplinary advisory council of nationally renowned experts and developed partnerships with leading nonprofits that were addressing early childhood education through initiatives such as Head Start and *Sesame Street*. One key goal was to convince policymakers at the state and federal levels not to dismiss early childhood education as "glorified day care" but instead to treat it as a serious concern with real influence on workforce and economic issues.

Although some states have aggressively supported early childhood programs, in 2003 PNC's home state of Pennsylvania still did not fund early childhood education at all or supplement Head Start funding. The personal advocacy of Rohr and of the firm's regional presidents in that state contributed to the passage of $75 million in funding for a Pennsylvania program called Pre-K Counts, funding that resulted in an additional 12,000 children receiving preschool education. In other states PNC regional presidents participated in similar advocacy forays, aided by Tom Lamb, PNC's senior vice president and manager of government relations, who, in addition to handling corporate lobbying for the firm, tracks early education policy issues and helps train and support executives.

Today PNC is more than halfway through its Grow Up Great program and initial results are promising. In March 2005, Pennsylvania governor Edward Rendell invited Jim Rohr to serve with him in chairing the Partnership for Quality Pre-Kindergarten, and Rohr accepted. This public-private partnership funds block grants that help school districts with a high percentage of at-risk children to create or improve their pre-K programs. In 2006, the group's name changed to Pre-K Counts, and Jim Rohr continued to cochair with Governor Rendell. In 2009, Pre-K Counts evolved into the Pennsylvania Early Learning Investment Commission.

Again, Rohr served as honorary chair with Rendell. Made up of business leaders from across the state, the commission seeks support for public investment in early learning.

These achievements come at a time when, since Rohr first took the helm, PNC as a whole is also doing much better. PNC is one of the few financial firms to have avoided involvement in the collapse of the subprime mortgage market, and it was in such a strong position at the time the recession of 2008 hit that it was able to acquire its larger competitor, Cleveland-based National City Corporation, becoming the sixth largest bank in the United States. Even though there was risk, PNC's efforts to advocate for change as well as fund early childhood education programs appear to be paying off.

THE DOWNSIDE OF CORPORATE LOBBYING

Despite PNC's successful forays into advocating for early childhood education, most companies and their foundations are not often to be found acting as leading advocates for important public causes. Mention *corporate* and *lobbying* together in this post-Enron world, and images of backroom deals by slick industry lobbyists flash before people's eyes. And even those corporations with kinder, greener practices sometimes support legislation that directly contradicts their socially responsible images. For example, Toyota, creator of the eco-friendly Prius, joined other carmakers to lobby against tougher fuel economy standards in the United States.[13] When it comes to advancing the public good, nonprofit advocates are often the lonely frontrunners in the fight for policy change.

This is unfortunate because corporations, with their carefully cultivated connections, wider lobbying leeway, and proficiency in influence, are often better equipped to make the case for causes than their nonprofit counterparts are. Consider that in 2006 alone, U.S. companies spent a record $2.6 billion on federal lobbying. Meanwhile, for the entire period between 1998 and 2004, nonprofit organizations spent only $222 million on federal lobbying.[14] Spread over six years, that's a pittance for lobbying toward the public good compared with the amounts spent on promoting corporate industry interests.

In contrast to most nonprofits, companies often represent thousands of voters—their employees—and help to create the tax base on which governments run. They can leverage their vast brand recognition and marketing channels to broadcast policy messages. They can reach beyond their own operations to mobilize entire industries, including supply chain partners and downstream buyers. They can multiply the power of their social advocacy by forming business coalitions. And ironically, they can lobby more liberally than nonprofits and private foundations, which face tighter governmental restrictions[15] (see Table 3.2).

TABLE 3.2. Summary of Legal Restrictions on Advocacy in the United States.

	What They Can and Cannot Do	What They Can Fund
Private foundations	• *Cannot lobby.* • *Can conduct nonpartisan research*; discuss broad social issues without referencing specific legislation; *perform self-defense lobbying*; *provide technical assistance*, including legal testimony related to specific legislation.	• *Cannot make grants earmarked for lobbying activities.* • *Can make grants to organizations that lobby*, such as general support grants and grants designated for a specific project that involves some lobbying as long as the grant is less than the amount budgeted for the nonlobbying parts of the project.
Corporate foundations	• Have the same restrictions as other private foundations (see above). • Corporate giving program employees are not subject to these lobbying restrictions and may communicate with public officials about legislation of interest to the company.	• Have the same rules as private foundations.

TABLE 3.2. SUMMARY OF LEGAL RESTRICTIONS ON ADVOCACY IN THE UNITED STATES (*continued*).

	What They Can and Cannot Do	What They Can Fund
501(c)(3) public charities (community foundations and nonprofits)	• *Can engage in lobbying* as long as "no substantial part" of their activities consists of lobbying. • The IRS has not made a clear ruling about what constitutes a "substantial part," and thus public charities can opt to be governed by the IRS's lobbying expenditure test (Section 501[h] of the Internal Revenue Code), which provides concrete guidance on what a charity can spend on lobbying.	• Community foundations are governed by the same restrictions as 501(c)(3) nonprofits.
501(c)(4) advocacy organizations (for example, the Sierra Club)	• *Can engage in lobbying* or political campaigning.	• N/A.

Source: Grantmakers Forum of New York. *How Can Foundations Engage in Advocacy & Lobbying?* (Rochester, N.Y.: Forum of Regional Associations of Grantmakers, 2006).

Of course, companies aren't compelled to advocate out of pure altruism. For example, in exchange for its efforts, PNC has not only gained the satisfaction of advancing the educational and life chances for children, it has also garnered new opportunities to get to know elected officials outside of its regular course of industry lobbying. Internally, advocacy campaigns provide a big boost to employee morale. And sometimes, a company's campaigns for the greater good can directly improve the organization's financial bottom line.

COMMUNITY FOUNDATIONS: AN EMERGING FORCE FOR POLICY CHANGE

Community foundations occupy a unique position in the philanthropy world. In some ways they are more akin to nonprofit agencies than to their private and corporate foundation peers. Unlike most endowed private foundations or corporate philanthropies that receive funding from a single source, community foundations raise funds from multiple donors year to year (just as operating nonprofits do). They are therefore accountable to multiple stakeholders—their many donors, the nonprofits that they fund, and the community members who live in their region. Despite the fact that community foundations, as public charities, have more leeway to lobby than private foundations do, community foundations face perhaps the steepest barriers to advocacy. As one CEO put it, "Community foundations are sensitive to wanting to be loved and not take risks."[16]

That barrier notwithstanding, one of the funders most skilled at advocacy and policy change is the New Hampshire Charitable Foundation (NHCF), a statewide community foundation. The foundation engaged in advocacy campaigns under the leadership of foundation president Lew Feldstein, fostering remarkable policy wins in a political environment that was not always friendly to progressive policy reform. To understand why these efforts were so noteworthy, it's important to understand two key parts of the backstory: the state and the man.

The frugal, no-nonsense, fiercely independent "Live Free or Die" State of New Hampshire has historically been main street conservative. In recent years New Hampshire has shifted to swing state status, albeit with a distinct libertarian flavor.

The man, Lew Feldstein, is a self-described "liberal Jew from New York," appointed president of NHCF in 1986. Feldstein was a veteran of the civil rights movement in Mississippi who had worked for liberal New York mayor John Lindsay. Feldstein had moved to New Hampshire during the back-to-the-land movement to raise his family.[17] During his job interview with NHCF foundation trustees, Feldstein described his passion for social justice and his policy credentials. With the support of a segment of the board open to risking new approaches, Feldstein went on to transform what was essentially a traditional community foundation that funded primarily local direct-service nonprofits into a powerful force for public policy change.

Beginning in 1987, Feldstein played a major role in creating funding and building political support for the Trust for New Hampshire Lands, which ultimately resulted in the conservation of 100,000 acres across the state. The effort doubled the total area of protected land outside the White Mountains. "Not since the creation of the White Mountain National Forest in 1911 had there been such an ambitious conservation undertaking in New Hampshire," says an Aspen Institute case study.[18] The trust launched a public-private partnership that protected the land, using $50 million in public funds and almost as large an amount of private matches in cash and contributed land.

Feldstein and the foundation went on to tackle other issues, such as teen alcohol abuse, which was the number one problem facing New Hampshire teens. Through savvy policy work, by 2001 NHCF had helped to secure a 180 percent increase in the allocation of state funds for treatment and prevention of underage drinking. Feldstein and other senior NHCF staff eventually even registered as lobbyists. These state-funded programs and major policy changes were tough sells in the Granite State, where periodic protests are still mounted to resist seat belt and motorcycle helmet laws, and broad-based taxes are simply not tolerated.

How did Feldstein do it? "I don't want to overstate my role," explains Feldstein. Many players from public, private, and nonprofit organizations contributed to these and other policy pushes. In the case of the land trust, it was the then-president of the Society for the Protection of New Hampshire Forests, Paul Bofinger, who devised the plan to create the trust. The community foundation provided the seed money but also, equally important, brought "the foundation's connections and Feldstein's political know-how to help secure the support of the governors and the legislature."[19] Feldstein personally testified before the legislature and chaired the task forces that would establish criteria for which the land could be saved. He also joined in conversations with then-governor John Sununu.

FOCUS ON THE CAUSE

A key lesson Feldstein learned was that placing advocacy at the center of a community foundation's agenda required diplomacy. Feldstein had catapulted into action in his first year on the job, meeting with policy leaders across New Hampshire and boldly stating his intention to pursue policy change. His pronouncements were not well received. Feldstein recalls his board chair telling him about receiving calls from constituents saying, "Why did you hire this guy? We didn't give our money to the foundation to spend it on government issues."[20]

He gained traction when he focused attention on the desired outcome—preserving the land Yankees loved—rather than the process of changing policy. "It was instructive that the same people who were furious at me for the general proposition of the Foundation being involved with public policy thought that it was perfectly all right for us to be involved with advocacy for public lands," reflects Feldstein.[21] That's when it clicked. By focusing on the cause—in this case, land identified by the public as significant—Feldstein was able to accomplish much more than when he touted the general concept of advocacy, which was perceived as threatening when it was divorced from its purpose.

This lesson is so ingrained at NHCF that today there is scant mention of policy advocacy in the foundation's materials. "Now [it's] called 'civic leadership,' not public policy," explains Feldstein. For a case in point visit the foundation's Web site, where you will see that there is not a single mention of "advocacy" or "public policy" anywhere on the home page or several layers into the site. Click on the home page tab labeled "Civic Leadership," and the following description appears: "For two decades, the foundation has been engaged in public issues, from substance abuse to land use. Our approach is apolitical and nonpartisan. Our only interest is improving quality of life."[22] This is diplomatic language for an "apolitical" approach that has been a powerful (if sometimes invisible) force for significant legislative change in the great independent state of New Hampshire.

It's also instructive that NHCF achieved success on a range of policy issues—from the environment and teenage drinking to prison reform, public education, affordable housing, energy policy, and state park management, among others. It shows that donor advocates need not be subject-matter experts in their issue area and that a foundation can advance more than one cause over time. Feldstein advises: "When you pick the issue, it's less important to do a huge macro needs analysis—there could be 20 or 30 issues that are important. Pick one to start and pick one that will work ... [one that you know will have] good partners, a history of concern, some momentum around the issue."[23]

Feldstein also observes that advocacy can occur in degrees. "This is not an 'on-and-off' switch. Even when you do grant-making, you're involved in policy to some degree through your funding decisions.... It's more like a dimmer switch."[24] Moving up the advocacy scale entails ascending steps of involvement, which we summarize for this practice and the others in Appendix E, "Getting Started with Catalytic Philanthropy."

LARGE PRIVATE FOUNDATIONS: A LONG POLITICAL HISTORY

One type of foundation is more prone than the others to support advocacy—the elite class of very large private foundations that operate from asset bases of $1 billion or more and give away tens or hundreds of millions in grants each year. These enormous philanthropies are robustly staffed, led by mostly nonfamily members, and governed by boards made up mainly of diverse professionals. Well-known U.S. examples include the Ford, MacArthur, and Rockefeller Foundations, and some examples in Europe are the Wellcome Trust in the United Kingdom, the Robert Bosch Stiftung in Germany, and the Calouste Gulbenkian Foundation in Portugal. The Bill & Melinda Gates Foundation and the David and Lucille Packard Foundation are also in this category; they are also family foundations, with donors or family members controlling their boards. Large private philanthropies like these tend to be more comfortable with funding advocacy because they have relatively big staffs of trained professionals who often possess deep issue expertise and social sector experience, so they are often quite familiar with the inner workings of the social sector.

The Ford and Mott Foundations are noted leaders in funding social policy change. Both were featured in Crutchfield and McLeod Grant's book *Forces for Good* as significant supporters of high-impact nonprofits like National Council of La Raza, Youth-Build USA, and the Center on Budget and Policy Priorities, each of these nonprofits engages both in policy advocacy and in running direct-service programs on the ground. In the peer survey conducted to surface nominations of catalytic funders for this book, the Ford Foundation was highlighted particularly for the time from 1979 to 1996 when it was under the leadership of Frank Thomas and for providing significant funds for groups leading the civil rights movement and seeding much of the community development field. The foundation's involvement was so extensive that its activities motivated the U.S. Congress to pass the 1969 Tax Reform Act, which for the first time taxed and regulated U.S. foundation grantmaking activities.

Of course with great heft come trade-offs: it's hard to steer big bureaucracies through a few narrow issues channels, and large foundations will often spread their funding across a range of issues and causes—resulting in the continued scattered giving approach of many foundations. The Robert Wood Johnson Foundation is a notable exception, as it has maintained a focus on advancing health and well-being since its inception, and the Gates Foundation is famously trying to tackle a few key issues in global health and U.S. education. But even with a strategic focus, it's difficult to harness all of a foundation's programs and steer them toward achieving significant outcomes that entail not just *funding* but also *actively participating* in advocacy, as The Tow Foundation, New Hampshire Charitable Foundation, and PNC examples illustrate.

To overcome the advocacy obstacles faced by large bureaucratic foundations, the pioneering Pew Charitable Trusts took a radical step and legally changed its charitable status from foundation to public charity. The Pew Charitable Trusts wanted to focus on solving problems and to engage only in those activities that would "move the needle" on key social and environmental issues, according to its president Rebecca Rimel.[25] (Pew qualified as a public charity due to its unique circumstances—seven charitable trusts had been established by four siblings; that makes Pew unlike most private foundations, which are funded by a sole source.) As a result of this change, instead of *outsourcing* its social and environmental change efforts to nonprofits by giving out grants, Pew could *insource* projects and take on campaigns itself. Like the

"Artist formerly known as Prince," who shed his legal name to gain greater control of the proceeds of his artistry, Pew adopted a new legal status so that it could exert more operating and advocacy muscle.

CONCLUSION

So what do The Tow Foundation, PNC, and New Hampshire Charitable Foundation cases reveal? Individually, they show that

- A small Connecticut family foundation can make a big impact on how at-risk young people are treated by a state-wide system.
- Government affairs and corporate foundation leaders can leverage their vast resources, political connections, public goodwill, and brand recognition on behalf of important social and environmental causes.
- Community foundations can fund and conduct policy change campaigns without alienating their supporters.

Collectively, these stories demonstrate that there are many paths to advocacy and that, no matter what the starting point, leaders can move their foundations from no or low levels of policy activity to higher ones. Even though advocacy may still not be comfortable for every donor, it is possible for philanthropists to proactively advocate for systemic change in ways that fall well within U.S. legal limits. For donors new to advocacy, Appendix E offers examples of beginning steps that can help you to put a toe in the water; this step can be as simple as removing restrictive language from grant award letters or providing general operating support to groups that advocate as well as provide direct services. Suggestions for experienced donors on diving into more advanced, sophisticated campaigns are also included there. Of course a donor's ability to achieve success requires that he or she can skillfully execute advocacy-related activities, but we believe that these skills can be *learned*. What's *essential* is a donor's willingness to commit to a cause and openness to deploying advocacy in a critical line of attack against a pressing problem.

KEY PRINCIPLES FOR DONOR ADVOCACY

1. **Previous policy experience is not required**. Although some
   donors may go so far as to register as lobbyists or may already
   have extensive legal experience, most foundation leaders bring
   no prior policy experience. But this does not need to hold you
   back from becoming involved with advocacy. Funding research
   to reveal new facts or perspectives on an issue and hosting
   speakers and educational seminars for key political decision
   makers are two ways donors can have a significant impact on
   policy initiatives without engaging in direct lobbying.

2. **Relentless persistence and a long-term view are required**.
   Policy change does not happen overnight; it can be fraught
   with delays. Political officials and appointees change or are
   voted out of office and public attitudes and priorities can shift
   almost spontaneously, so donors who aim to achieve policy
   wins must remain committed with their funding, their time,
   and their mind-share. Additionally, a thick skin and
   perseverance in spite of failure are helpful traits; many donors
   make blunders in their first attempts at policy change but they
   keep trying and often are successful in subsequent campaigns.

3. **Leverage every asset—not just the financial ones**. The
   foundations and corporations described in this book drew as
   much on their political and social connections and their
   growing knowledge of issues as they did on their financial
   coffers. For instance, corporations often possess enormous
   scale, clout, high-level connections, and a broad geographical
   footprint, things that nonprofits often lack (an issue we
   explore further in Chapter Four). Corporate foundations can
   leverage those nonfinancial assets to garner favor with political
   leaders. Likewise, trustees of private and family foundations
   operate from a position of wealth and prestige, so they can
   often obtain access to decision makers when local nonprofits
   cannot.

4. **Make lobbying just one arrow in the donor advocacy quiver**.
   Funders can support research, educational seminars, and
   other events that build awareness and increase understanding
   of an issue among the public and policy leaders. In Chapter
   Five we explore how donors forge and participate in peer
   networks with nonprofits and other funders to achieve more

impact. Networks are essential to running effective advocacy campaigns—including lobbying for specific policy changes—and also to building awareness and other general advocacy activities.

5. **Give credit where it is due—to the collective**. Donors can grow accustomed to hearing platitudes such as "your grant made all the difference," or "we wouldn't be here without you." Really? Although these expressions of gratitude might be genuine and they make you feel good, it's rarely true that a single donor has been responsible for the success of any one nonprofit or initiative. Advocacy campaigns succeed because of collective contributions. So donors seeking the immediate gratification of direct praise for their grantmaking and on-the-ground efforts will be disappointed. But donors who take their gratification when laws are remade, entire systems are changed, and better outcomes achieved will be happy with advocacy. The name of the game in policy change is *contribution* not *attribution*, as it is for most work that entails changing systems. (We explore how this affects foundation evaluation in Chapter Eight.)

CHAPTER FOUR

PRACTICE 2
Blend Profit with Purpose

The power of private enterprise can be harnessed to drive social and environmental impact when businesses use the scale, the clout, and the political connections that their nonprofit counterparts sometimes lack.

It used to be simple: if you wanted to make money, you invested in business; if you wanted to solve social problems, you contributed to charity. Unfortunately, if social issues ever divided quite so neatly, they certainly don't anymore.

The fact is that you can increase the funding and effectiveness of the nonprofit sector as much as you like, but you can't solve most social issues without engaging business. You can't lift people out of poverty without creating jobs, and you can't create jobs without growing profitable and competitive companies. You can't fight global warming by reducing greenhouse gas emissions without persuading utilities and transportation companies to change their behaviors. And you can't improve health care without the cooperation of pharmaceutical companies, insurance companies, and health care providers—nearly all of whom are out to make a profit.

You might think it is unfortunate that social problems can't be solved by the nonprofit sector alone, but it turns out that business has a lot to offer as a vehicle for social progress.

TABLE 4.1. DONORS ENGAGE BUSINESS IN THREE WAYS.

	Tap Corporate Know-How	Create Shared Value	Invest for Impact
Description	• Deploy business skills, knowledge, and other nonfinancial resources for social impact.	• Pursue profit in ways that advance social and environmental objectives.	• Invest capital to generate financial returns from enterprises that create social and environmental impact.
Types of activity	*Partner and coach.* Provide technical help to grantees or investees. *Extend corporate skills.* Deploy core corporate skills such as Six Sigma processes to solve social problems.	*Build businesses that solve social problems.* Pursue for-profit opportunities that address issues such as access to clean water, energy efficiency, or employment creation in vulnerable communities.	*Invest in conventional instruments* that produce market-rate returns while screening for negative impact on mission goals. *Subsidize investments* that generate below market-rate returns but advance mission goals. *Make transformative investments* that are risky or innovative but could yield market-rate returns while advancing mission.

First, it is sustainable—a profitable company doesn't need ongoing government or charitable support to keep doing what it does. Second, it can attract the capital to grow faster and larger than any nonprofit ever has. Third, the pressure of for-profit competition has led to innovations in technology, management, and communications that offer tremendously powerful tools to solve social problems.

That's all well and good, you might say, but business has also depleted our natural resources, polluted the air and water, exploited people by forcing them to work in inhuman conditions for inadequate wages, and created vast inequalities of wealth in the world. True enough. Business may not carry the mantle of virtue that endows nonprofits, but that's no reason to write off the positive impact it can create. After all, catalytic philanthropists are trying to use every tool at their disposal to create social progress. Leveraging corporate resources is no exception.

Donors can engage the tools of business in three ways: They can tap corporate know-how to create direct social impact, they can create shared value through profit-making initiatives that serve social objectives, and they can use their investment capital to further their social impact. We will examine each of these approaches and show how a variety of donors—family, private, and community foundations as well as corporate foundations and even corporations themselves—put them into practice.

TAPPING CORPORATE KNOW-HOW

Every successful company counts corporate know-how as one of its strategic assets. This know-how includes the knowledge, skills, and abilities of employees as well as company systems and processes; intellectual property such as patents and trade secrets; and other assets. Know-how drives profits, but it can do more—it can also be deployed to advance social and environmental concerns. Let's look at how three very different types of donors—General Electric, a Fortune 500 company; the Shell Foundation, a $250 million private foundation (initially endowed by Royal Dutch Shell plc); and software entrepreneur Tom Siebel, a high-net-worth individual with a family foundation—tap corporate know-how to drive change.

The Big Company Approach: General Electric

Consider what happened when one of the world's largest corporations, General Electric Company (GE), decided to apply its technology, management skill, and other resources to transform the neonatal intensive care unit (NICU) of the national hospital in Tegucigalpa, Honduras.[1]

Two years ago, if you had walked into this NICU you would have been appalled by what you saw: seventy crying babies, disfigured by severe birth defects, crowded into several shabby rooms. Tiny underweight infants, born prematurely, stacked sideways so that three could be wedged into an incubator designed for one. Broken pieces of donated equipment rusting in the corners. A doctor rarely present because there was little he could do. Look into the eyes of one of the mothers sitting on the hallway floor, and you would know immediately that this was not a place babies were brought to be cured. It was a place for them to die.

Today the NICU operates with world-class standards. The first thing you notice is a central nursing station with enough monitors to track the health of every baby. Look through the glass window and you can see the same doctor, now operating on an infant in a fully equipped surgical theater. The broken and discarded equipment has been replaced by shiny new X-ray and ultrasound machines. Well-trained medical technicians are interpreting ultrasound results wirelessly transmitted from remote rural health clinics, sending back advice that has cut in half the number of premature births that would need to be treated here. The NICU hums with life and hope, and for good reason: today, despite the severity of their birth defects, three-quarters of the babies who come here *survive*.

GE donated money and equipment, of course, just as any donor could. But GE did more than give. The company is a major manufacturer of health care equipment, providing its employees with the expertise to conduct a needs assessment to determine exactly what equipment would best serve the local conditions, the technical capability to ensure that the equipment was properly installed and maintained, and the knowledge to train the staff in how the equipment should be used. Equally important, GE possessed the clout to negotiate with government leaders to provide a budget for the necessary ongoing staffing and maintenance to keep the NICU operating.

Even more compelling is GE's ability to quickly scale up its philanthropic efforts. In the last seven years GE has built or refurbished thirty-seven clinics and hospitals and retrained local staffs in poor communities in Africa, Asia, and Latin America, all without charge. The company continues to open a new clinic every month as part of its $90 million annual budget for philanthropy and product donations. Ask Bob Corcoran, who heads the GE Foundation, why the company decided to take this route, and he'll tell you that they tried to work through nonprofits at first, but they see better, faster, and more sustainable impact on the ground when they leverage GE's know-how to do the philanthropic work themselves.[2]

Every company has powerful assets that can create social impact far beyond what it could produce by just writing checks. A company often has deep expertise in its field, skilled employees, a network of suppliers and other relationships, and in cases like GE's, a global footprint that no foundation or nonprofit could match. When companies use their core business capabilities to tackle social problems, they can often achieve as much or more than any nonprofit. As obvious as this may seem, corporations like GE have only recently begun to embrace their powerful potential as agents of social progress.

The Private Foundation Approach: Shell Foundation

At first glance, Chris West, director of the London-based Shell Foundation, does not appear to be an obvious choice for the directorship of a $250 million endowed foundation spun out of one of the world's most profitable extractive resource companies. When he joined the Shell Foundation as deputy director in 2001, at the age of forty-one, he brought neither expertise in philanthropy nor experience in working for large corporations. His résumé is distinctly devoid of any stint at Royal Dutch Shell plc (the corporate entity that funded the Shell Foundation) in particular.[3]

What West does possess, however, is experience with successfully building and growing small companies and a keen interest in the environment and international development. He started an environmental services sector business in 1984, which expanded across the United Kingdom and internationally. Later, he joined the U.K. Department for International Development as senior environmental advisor. This combination of business know-how and global development experience, as it turns out, prepared him well for heading a foundation that at its core believes in using business savvy to create jobs and improve the standard of living in economically depressed areas.

One of the Shell Foundation's most notable initiatives has been the launch and spin-off of GroFin, a for-profit service provider to small and medium-sized enterprises (SMEs), with a focus on sub-Saharan Africa. Since 2004, GroFin has financed loans to almost 200 businesses—98 percent of which are still operating—along with offering business development assistance to more than 1,200 entrepreneurs, while maintaining an overall default rate on its loans of less than 1 percent. Its success translates into significant socioeconomic benefits: nearly 5,000 sustainable jobs created and maintained and approximately 30,000 improved livelihoods.

What's more, with funds under management today of $250 million, GroFin has effectively established an important new source of financing for start-up and emerging businesses in emerging economies that would otherwise have fallen into the financial market's *missing middle*. After all, large established companies can easily access banks for capital. And so-called barefoot entrepreneurs can now access microfinance—at least since Nobel laureate Muhammad Yunus sparked the worldwide microcredit lending movement with the creation of the Grameen Bank. But not everyone is an entrepreneur, and the jobs created by SMEs are turning out to be one of the key drivers of economic advancement in every economy in the world. The problem is that SMEs fall into the missing middle—they need more money than microfinance can provide, but they aren't yet established enough to be attractive to commercial banks, and they lack the rapid growth potential that might attract venture capital. This "means small and medium-sized businesses are unable to grow, and Africa misses out on a potential engine of economic growth and job creation," explains West. Through GroFin, the Shell Foundation hopes to achieve for SMEs what Yunus created for microentrepreneurs: the creation and promotion of *growth finance* as a new commercial asset class to bridge the missing middle in emerging economies.

What exactly is driving GroFin's success? Chicken feed, for starters. One of GroFin's leading investments is Lima Feeds, a company founded in 2005 by Kenyan entrepreneur Charles Githuka Ngugi. Lima Feeds manufactures food for chickens, pigs, and dairy cows and supplies it to wholesalers, retailers, and individual farmers based in and around Nairobi, Kenya's capital. Each product is a unique mixture of maize, cotton seed, bread dust, coconut cake, and other ingredients. When GroFin first invested in Lima Feeds in 2006, the company was producing about 1,500 70-kg bags animal feed per month—a respectable amount for a small business new to the industry, but not nearly enough to compete with bigger rivals and meet customers' demands. So GroFin staff worked closely with Ngugi to overcome obstacles that were holding his business back.

GroFin gave Lima Feeds loans totaling about US$ 95,000, and GroFin's expert staff provided crucial business guidance that made perhaps an even bigger impact (which we explore further in the next section). With this financial and technical help Lima Feeds grew: Ngugi purchased a delivery truck that he needed to expand sales, and he hired four new staff members—two salespeople, an accountant, and a driver for the truck. As a result, the production and revenues have grown. By 2007, Lima Feeds was producing 2,500 70-kg bags of feed per month and had added several new clients, and sales grew substantially.

Looking ahead, the Shell Foundation has big plans to build on GroFin's early success and to expand to new markets, as it aims to solve Africa's missing middle problem altogether (West prefers not to say *missing middle*, supplanting it with the term *growth finance sector*—a twist of terminology that emphasizes the upside of growth rather than the gap).[4] Following the closure of the US$170 million GroFin Africa Fund in 2009, which enabled the firm to support SMEs in seven countries—Kenya, Uganda, Tanzania, Rwanda, South Africa, Ghana, and Nigeria—the Shell Foundation is currently working with GroFin to expand the provision of growth finance into countries in the Middle East, North Africa, and India, as well Africa.

Of course many private foundations aren't as closely connected to their benefactors' company (or the company that initially endowed the foundation) as the Shell Foundation is to Royal Dutch Shell. But other private foundations can still take advantage of business know-how by hiring the right people with business backgrounds. In later chapters we will discuss the John S. and James L. Knight Foundation's efforts to build informed and engaged communities. The Knight Foundation has no connection to the Knight Ridder company, the newspaper conglomerate that generated the wealth that led the Knight brothers to establish their foundation. (Knight Ridder was bought by the McClatchy Company in 2006 and no longer exists.) So now the Knight Foundation taps into business know-how to advance its mission by hiring and employing former journalists, publishers, and executives from the media industry to lead many of its programs.

THE HIGH-NET-WORTH INDIVIDUAL APPROACH: TOM SIEBEL

Business know-how isn't always institutional, however. Many high-net-worth donors achieved that status because of their own savvy knowledge of finance, management, or marketing, and they have decided to use their experience to guide nonprofits toward greater effectiveness. There's nothing new about business leaders serving on nonprofit boards, but outside the audit and investment committees, most board members seem to leave their business hats at the boardroom door. The tough negotiations, rigorous business plans, and demanding performance reviews that these executives expect in their day jobs are often completely absent from the nonprofit board meetings they attend in the evenings. It sometimes seems as though the good intentions and hard work of nonprofit managers give them a free pass when it comes to financial discipline and measurable results.

Some high-net-worth donors have sought results by creating entirely new nonprofit organizations to design and implement the programs they have devised. Tom Siebel is the founder of the software company Siebel Systems, Inc., and a major philanthropist. While spending time on his Montana ranch, Siebel became concerned about the epidemic of methamphetamine (or meth) abuse in that state. Meth is a highly addictive and physically destructive drug, and at the time, Montana had the fifth worst level of meth abuse among all U.S. states. Half of the state's prison inmates were serving sentences for meth-related crimes, and the direct cost to the state was estimated at nearly $300 million per year. The cost in human lives and suffering was far greater.[5]

Rather than just writing a check to a local nonprofit, Siebel took the time to find out why people become addicted to meth. After learning that first-time users were typically teenagers who were unaware of meth's risks, Siebel decided to create the Meth Project, an initiative to change teenagers' perceptions about the drug. As a long-time marketing expert, Siebel knew how to manage an ad campaign to influence public opinion. By focusing on prevention rather than treatment, Siebel was playing to his strengths. Helping to rehabilitate those already addicted, although an equally important issue, was not an area where Siebel's advertising savvy would have helped. So he brought together top experts from across the country and hired a major San Francisco advertising agency to develop a hard-hitting campaign that would reach 80 percent of Montana teens with at least three media impressions every week.

The ads were world-class: with production budgets of $500,000 to $1 million each, they were directed by leading Hollywood directors such as Alejandro González Iñárritu, director of the Academy Award–nominated film *Babel*. Altogether, the ad campaign has won forty-three awards in national and international advertising competitions, including the Bronze Lion Award at the Cannes International Advertising Festival.

The ads were also gut-wrenching: tested in focus groups to ensure that they would capture a teenager's attention, they were far more brutal than anything the community had seen before. The graphic and often disturbing thirty-second spots begin with an ordinary teen whom kids can relate to, and end by showing the badly scarred and disfigured faces and bodies that come from addiction to meth. Teens are shown attacking and robbing their own families, prostituting themselves, or dying from an overdose. In the voice-over of one ad, a boy describes how his mother has always been there for him, while the screen shows him stealing her purse, hitting her, and kicking her away as she pleads and desperately tries to grab his leg while he runs out the door.

Finally, the ads were pervasive. Because Montana is a relatively small media market, Siebel's $2 million annual advertising budget generated more than 45,000 airings of the TV ads and 35,000 of the radio ads, and ads appeared on 1,000 billboards in the campaign's first two years. That works out to nearly 60 TV ads and 40 radio ads every day during that period. Siebel became the largest single purchaser of advertising in the state, eclipsing even McDonald's Corporation's ad budget.

Between 2005 and 2007, meth use in Montana dropped 45 percent among teens and 72 percent among adults, and meth-related crimes fell 62 percent. Independent surveys showed that the percentage of teenagers who were aware of meth's dangers increased from 25 percent to 93 percent, and that teenagers had even begun to dissuade their friends from trying meth. Montana's ranking in meth abuse among U.S. states fell from fifth to thirty-ninth. And the annual costs of meth to the state dropped by an estimated $100 million.

Siebel has continued the saturation-level campaign for more than four years, renewing its impact by using teen focus groups to develop new advertising campaigns every nine to twelve months. He has convinced other funders to support the campaign, which is now self-sustaining, and he has encouraged schools and community organizations to sponsor anti-meth events. He has personally lobbied Congress to address the meth problem in the United States and has helped six additional states to adopt the Meth Project's program.

These are just a few examples of companies and individuals leveraging corporate know-how. Others are laced throughout this book. In Chapter Five we will explore how donors in the Cincinnati and northern Kentucky region addressed education reform through an initiative called the Strive Partnership. The same Six Sigma process that GE used in planning the renovation of an NICU in Honduras was also employed in Strive to look at the pipeline of systems and organizations that touch a child's educational life—from early childhood education to K-12 public schools to afterschool programs counseling—to help design appropriate shared goals, outcomes, and metrics. And in Chapter Seven we will explore how a community foundation engaged Boston-area hospital executives in applying their expertise to developing workforce solutions for low-income individuals.

CREATING SHARED VALUE

Using business skills and resources to help solve social problems isn't always philanthropically motivated. Much has been written about doing well by doing good, but companies large and small are increasingly awakening to the idea of creating shared value for society while they create economic value for themselves. Companies that create shared value adopt operating practices and pursue policies that enhance the competitiveness of the company while simultaneously advancing the economic and social conditions in the communities in which it operates.[6] Shared value creation is different from corporate philanthropy and social responsibility programs, which are often tangential to a company's core operations. A shared value approach, instead, entails reconceiving a company's product and markets, reinventing its value chain, and strengthening the productivity of the communities in which it operates.

For example, when senior GE executives directly engaged with the health problems of the world's poor through GE's new approach to philanthropy, they saw the tremendous range of opportunities for their business. The company couldn't sell the same products it sold in developed markets, but it could design new products that would meet the needs of the developing world. Innovations based on GE's core technologies, like an inexpensive ultrasound scanner that transmits its pictures over the Internet without a computer, are already changing the lives of women in rural villages across the developing world.[7]

In fact GE executives realized that the challenges of global health represented one of their company's greatest opportunities for growth in the coming years. The company is investing $6 billion to develop new, inexpensive products and treatments that meet the health needs of low-income populations around the world, with a goal of reaching 100 million new patients every year. It is also partnering with Grameen Bank, the microfinance institution founded by Muhammad Yunus that was mentioned earlier, to create a sustainable rural health model that can reduce maternal and infant mortality by over 20 percent—not as charity but to make money by finding the profits hidden under social issues. In short, GE has found a way to create shared value through products and services that advance its business by meeting social needs.

Other examples abound. Hindustan Unilever employs more than 45,000 women in deeply rural villages throughout India to sell soap and other hygiene products where normal distribution channels cannot reach. Unilever makes money from this, to be sure, but washing hands with soap is the single greatest factor in reducing the spread of diarrheal disease, one of the leading causes of death among children in developing regions. ICICI, a major Asian bank, has created a crop insurance product that is affordable by smallholder farmers earning as little as a dollar a day. It is a profitable division for the bank, but it also enables farmers to survive a drought or flood that might otherwise leave their families starving.[8]

There's no doubt that the primary goal of these companies is making money, but an ever-growing set of social entrepreneurs are choosing for-profit business models as the best way to make a social impact. Not all social problems can be solved in ways that turn a profit, but for those that can, the classic nonprofit dilemmas of growth and sustainability melt away. Access to commercial sources of capital enable these social enterprises to grow far more rapidly than most nonprofits, and the steady stream of earned income enables them to survive without charitable or government support. Catalytic philanthropists therefore sometimes find themselves funding start-up companies instead of making charitable grants.

Collecting garbage is a government concern in most countries, but in the slums of Bangladesh, the government leaves most garbage to rot on the streets, creating serious health hazards through the spread of disease and generating greenhouse gases that contribute to global warming. Two enterprising local engineers, Iftekhar Enayetullah and Maqsood Sinha, decided there might be a business solution to this problem, and they launched a hybrid company called Waste Concern—one part nonprofit and one part for-profit. Lions Clubs International and the United Nations Development Programme made small initial contributions to cover the cost of buying some land and equipment, and the engineers set about hiring some of the unskilled and unemployed women who lived in the slums to collect garbage and bring it to the Waste Concern facility. There the recyclables were separated out, and the rest was composted to make organic fertilizer and methane gas, which Waste Concern sold to local farmers. Fertilizer and gas sales didn't quite cover their costs, but they discovered that they could sell carbon credits through the UN in return for the greenhouse gases they eliminated. Soon they had a business model that worked: collecting the garbage cost $30 per ton and the combined sales of fertilizer, gas, and carbon credits generated $60 per ton in revenues.[9]

With that healthy profit margin, Waste Concern was able to grow rapidly. In less than a decade, the company has expanded to collect garbage in the five largest slums of Dhaka and from slums in fourteen other cities—even franchising its operations in Sri Lanka and Vietnam. In partnership with a major Dutch corporation, Waste Concern now has the capacity to serve 3.6 million people and to handle 700 tons of garbage per day. The company employs more than a thousand women, reduces health risks from festering garbage, recycles countless tons of trash, reduces greenhouse gases by 90,000 tons per year, and increases crop yields for small farmers through the sale of its fertilizer. Had its founders designed it only as a nonprofit, concentrating on social impact but not trying to create a profitable business model, it's hard to imagine that it could have raised enough money to expand its impact so rapidly.

Social enterprises like these have spawned a new type of venture philanthropy fund, the nonprofit Acumen Fund, that offers charitable donors an array of investments in profitable, scalable, and sustainable business models. Launched in 2001 by the energetic and charismatic Jacqueline Novogratz, with seed funding from The Rockefeller Foundation, Acumen has raised more than $80 million in charitable contributions and invested the money in more than thirty enterprises throughout Africa and India and across industries ranging from housing and health care to energy and water purification. In fact, Waste Concern is one of Acumen's lead investments.

The enterprises like Waste Concern in which Acumen invests are motivated primarily by their social impact, yet they have found that they can scale up and sustain their operations more effectively by relying on a profitable business model rather than by raising charitable or government funds. Companies like GE and Unilever are motivated primarily by profit, yet they have found that they can serve rapidly growing markets in developing countries, earning attractive returns by delivering products and services that create important social benefits for millions of people. Ventures like these sidestep the age-old debate about whether business is good or evil. They don't redeem the harms that many businesses cause, nor do they imply that all social problems can be solved by capitalist solutions. Catalytic philanthropists aren't trying to pass judgment on either the corporate or the social sector. They just want to solve social problems in the most effective way they know how, and engaging business know-how, resources, and the profit motive turns out to be an important part of many solutions.

Investing for Impact

Traditionally, most endowed foundations, as well as family and individual investors, have maintained a rigid division between how they managed their financial investments and how they supported charitable causes. Typically, a donor would give grants to nonprofits to achieve charitable goals on the one hand and would invest endowment and personal income to maximize financial return on the other hand. As the two hands have operated separately, donors missed the opportunity to drive their charitable goals with the largest and most powerful financial resource they have—their investment capital.

Yet this is beginning to change. Let's take a look at two important ways that you (or your organization), as a catalytic donor, can strategically apply your investment capital to make progress toward your chosen causes: (1) using your vote and (2) using your cash.

Using Your Vote

The simplest way to use investment capital for social purposes is to vote the shares of stock you own in ways that encourage companies to exercise more social responsibility. After all, not all companies are as enlightened about creating shared value as our examples in this chapter are. The lure of short-term profits still leads many companies to ignore the environmental degradation, unsafe labor conditions, or deceptive consumer practices that may lie beneath their glossy corporate responsibility reports. Even these laggard companies can be moved to action, however, when catalytic philanthropists step into action.

The Nathan Cummings Foundation, a family foundation established by the founder of the Sara Lee Corporation, is by far the most sophisticated practitioner of shareholder advocacy among U.S. foundations. The family has long had a strong interest in the protecting the environment. Through its grantees, the foundation has, for example, supported initiatives to fight the devastating pollution from the waste generated by large-scale commercial hog and cattle farms. In 2003, after several years of grantmaking to nonprofits that fought this specific issue, the foundation was surprised to discover that through sheer coincidence, its investment advisor had purchased 32,000 shares of stock in Smithfield Foods, Inc., the largest pork processor in the United States and one of the worst polluters in the nation through its 2,300 owned or contracted pig farms.[10]

The foundation's first thought was simply to divest the stock in protest and thus avoid the conflict between its grantmaking and investing. But the foundation's CEO, Lance Lindblom, realized that selling the stock would accomplish nothing beyond ending the foundation's internal embarrassment. If the foundation was serious about creating social impact, Lindblom reasoned, it should use its status as a stockholder to pressure the company to change its environmental practices. So, for a start, the foundation decided to file a shareholder resolution requesting more complete disclosures of environmental impacts in Smithfield's annual sustainability report. At first Smithfield fought back and persuaded the Securities and Exchange Commission to disallow the resolution. The foundation continued to file resolutions each year, however, and by 2006 its resolution had attracted 29 percent of the shareholders' votes, and the company eventually began to negotiate with the foundation. Seeking greater expertise, the foundation brought its grantees into the negotiations. Ultimately, a working relationship was formed among the foundation, the company, and several nonprofit organizations that led the company to track and report environmental indicators relating to its contract farms.

The Cummings Foundation has since adopted shareholder advocacy as one of its core tools for social impact, with a full-time director of shareholder activity on staff. Since that first resolution was filed in 2003, the foundation has filed more than eighty stockholder resolutions at a variety of companies and has used its network in the foundation and investment communities to encourage other shareholders to vote their shares in support of the foundation's campaigns. Although these resolutions rarely attract a majority of the votes, they reliably engage the attention of senior management and have frequently led to substantial changes in environmental policies at a number of major corporations.

The Cummings Foundation's commitment to shareholder advocacy is unusual; few other foundations have employed this tool as aggressively. But the nonprofit organization Ceres, together with the As You Sow Foundation and Rockefeller Philanthropy Advisors, has orchestrated a campaign in recent years to advise foundations and other donors—along with pension funds, universities, and other nonprofit holders of major endowments—on voting their shares to advance social objectives. It is an effective tool that nonprofits rarely have the resources to employ but that offers funders yet another opportunity to engage with businesses on social issues.

Using Your Cash

An even more immediate way to use your capital for social impact is to invest directly in enterprises that deliver social benefits. Foundations have made low-interest or no-interest loans to grantees for decades. Often these loans qualify as *program related investments* under the U.S. Tax Code, which means that the lending foundations can count these loans as part of their payout requirement. Although funders often assume that loans to nonprofits are risky, a study by FSG in 2007 found that these loans had surprisingly low levels of risk, with 96 percent repayment of principal and interest.[11] After all, what grantee wants to default on a loan from one of its donors?

Making capital available at subsidized rates of interest can certainly help a nonprofit organization bridge a short-term downturn or launch a new enterprise that will generate revenues to repay the loan. It also enables the foundation to "recycle" its money, using the same funds multiple times to achieve social impact instead of making a one-time grant that is used up on a single project. It can also help smaller nonprofits establish financial discipline and commercial credit. But the pool of subsidized capital remains limited because few donors want to give up market-rate returns on their investments.

Fortunately, you don't have to. It turns out that there is a host of market-rate impact investments—it may take a bit more effort to find them, but the risk and return are comparable to—and often better than—the equivalent conventional investment. Take the New York–based F. B. Heron Foundation, which has committed more than a third of its $240 million in assets to equity investments and loans, most of which deliver market-rate returns while directly furthering the foundation's mission to help people overcome poverty.[12] The Heron Foundation was an investor in Market Creek Plaza, the neighborhood revitalization project of the Jacobs Family Foundation profiled in Chapter Two, which has returned 10 percent to its community investors every year since the close of the offering.

Heron has also invested in the Yucaipa Corporate Initiatives Fund, a $577 million private equity fund based in Los Angeles that invests in businesses that locate in or expand their operations in underserved rural and urban communities throughout the United States. The fund has created thousands of jobs through its investments in three hundred stores, fourteen manufacturing facilities, and fifty-four distribution facilities, all in economically depressed areas. At the same time, the fund aims to generate a risk-adjusted rate of return. And Heron has also invested in the Community Reinvestment Fund, based in Minneapolis, which increases access to capital for community development lenders through the creation of a secondary market for loans to small business owners.

All told, 70 percent of the Heron Foundation's impact investments deliver market-rate returns, which the foundation meticulously tracks against the relevant conventional indexes. And in 2009, when the economy bottomed out at what economists hope will be the great recession's lowest point, the foundation's impact investments substantially *outperformed* the foundation's conventional portfolio.

Another foundation that has taken a leading role in impact investing is the David and Lucile Packard Foundation, the family foundation started by David Packard, the cofounder of the Hewlett Packard Corporation. The foundation found a way to use mission investing as part of a broader, market-driven strategy—in one case, to help the environment. The Packard Foundation has long been committed to protecting and enhancing ocean health, and through its Marine Fisheries program, one of its major efforts has been to encourage consumers to make more eco-friendly choices when they purchase seafood. But increasing consumers' appetites for sustainably sourced fish would do no good if consumers couldn't identify at the point of sale which fish were sustainably caught. And even though a growing number of fishing companies were catching or farming fish in more sustainable ways, unfortunately, wholesale seafood distributors didn't differentiate between those fish that were sourced sustainability and those that were not—the wholesalers basically dumped all the fish into the same bins for distribution. The result was that average consumers had no reliable way to know which fish in their grocer's freezer were sourced in an eco-friendly way, and so they couldn't signal their preference through their purchases.[13]

An enterprising young company based in Maine saw this gap and prepared to pounce. The founders wrote a plan to launch a seafood wholesale company that would segregate and certify fish as sustainably sourced. But the venture capital community was reluctant to fund them. So the Packard Foundation committed $10 million as the first money in, and agreed to take the risk of first loss and a lower return, an arrangement that enabled the company to attract substantial venture capital from traditional sources. The result has been a quadruple win: The venture proved successful for the founders, the Packard Foundation recovered its capital in full, consumers now have a more reliable means of choosing sustainably caught fish, and most important, market forces are now more aligned to protect rather than exploit vulnerable ocean populations.

Donors who are willing to be daring in the hopes of greater social impact are in a unique position to pioneer and test transformative financial instruments that can contribute to solving social problems on a global scale. After all, if someone had tried to persuade you, twenty years ago, that you could make a $50 loan to a poor farmer in Africa and ever expect to see the money back—let alone earn an attractive rate of interest after paying for all the transaction costs involved—you'd probably have laughed them out of your office. It took early risk capital from the Ford Foundation to test Muhammad Yunus's idea that microfinance loans were possible. Once the concept was proven to deliver reliable returns, however, it opened the floodgates to billions of dollars in commercial investment from large investors such as the World Bank and Deutsche Bank, investment that provided a pool of capital vastly larger than philanthropic dollars could produce. Today even individual donors—whether of high net worth, low net worth, or somewhere in the middle—can participate through online organizations like Kiva to raise the living standards of the world's poorest through microfinance. In fact Kiva users alone had lent more than $100 million in microloans by 2010.[14]

Microfinance is only one example of transformative investments that at their outset are perceived as too new or risky to access traditional capital markets yet that have the potential to yield market-rate returns. Philanthropy is uniquely position to absorb early risks and demonstrate the reliability of these investments over time, paving the way for much larger amounts of conventional capital to follow.

Clackamas County, part of the greater Portland metropolitan area in north central Oregon, is better known for its densely wooded hiking trails to the top of Mount Hood than for innovative financial instruments. Yet with the support of a local foundation, the Meyer Memorial Trust, this small county is pioneering a new way of financing energy conservation that could have national repercussions. Retrofitting all county buildings with state-of-the-art, energy-saving equipment would dramatically reduce greenhouse gas emissions, but the county had no way to borrow the $10 million it would cost. The retrofit would also save a great deal of money on future energy bills, but without increasing taxes, taking out a loan, or issuing a bond—all of which were politically impossible—the county had no way to pay for the improvements.[15]

Instead, the Meyer Memorial Trust agreed to put up the $10 million, as an impact investment, to pay for the installation. Once the equipment was installed, the county worked with a financial intermediary to sell the equipment together with a long-term power purchase agreement to a pool of private investors. The county now pays two energy bills each month: one to a utility company for the actual energy consumed and the other to the investors for the energy savings, enabling investors to recoup their capital with a reasonable return.

Selling the equipment and savings to the investors enabled the foundation to immediately recoup its original $10 million in capital, which can now be used for additional building retrofits rather than being tied up for over a decade of slow repayments. From the county's perspective, the arrangement is just another purchasing contract requiring no legal authorization for loans or bond issues. If this model of securitizing the energy savings proves successful, it could expand rapidly, creating a powerful new type of security that finances energy-saving equipment for both private and public properties across the country. It required a transformative investment from a foundation, however, to test the concept.

Donors certainly don't want to emulate the many Wall Street bankers who with wild abandon invented precarious financial instruments just to enrich themselves. Yet for all the creativity that is poured into financial innovation, few people spend their days trying to invent financial instruments than can solve—rather than cause—social problems. The availability of financing, however, can drive profound social change—whether through microfinancing in Africa or consumer credit in the U.S. Catalytic donors have the vision and daring to engage businesses by testing innovative financial instruments that can serve social purposes and, if successful, can be scaled up to national or global impact.

CONCLUSION

Even as recently as ten years ago, corporations and the nonprofit world had very little interest in mixing together. Businesses were typically viewed as self-serving organizations, pursuing profit in ways that were indifferent to the impact on human culture and well-being and on the environment. And nonprofits were typically viewed as altruistic, charged with identifying and solving the world's problems and acting as public watchdogs to raise the alarm about harmful business activities, but rarely if ever engaging with and in profit-making enterprise. Yet today we have entered an age in which all sectors—corporate, philanthropic, government, and nonprofit—are awakening to the power of engaging business resources in the service of solving social problems.

The foundation community is embracing impact investing with remarkable speed. The Bill & Melinda Gates Foundation recently committed $400 million to impact investments, and The Rockefeller Foundation launched the Global Impact Investing Network to encourage impact investments by pension funds and wealthy families as well as foundations. Fueled by new innovations in socially oriented financing mechanisms, entrepreneurs are even experimenting with the development of *social stock exchanges* in the United Kingdom and Singapore, to provide investment opportunities and liquidity for impact investments.

What catalytic donors recognize is that both business and nonprofit organizations can create positive impact, and that working through both sectors at the same time often produces greater results than working through either one alone. Catalytic donors look for opportunities to marry charitable purposes with private enterprise in ways that leverage market forces for the greater good.

Of course it would be a mistake to think that the pursuit of profit can always be perfectly aligned with solutions to social and environmental problems—just as it would be a mistake to assume that market forces always run counter to the greater good. Neither nonprofits nor businesses nor the donors that often broker between them have all the answers to society's problems—but where they can work together, they create tremendous opportunities for impact.

Key Principles for Blending Profit with Purpose

The clear line so often drawn between for-profit businesses and nonprofit organizations is becoming increasingly blurred as catalytic donors experiment with new ways of blending profit with purpose. Catalytic donors leverage the power of private enterprise for social change by following one or more of these principles:

1. **Apply business know-how.** Corporate leaders and all types of donors can apply business skills, knowledge, and other nonfinancial resources to help nonprofits achieve greater impact. Depending on what size and type of business you run, you can apply know-how in different ways. For example, large Fortune 100 companies, such as General Electric, can apply technical and management skills to develop new products designed to serve customers in emerging or nontraditional markets. Private foundations, like the Shell Foundation, can tap into parent company resources to leverage capital and business knowledge to help finance and grow emerging businesses in Africa. (Funders that aren't closely associated with a company can hire business talent.) And individual funders, such as Tom Siebel, can apply their marketing and management prowess to tackle issues such as meth abuse in communities closer to home.

2. **Create shared value.** Unlike corporate philanthropy and social responsibility programs (which are often tangential to a company's core operations), creating shared value is an essential part of a company's competitive positioning. For example, Hindustan Unilever recruits, trains, and employs more than 45,000 impoverished women in deeply rural villages to sell hygiene products. This business generates triple bottom-line returns: it creates jobs for unskilled Indian women (a population traditionally excluded from earning income), it advances public health (hand washing is one of the easiest and least expensive ways to help prevent the spread of disease), and it generates profit for the company.

3. **Invest for impact.** Endowed foundations, individuals with investment portfolios, and corporations alike can use investment capital to advance social and environmental goals. One approach available to any donor who holds shares in public companies is to influence those companies through shareholder advocacy and proxy voting. Other examples of impact investment include providing low-cost capital to social ventures, investing in market-rate opportunities that further

mission objectives, and testing innovative financial instruments that serve social objectives. These types of approaches enable donors to put to work capital reserves that are usually significantly larger than the sums they donate to charitable pursuits each year.

CHAPTER FIVE

PRACTICE 3
Forge Nonprofit Peer Networks

*Donors are uniquely positioned to see needs across
entire fields as they broker alliances and foster
collaboration between nonprofits that otherwise might
be locked in a competitive race for scarce resources.*

Facebook. LinkedIn. Twitter. You can't click on a news site or thumb through an old-fashioned magazine these days without reading some post or article about the ways in which social networking sites are revolutionizing our lives. Nonprofits are tapping into this trend, leveraging online networks to raise more money, make new friends, and build broader awareness of their causes. And donors benefit, too—now a contributor can make a microloan to an entrepreneur in Kenya as easily as she can drop a few dollars into a church collection plate.

But the significance of online networks to philanthropy isn't only that they lubricate the fund- and friend-raising efforts of countless global causes. It's actually the architecture undergirding online networks that is informing how social change happens in new ways. What's interesting about an online network is not just that anyone can tweet or post a personal page; it's the fact that another person can establish a link to that page and so can another person and so forth. What emerges is a web of formerly unconnected individual nodes now threaded together by links, across which information can be shared and actions instantaneously coordinated. What is key is the relationship *between* things, not just the objects themselves, as network theorist Duncan Watts notes.[1]

And it's in the relationship *between* nonprofits—off-line as much as online—that catalytic donors find fertile ground for advancing impact.

In Chapter One, we introduced the notion that funders typically engage in a linear grantmaking process that centers on giving money to individual organizations. But catalytic donors work with nonprofits in a different way. Instead of focusing on a single group, they look at the entire suite of nonprofits involved in a given issue, and then invest resources to help establish connections and foster collaboration *between* the groups.

When this is done successfully, nonprofits and funders collectively work together to solve problems and advance causes, rather than continuing the situation in which each nonprofit promotes its particular programmatic solution and each funder handpicks what he or she perceives to be the best grantee. As a result, catalytic funders find themselves in the business of *building nonprofit networks*, rather than just funding nonprofits. And at first, funders may find it strange. Most networks are informal, and so they're hard to see—and even harder to foster. They don't always come with 501(c)(3) tax-exempt status, or submit applications in response to a request for proposals. And yet when they are created and nurtured in the right way, networks are one of most powerful tools for solving social and environmental problems that a donor can deploy.

To see how one works in action, let's explore the case of The Strive Partnership—a network based in Cincinnati, Ohio, that is increasing achievement and life prospects among urban core public school students in remarkably short order.

THE NETWORKED SOLUTION

In 2005, The Strive Partnership, which is a nonprofit subsidiary of the KnowledgeWorks Foundation, successfully forged a network of more than three hundred local leaders to tackle the student achievement crisis and improve urban education in greater Cincinnati and northern Kentucky. In the four years since this network was formally launched, Strive partners have been able to improve student success in dozens of key areas in three public schools districts (Cincinnati plus Covington and Newport in Kentucky). Reading and math scores of fourth graders have increased steadily since 2005, up anywhere from 7 to 16 points for reading and 14 to 30 points for math. High school graduation is up 7 to 11 points in two of the three K–12 systems. The average level of preparation among preschoolers entering kindergarten has increased by approximately 10 percent since 2005. Of the fifty-four success indicators that Strive systematically tracks and measures, forty had already demonstrated positive trends by the end of academic year 2008–2009.[2]

How have so many systemwide achievements been accomplished so quickly?

To understand the change, we need to go back to the program's beginnings. Chad Wick, a founding member of Strive and CEO of KnowledgeWorks—the largest education funder in Ohio—was frustrated. He had been making grants to well-intentioned nonprofits running various afterschool, teacher training, and curriculum reform efforts, many of which were individually promising. But they weren't adding up to better academic outcomes in Cincinnati. Meanwhile another founding Strive member, Nancy Zimpher, then president of the University of Cincinnati, was also fed up. She and her colleagues at leading neighboring universities were concerned that the state's poorly performing secondary schools were graduating fewer and fewer students and that those who did graduate were largely ill prepared for college.

Wick had mounted several attempts to confront the school system directly. Before Strive, he says, KnowledgeWorks had tried to meet with Cincinnati public school leaders and bargain for change, but "we couldn't penetrate [the school district]. We just couldn't get the trust, we couldn't get inside to talk about effective teaching and leadership. . . . It was a classic case of, 'immovable force meets irresistible object.' It was a fortress."[3]

THE NETWORK STRATEGY

Instead of throwing their hands up at the problem or continuing to go it alone, Zimpher and Wick attempted a different strategy.

They joined forces and decided to build a network focused on student achievement. "We rounded up everybody—United Way, Head Start, Every Child Succeeds, Success by Six and 15 other entities," Zimpher explained to a local news outlet. "And we said, 'Let's get focused. Let's prioritize what we're going to do.' We ended up doing two things, not 30."[4]

Major funders and foundation leaders shared their frustration and eagerly joined in. Rob Reifsnyder, CEO of the United Way of Greater Cincinnati, had already laid the groundwork for a comprehensive system reform strategy like the one Strive had in mind. He had launched the Success by Six program, which promoted better early childhood education for low-income preschool students. This powerful United Way—the fourth largest in the country—had thus already sensitized area leaders and donors to the need for better overall outcomes for kids. Kathy Merchant, president and CEO of The Greater Cincinnati Foundation, was another early adopter and now serves as chair of the Strive board.

By the time Strive was formally launched in 2006, the network of education-related providers and advocacy groups had swelled to three hundred members, and Strive's board grew to include leaders from four key local private and corporate foundations, four school districts (three public and one diocesan), and the CEOs of eight universities and community colleges. Strive's mission was holistic and ambitious. They aimed not just to reform K–12 education but also to change opportunities at *every* stage of an urban young person's life cycle, assisting youth with "cradle to career" support so that they could succeed from birth through attending some form of college and on into finding a meaningful career.

Strive homed in on the five critical transition points when young people most need help—kindergarten, starting middle school, starting high school, graduating from high school, and the first two years of college. Through a rigorous research process, Zimpher and her colleagues at the University of Cincinnati developed a set of clearly defined, outcome-oriented goals for these critical points, a result of the Six Sigma process. Beyond agreeing to achieve the goals, it was then up to each member of the network to determine how best to reach them. The catch: members had to agree to evaluate and report on their progress using common measures. That way, providers would understand how well they were doing collectively in achieving district-level outcomes, in addition to understanding whether or not their particular program was effective.

Take the preschool program members, for example. There were dozens of nonprofit education groups, Head Start centers, child-care agencies, church-based nursery schools, prekindergartens, and other types of organizations serving preschool kids. Each had its own method of educating children and measuring results. Strive members learned that regardless of the type of program they have been receiving, almost all children regress during the summer break before kindergarten. This presented a major barrier to learning, especially for low-income students who enter kindergarten underprepared and find it difficult to catch up—a problem that only compounds over time. So the Strive preschool members launched an innovative *summer bridge* session, a technique more often used in middle school. The result? Strive partners increased the average kindergarten readiness scores throughout the region by 10 percent in a single year.

IN SYNC WITH STRIVE

Had each preschool and day-care initiative continued to operate independently, focusing on running its own programs and using separate yardsticks of success, everyone involved would have failed to realize that although each program might have seemed to have been performing just fine individually, the system as a whole was faltering.

In the two years after Strive's launch hundreds of member organizations met approximately every two weeks in subgroups called Strive Student Success Networks. Despite the promise of better outcomes for kids, the amount of extra effort involved might have made it tempting for some nonprofits or school districts to drop out or slide back into their former, uncoordinated ways.

That's where money matters. Between KnowledgeWorks, The Greater Cincinnati Foundation, the local United Way, the General Electric Company, and later the Haile/US Bank Foundation, Strive had locked up the biggest education funders in the state. And even though no grants pass through Strive, these donors have subscribed wholesale to Strive's cradle-to-career agenda. The Greater Cincinnati Foundation realigned its education goals to sync with Strive's and adopted Strive's annual report card as the measure of success. Procter and Gamble, a major corporate player based in Cincinnati, targeted early childhood with much of its giving budget as part of its Live, Learn & Thrive program. Duke Energy, according to Wick, said that every time someone applied for a corporate grant, staff asked, "Are you part of the [Strive] network?" And when a new funder, the Haile/US Bank Foundation, expressed interest in education, it was told by other Cincinnati area funders that the most effective way to influence local education was to get on board with the Strive agenda.[5]

So many powerful funders acting in lockstep created an important effect. Rather than fueling hundreds of different nonprofits with their varied strategies, they instead aligned grants to support the five goals advanced by Strive. They said no to well-intentioned proposals that fell outside Strive's goals in order to say yes to in-network approaches. The bottom-line result has been that all three hundred participating organizations—with their combined annual budgets of $7 billion in philanthropic and public resources—are now focused on the same five key goals.

Strive's success hasn't hinged on convincing donors to throw more money than before at the problem of student achievement. And Strive hasn't added any new nonprofits into the mix of hundreds of organizations already tackling the issue. Instead, Strive got funders and nonprofit leaders to do what they were already doing, just in a different, more collaborative way. And so where countless foundations have largely faltered, this on-the-ground local network has persevered—and in relatively short order.

"Give me a lever and a place to stand, and I will move the world," said Archimedes. By forging a lever from a vast peer network and centering it on the fulcrum of better student outcomes, Strive members could plant their feet and hoist thousands of urban kids into higher levels of learning and life success. In so doing, Strive is forcing mighty public systems to change by applying an equally mighty counterpressure. Its success is a testament to the power of networks, and reveals how a carefully orchestrated, intensely focused, collaborative campaign can result in a whole that is greater than the sum of its disparate parts. *E pluribus unum*—out of many, one.

THE COLLABORATIVE CHALLENGE

It may not be surprising that a collective action network like Strive proved a powerful force for social change. Indeed, it's the story behind every successful movement—social, political, cultural, or otherwise. It makes sense that many organizations working together toward a common cause can achieve more than a single person or nonprofit could alone.

"What is surprising, however," write Kania and Kramer in a recent article, "is that hundreds of different organizations that were traditionally separate, at times competitive, and even sometimes antagonistic, have actually joined together to achieve collective impact. It doesn't happen often—not because it's impossible—but because it is rarely attempted."[6]

When it is tried, it is enormously difficult. Imagine coaxing more than three hundred formerly disparate donors, universities, public school officials, and education leaders to collaborate in unison, each sacrificing some individual authority and compromising singular points of view to advance a larger cause. It's no wonder that donors traditionally steer clear of the effort—it's not for the weak willed or the charitable dabbler.

Forging successful collaborative networks is just as challenging for nonprofit leaders as it is for donors. The networking phenomenon was one of the most counterintuitive findings in *Forces for Good*. Crutchfield and McLeod Grant observed that the most successful nonprofits work *with and through* their peers to achieve high levels of impact. They collaborate rather than compete with other nonprofits. This trait distinguishes them greatly from other, average-performing nonprofits. It's what makes great nonprofits great.[7]

It's easy to see why collaboration is difficult for most nonprofits. With so many needs to address and society's limited resources, the average nonprofit scrambles to raise funding, grab media airtime, and gain recognition for its programs and services. This forces nonprofits to emphasize their unique contributions and claim credit whenever possible in the never-ending race to secure resources for their cash-strapped, overworked organizations. It often just doesn't pay to spend time working on another organization's problem or to share your hard-won learning with a group that just might become the recipient of what was to be your next grant.

This raises an interesting question: Why don't more foundations actively collaborate with their peers? Donors don't need to compete with each other for resources. Most private foundations operate on endowments that will keep them in business in perpetuity. And although one donor may envy another's greater media exposure or higher billing on a gala program, the next donor actively shuns the limelight. It seems that little holds donors back from working in alliance with their peers—and yet at first, Strive found it harder to get donors on board than to engage the nonprofits who compete so fiercely for funds. "It's very difficult to get independent-minded, wealthy, and well-intentioned people [to collaborate]," explains Strive board chair Kathy Merchant. "They would be happy to invest in more tangible things closer to their heart. These bigger, mind-boggling system change initiatives can be overwhelming."[8]

On one level there are many examples of philanthropic collaboration. It's trendy for donors to say they *partner* with their grantees and that they seek ways to work cooperatively with peers. For example, foundation executives often remark on the extreme openness of their philanthropic peers. Their colleagues are eager to meet with them, and freely share grant agreement templates, legal documents, and due diligence formulas. Donors enjoy helping each other in making the business of running their foundations easier.

Funders also coordinate around causes. Today there are at least thirty-seven donor *affinity groups* recognized the by the Council on Foundations. Members of each group periodically gather and share knowledge and best practices in their issue area, for example, health, environment, education, or civic participation. One affinity group focuses exclusively on harm reduction (that is, drug abuse prevention). There is even an affinity group of affinity groups—the Joint Affinity Group. Members of these loosely affiliated donor networks may also commission research to see which nonprofits and interventions receive the most support and thus to reveal gaps or opportunities in the field. But beyond that, most affinity group members are free to make grants in any way they wish. What these loosely affiliated groups rarely do is collectively decide on a discrete set of priorities and then modify their donating strategies to exclusively support those targets. That's the difference between, for example, Grantmakers in Education—an affinity group that studies and shares knowledge about funding trends in school education reform among other items—and the Strive network, whose members align their education giving with the five priority areas set by the collective.

THE SPECTRUM OF COLLABORATION

Part of the complexity of explaining the varieties of collaboration has to do with terminology. *Partner* and *collaborate* are buzzwords used ad nauseam. In practice *partnering* and *collaborating* could perhaps be better described as *cooperation* or *loose coordination*. They imply simply being nice, rather than strategic, and lack the force of mutual accountability that exists when each participant is equally invested in a cause and equally shares the risk. This is not to say that forming partnerships and coordinating among donors is completely useless—these activities can be very productive. The efficiencies gained from donors' sharing issue-based knowledge and trading best practices can prevent duplication of effort and unnecessary mistakes and can produce other benefits.

It is useful to think of collaboration as a spectrum of activity that ranges from loose coordination and informal information sharing to intense, focused collective impact campaigns (as outlined in Figure 5.1).

As donors move across the spectrum of collaboration from left to right, they increasingly engage in activities that extend beyond grantmaking, and their commitment to shared objectives intensifies. At the right end of the spectrum, "Collective Impact," the donor is fully committed to achieving an outcome, both funding and participating in collaborative activities that share common metrics of success and to which all participants hold themselves accountable.

In Strive's case, the participating foundations and nonprofits engaged in activities at each end of the spectrum: they met

FIGURE 5.1. THE DONOR COLLABORATION SPECTRUM.

Informal cooperation between donors	Coordination among donors within an issue	Participation in coalitions and alliances	Collective impact through peer networks
Example: Donors share grant agreement templates and evaluation best practices.	*Example:* A donor joins an issue affinity group, learns about and shares knowledge, and embraces best practices.	*Example:* A donor funds and joins a coalition and writes an op-ed advocating for the group's policy agenda.	*Example:* A donor funds, joins, and actively participates in collective action and holds itself and its peers accountable to common goals using agreed-upon metrics.

frequently and shared knowledge and best practices in youth development and academic success. Donors made grants to nonprofits; many joined boards. But their collective efforts went beyond information sharing and a common concern for kids. They agreed to a short list of priorities and adopted a single set of measures for marking their progress. This mechanism for mutual accountability forced the foundations and nonprofits alike to make decisions that they might otherwise not have made.

Think of a wagon drawn by several horses. Without a central harness connecting them, each horse could lunge in any direction it liked, and the wagon would go nowhere. Education reform—and many social problems—are like that wagon. The horses are nonprofit leaders, each with its own strengths and strong sense of direction. Unbridled, two leaders might lunge in opposite directions—one gallops east while the other charges west—effectively negating each other's efforts. Or a subgroup of the leaders may spontaneously head north, and so the wagon slowly veers in their direction. This is the way of many social change movements. Hard-won but incremental progress made by a sprawling network of loosely affiliated groups and individuals. The trick is to fashion a sturdy harness to guide them in one unified direction, as the Strive network has steered its participants forward.

Defining *Collaboration*

"True collaboration requires a commitment to shared goals, a jointly developed structure and shared responsibility, mutual authority and accountability for success, and sharing of resources, risks, and rewards," write Carol Lukas and Rebecca Andrews in "Four Keys to Collaboration Success."[9] True collaboration is much more than simply getting together to talk about issues. It is often difficult to achieve, but many believe that it is the best way to effect lasting change.

Adopting a Peer-Network Mind-Set

As the Strive example shows, forging a network of peers and marshalling a successful collective impact campaign requires sacrifices and an intense commitment by member donors. They contribute time, intellectual expertise, political chits, and social connections, and they must align their grantmaking decisions to advance the collective agenda. But the benefits can be significant. The power that results when groups lock arms to collectively crack society's toughest problems is much stronger than the power that any single entity could hope to contribute.

Full participation in collective impact requires a mind-set shift on two levels:

First, donors must change the way they view their role in the process of creating social change. They must shift their operating mind-set so that instead of acting like a tax-exempt ATM machine, programmed to dispense cash to worthy charities, they become a contributing partner capable of catalyzing change.

Second, donors must reset their focus from funding individual nonprofit programs to supporting (in many ways) progress toward a larger cause. They need to look for the forest through the trees.

Today most donors operate in a traditional bilateral mode. The donor defines himself or herself as *grantmaker* and the chosen nonprofit as *grantee*, and together they engage in a linear relationship that starts with a site visit and concludes with an end-of-year report. Funders see their main challenge under this paradigm as choosing a few grantees out of many applications. The more sophisticated donor will try to ascertain which nonprofits seem to be making the greatest contribution toward the causes he or she cares about, and then will fund only those.

Potential grantees, in turn, compete to be chosen by the donor, each emphasizing how its discrete activities have the greatest effect. Each nonprofit is judged on its individual potential to achieve impact, independent of the numerous other nonprofits tackling the same cause—let alone other corporations, governmental agencies, and individual actors that are likely also having an impact. And when a funder asks a grantee to evaluate its impact, every attempt is made to isolate that grantee's individual influence from all the other various influences in order to demonstrate that whatever improvements occurred were caused solely by that grantee's intervention. This is a mode we call "the paradigm of isolated impact."[10]

Figure 5.2 contrasts this common perspective with a catalytic one. Catalytic donors operate in a different mode. Instead of defining their main objective as picking the right grantees, their vision broadens to questioning how they and the potential grantees can collectively help solve the problem at hand. To achieve this broader vision, donors can forge or join peer networks. In so doing, they move across the spectrum of collaboration, starting with sharing best practices and escalating up to participating in networked collective campaigns.

Again, examples of donor-led change on the collective impact side of the collaboration spectrum are rare—but they exist. And they don't always require the depth and breadth of complexity of an initiative like Strive. In the next section, we explore how a Latin American foundation, Fundación AVINA, forges peer networks among its allies (also known as grantees) to more effectively protect the Amazon rainforest. Then, we investigate how the United States–based Knight Foundation taps into community foundation networks to cast a collective response to the newly

FIGURE 5.2. COMMON VERSUS CATALYTIC DONOR VIEWS OF NONPROFITS.

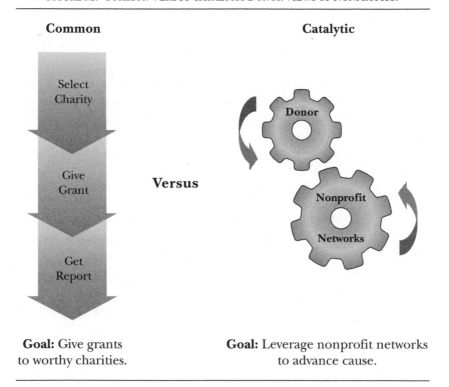

Goal: Give grants to worthy charities.

Goal: Leverage nonprofit networks to advance cause.

breaking problem of disappearing community-based news and diminishing investigative journalism. Both of these examples show how donors, when they move toward the right-hand side of the collaboration spectrum and focus on forging networks, achieve greater impact and advance causes further than if they only funded nonprofits on a one-off basis.

AMAZONOMICS

It seems you can help save a rainforest with nearly every purchase you make these days. Kick-start your morning with a grande Fair Trade Certified™ coffee—at Starbucks your barista may recommend the Café Estima Blend® as "bold and roasty-sweet"—and for a few cents more than you would pay for the house blend, you can rest assured that the Latin American coffee growers received a good price for their beans and that they didn't scorch a patch of rainforest in order to grow them. Or browse the furnishings in Pottery Barn's new Earth-Friendly Shop and choose a table hand-crafted from pine originally used for shipping crates or a chair made of woven sea grass and abaca. These materials are either reclaimed or are rapidly renewable (which means they regenerate in a relatively short time), so you won't worry that your acquisition contributed to extermination of an exotic species or killed one more tree. Not so long ago a consumer's only option for slowing deforestation and preserving biodiversity through a commercial purchase was to indulge in a pint of Ben & Jerry's Rainforest Crunch.[11]

Coupled with the millions of outright charitable donations made each year to environmental organizations such as Green-peace, World Wildlife Fund, and Rainforest Action Alliance, how much rainforest have eco-friendly purchases like these helped save? As much as these enterprises are prime examples of the practice of blending profit with purpose (discussed in the previous chapter)—and despite the dedicated efforts of numerous non-profit groups and activists—the majority of the world's rainforests are worse off today than two decades ago.

It's not that demand-side strategies don't work—dampening the appetite of consumers worldwide for unsustainably harvested goods can help stem the pace of deforestation. But in this case the roots of the problem are entangled in complex cultural, political, and economic dynamics on the supply side of the equation. To understand what's at stake on the supply side, you need to go straight to the source.

Roots of the Problem

Let's focus on the Amazon rainforest, as it represents more than half of the planet's remaining rainforests, encompassing 1.4 billion acres—a region larger than the whole of Western Europe. Almost 20 percent of the Amazon rainforest has been permanently destroyed as residents and companies burn or clear-cut the land and develop it for cattle ranches, mining, logging, or subsistence agriculture. At the current rate of destruction, experts predict that this biome is at risk of collapse in the next fifteen to twenty years.[12]

The biodiversity loss would be significant, as the Amazon is among the most species-rich tracts of tropical rainforest. Deforestation is also a major contributor to climate change. In Latin America, more than 60 percent of greenhouse gas emissions result from deforestation, with a significant proportion of these emissions being generated in the Amazonian region, where fewer plants are now absorbing harmful carbon dioxide and where there is pollution caused by fires as local farmers and developers burn or clear-cut their way through millions of acres every year.

Who is responsible for all this destruction? Although it's easy to target logging companies and big agribusinesses such as cattle ranchers, the single largest of cause of deforestation is the combined actions of countless small-scale farmers eking out a living in the Amazon biome.[13]

They are farmers like Nelci Aparecida de Queiroz, who lives in the Brazilian state of Mato Grosso.[14] Every year during the dry season, de Queiroz sets fire to her small property in order to plant corn and coffee. She knows that fire does not make her soil more fertile, but it is the only way she knows to clear the land. Aparecida de Queiroz is one of many contributors to the Amazon's rapid deforestation profiled in the online series *The Route of the Smoke*, which tracks the causes and effects of the burning. There are alternatives for people like Aparecida de Queiroz. She could clear her land with a tractor, but most residents of Brazil can't afford to purchase a tractor and the government does not provide them. Or she could clear it by hand—a hard, laborious approach that most farmers would understandably avoid. And then there is the intangible but real influence of cultural traditions—Brazilians have been clearing the land this way for a century or more. Why change now?

In the nine Latin American states that border the Amazon rainforest, policies are in place to prevent farmers and squatters from burning the forest. But because the region is so sparsely populated and the Amazon is essentially open terrain, it's virtually unpoliceable—even if the municipalities had allocated sufficient funding to enforce the law. Meanwhile, substantial portions of state budgets go toward subsidizing the agribusinesses that help these developing economies grow. Further, successive overlays of land reforms have not succeeded in solving historical land tenure problems. The result is that most states' economic practices enable rather than prevent further destruction. And so no matter how many fairly traded grande lattes or sea grass chairs consumers in the north may purchase, stronger market forces prevail in the south.

To overcome these barriers, Fundación AVINA has enlisted a force of a different nature: locally grounded, continentally coordinated nonprofit networks.

In 2007, AVINA had chosen as one of its five key strategies to focus on protecting and preserving the Amazon rainforest, as one of Latin America's most significant contributors to the global challenge of climate change. With one hundred staff members dispersed across offices in every major Latin American state, the foundation was uniquely positioned to take a pancontinental view of the problem. AVINA representatives in five of the nine countries that border the Amazon basin—Columbia, Peru, Brazil, Ecuador, and Bolivia—convened an informal working group, later called the Amazon Regional Alliance (ARA), whose initial members were thirteen nonprofit organizations in the region. They later added to ARA Venezuelan and Guyanese organizations from the Orinoco basin of the Amazon rainforest. The main objective of ARA has been to mitigate climate change produced by deforestation.

Rather than function as a loose alliance of nonprofits connected by concern for the Amazon but effectively operating independently in their own states, the ARA members have acted as an AVINA network committed to collective action. One of their first goals was to map and understand the full extent of the deforestation problem and to pinpoint where and why the worst destruction was occurring. This had previously been seen as a nearly impossible task, given the vast size of the Amazon region. But that situation was now changing with the advent of accessible GIS (geographic information system) remote sensing technology. AVINA representatives saw the potential impact of this new technology, so the foundation supported the Amazonian Network of Socio-Environmental Geo-referenced Information (or RAISG, a previously existing network) to create a GIS map of the entire Amazon region. Until that point, a comprehensive map did not exist. "We had local maps produced by traditional means, but we hadn't yet produced an updated, digital map that could be used to respond for the whole biome," explains AVINA representative Federico Bellone.[15]

By 2009, the first pan-Amazonian map of conservation areas and indigenous reserves in the nine countries of the watershed was published. Based on this innovation, AVINA went on to connect the ARA and RAISG networks, so members of each could use the other's information to influence policymaking at a national level. AVINA also brokered meetings between RAISG and Google Earth engineers, which became a building block for the creation of Google Forests, a global, online deforestation-monitoring tool.

The map changed everything. Suddenly, the nonprofit leaders in the network could see that about half of the Amazon land was protected, whether as national forests or parks or indigenous land. The other half was subject to market forces—mostly ecologically harmful ones, including the burnings by small land holders like Nelci Aparecida de Queiroz, described previously. Now members of the ARA network could take the images back to their home states and use them to pressure governmental agencies and businesses to change. For instance in Brazil, where most of the deforestation is caused by small farmers and squatters, municipal governments weren't enforcing the environmental protection laws already on the books. But through monthly GIS updates, nonprofit leaders were able to show public officials exactly which municipalities hosted the worst offences. Soon the media published a list of the thirty biggest infractions. "The list led immediately to cabinet meetings with senators and congressmen doing flyovers to make sure the information was correct," explains Bellone. "Government couldn't put that [information] under the carpet."[16]

Maps like these have proven to be crucial links to sparking change at the global level as well. ARA and RAISG members presented the map at the 2009 Copenhagen Climate Conference, along with Brazilian senator and then-presidential candidate Marina da Silva. This action and other AVINA partners' campaigns to make Brazil commit to emissions reductions were instrumental in Brazil's announcement at the conference of an unprecedented shift in its climate policy: it committed to cutting emissions 36 to 39 percent against BAU (business-as-usual) levels by 2020—one of the few breakthroughs that resulted from the Copenhagen conference.[17] What began as a pancontinental innovation created by networks supported by AVINA had become a tool for advocates to effect change at both national and global levels.

What It Took

The ARA network started with a few simple things: AVINA offered to pay for travel and other expenses associated with each meeting with grants of about US$20,000. Although the costs of the flights were not insignificant, the real burden was the sacrifice of time: given the enormous breadth of the rainforest at 1.4 billion acres, for any given meeting at least one member would have to fly more than 5,000 miles to get there. With so many challenges to confront at home, it's understandable that any single nonprofit executive would think twice about investing that kind of time.

But members of this network were able to see the bigger picture—if they wanted to protect and preserve the rainforest, they could continue to focus on their slice of it or they could tackle the larger cause. AVINA made it easier for them to sacrifice some of their time and autonomy to approach the problem in a holistic, pancontinental frame, yet in the end it was the members of the network who collectively produced something that individually would be nearly impossible.

Bellone is careful to point out that AVINA's role in the network is that of active facilitator, rather than that of passive convener or top-down leader. AVINA representatives have learned that it's not the funder's role to set the agenda in any of the networks AVINA supports, but rather to *create the conditions* under which the leaders can come together. At the same time, AVINA representatives participated as peers in the process. And their participation has been crucial, because what AVINA brought in this case was a pancontinental view and a focus on protecting the Amazon region as a whole.

A broad vantage point is something that funders are often uniquely situated to adopt. Unconstrained by the day-to-day fire-fighting and organizational issues faced by direct-service and advocacy-oriented nonprofits, donors are free to focus on the bigger picture and what it collectively might take to solve the problem. Then they create the conditions that allow nonprofits to act effectively within that larger framing—a trait that we'll explore more in Chapter Seven.

AVINA's network-building approach has had other positive effects. Because of this work, AVINA has gained a unique on-the-ground understanding of what is needed to stem the tide of deforestation, and it is now positioning itself as a partner to other foundations that want to have a significant impact on the rainforest. AVINA recently formed an alliance with the Skoll Foundation, the philanthropy of e-Bay's cofounder and independent filmmaker Jeff Skoll, who produced *An Inconvenient Truth* among other films. Skoll and AVINA agreed to make a joint investment of US$6 million over three years, by agreeing to match one another 1:1 to support a shared strategy. In addition to leveraging each other's resources, they also complement one another's strengths. Skoll has global experience in social entrepreneurship and in scaling up successful models for change. AVINA has on the ground presence and regional expertise in Latin America, and thus the ability to broker alliances with diverse stakeholders and to immediately react to opportunities and threats.[18]

This is an impressive example of a funder sharing significant power and decision making with a locally based funding partner in a quest to achieve the most significant level of shared impact. And it's a testament to the power of participating in and building networks as an effective strategy for solving problems.

BLUEPRINT FOR CHANGE

With today's advanced digital and aerial technologies, making a map probably doesn't sound so groundbreaking. But what is truly remarkable is AVINA's ability to foster effective networks for collective action around such technologies. Doing this kind of work doesn't require a whole lot of money, but it does require a substantial investment of time, staff presence, and sweat equity. And perhaps most important, it requires a change in thinking on the part of network members.

The need for this change goes back to the nature of complex social and environmental problems and the difference between providing technical solutions and making adaptive changes such as shifting beliefs and behavior. A technical solution—like a GIS map—doesn't by itself solve a problem like deforestation. It's only useful to the extent it is deployed by the right people in creative ways to persuade public officials, business leaders, and the public of the need for change. Thus in changing stakeholder minds and behavior, as AVINA allies (or grantees) needed to do in this instance, networks will almost always be at the center of the change. (We talk more about approaches to technical versus adaptive challenges in Chapter Seven.)

The AVINA Amazon basin program is one of more than fifteen initiatives in which the foundation has actively helped its allies build and develop peer networks. In so doing, the foundation stretches beyond grantmaking and leverages its monetary donations by creating conditions for collective success. Like most funders, AVINA went about the typical foundation business of making grants to its allies in the race for change. But unlike its more traditional peers, this catalytic funder doubled down on its investment, funding and joining collaborative campaigns to ensure that its allies—including its grantees—worked together to advance a cause much further than any single organization could do on its own. "It's not always a lack of resources that's a problem, but the alignment of such resources" explains AVINA's Bellone, "Funders often act independently, on a project-by-project basis that's linear as opposed to systemic."[19]

Beyond Just Filling the Room

In much the same way that KnowledgeWorks incubated and supported the Strive initiative, AVINA intentionally created the time and space for leaders to physically come together, share information, and cement trust. AVINA didn't try to dictate or even identify the solutions but instead focused on establishing the process that would enable the participating organizations to determine the solutions for themselves.

Most donors have no trouble filling a room with nonprofit leaders. But AVINA and the funders in Strive did more than simply create a space for information sharing; they created the conditions that would help nonprofits to deliberately coordinate their activities. Importantly, they created a space for grantees to clarify values, discuss conflicting perspectives, and reach a common understanding of the endgame. And they actively participated—dedicating staff time and intellectual energy in addition to funding—to ensure that true collaboration would happen. AVINA's approach in this instance presents a classic example of adaptive leadership (explored further in Chapter Seven).

These funders' approach also illustrates the difference between tightly networked collaborative campaigns and other forms of cooperation, such as learning circles, affinity groups, and the informal sharing of knowledge and best practices that goes on in various fields—for true collaboration requires "a commitment to shared goals, a jointly developed structure and shared responsibility, mutual authority and accountability for success, and sharing of resources, risks, and rewards."[20]

CREATING THE CONDITIONS FOR CHANGE

So far in this chapter, we've explored how foundations have helped to catalyze education and environmental change by forging and underwriting networks and creating the conditions for partners to truly collaborate. But sometimes a problem may be so new that there aren't any formal nonprofits or organized campaigns under way to sync up with. When this situation emerges, the role of the catalytic funder is not to create or join a collaborative network but rather to define and build the field into which networks can proliferate.

This was the context in which the John S. and James L. Knight Foundation found itself in 2005, at the same time as Alberto Ibargüen became its new president.[21] With locations in twenty-six U.S. cities, the Knight Foundation had long engaged in place-based grantmaking and in supporting journalism and education programs. But with the advent of the Internet, the nature of news and how it was created and consumed was shifting profoundly. Hardly detectable at first, the change had not yet shown how destructive the reduction of local news outlets would become to communities that would no longer have the information needed to hold local leaders accountable and fully participate in democracy. Ibargüen and other Knight senior staff knew the ground was shifting and they wanted to craft a response that could help communities create new modes of communicating important information to local constituencies. But they didn't know how. The only thing that the Knight Foundation staff knew at that point, says vice president Paula Ellis, was that they did not know the answer. "Like many social issues, this problem was emergent, complex, hard to define. There was nothing to even make a grant to—the traditional approach just wouldn't work in this case."[22]

The New News Network

One rainy Seattle day, Ibargüen was making final revisions to a speech he was about to give to a large group of community foundation leaders attending the September 2007 Council on Foundations conference. He was not happy. "I'd written it, and I was already bored with the speech and I hadn't even delivered it," says Ibargüen.[23] So he tore it up.

Instead of bending his audience's ears with some bland discourse on, say, leadership in the information age, he told the foundation leaders a personal story. He shared his passionate belief that the real victims of the Internet age would not be print newspapers and magazine publishers—although dozens of major metro dailies would soon implode. The ultimate victims would be the millions of people in communities across the country who would no longer have access to news that mattered—to them. "We're already in an era where it is more likely that a high school student can more easily access information about swine flu or the crisis in Darfur than corruption in city government or decisions about education in his town," as Ibargüen would later testify at a U.S. Senate hearing on the future of journalism.[24]

He then exhorted the members of his captive conference audience to understand that they could be part of the solution or be part of the problem. He acknowledged that many community foundation executives might not know how to use new media, might be scared of them, or just weren't paying attention to the issue. But soon *their* community would have no journalist doggedly asking questions of the mayor or writing about *their* school board's lack of concern about student achievement. Community foundations, said Ibargüen, could either rise to the challenge or not.

Ibargüen then did something even more extraordinary than discarding his own keynote speech: he spontaneously promised to fly every interested community foundation CEO in the room to Miami and to create a "new media learning seminar" tailored specifically for them.[25]

Five months later, more than two hundred community foundation leaders and trustees flocked south. Ibargüen made good on his promise and hosted the Knight Foundation's first Media Learning Seminar, which Knight staff designed to help community foundations learn about local news and information challenges and to foster discussion about possible solutions. The response from attendees was palpable. Ibargüen and the Knight Foundation were on their way to capturing the attention of, and enlisting leadership from, an entire network of community foundations that could collectively tackle the challenge of addressing community information needs. To channel all of this energy and enthusiasm, the foundation's staff developed the Knight Community Information Challenge, a $24 million initiative, of which $20 million would be given as matching grants to community foundations that discovered creative ways to use new media and technology to keep community residents informed and engaged.

HOMEGROWN SOLUTIONS

In the two years since the announcement of the Knight Foundation's contest, foundations both small and large have taken up a host of community information innovations.

In the Chicago metropolitan area, both major newspapers, the *Chicago Sun-Times* and the *Chicago Tribune*, had been scaling back and laying off reporters when the Chicago Community Trust conducted a community-wide landscape assessment of the "New News." The initiative uncovered not only the gaps in the information fabric of the city but also promising recent alternative news start-ups in the region. With this comprehensive research in hand, the trust approached other funders based in the region, including the MacArthur and McCormick Foundations, to collaborate on a local grantmaking initiative that has helped to scale both nonprofit and for-profit news models locally.

Meanwhile, in Colorado, although the Community Foundation Serving Boulder County (CFSB) had been compiling information on education outcomes of county students for a decade, residents didn't know what an "achievement gap" was, according to foundation sources. Using its research in a new way, CFSB launched an awareness campaign on the importance of early childhood education, targeted to low-income, Latino parents, who were the most likely to be negatively affected by a widening achievement gap and the least likely to have access to quality preschool experiences for their children. CFSB then began working on a campaign to pass new local policies that would fund universal preschool (the campaign was still underway as this book went to press).

For each of these foundations, addressing information needs in their communities was a new endeavor—and a direct result of Knight's program.

What was unique about the Knight Foundation's initiative was not the idea of a challenge grant. Lots of donors make grants with attached strings requiring the grantee to raise a match for the grant. It's one of the most common forms of leverage employed by funders. The uniqueness was that, first, Knight had not specified the actual programs to be funded and, second, that the program partners were other foundations. The Knight Foundation's instinct was to work *with and through community and placed-based foundations* to achieve its goals. It was a counterintuitive move because making grants in partnership with other foundations just doesn't seem as rewarding as working directly with grantees. Also, the decision effectively meant that Knight had relinquished some control over how its grant dollars would be spent. In a way, it was a surrender of power.

The community and place-based foundations developed some great new ideas, such as the two early successes that were described previously, whereas others flopped. Most of the picks were ones that the Knight Foundation might never even have considered had it been *requesting* proposals directly from its Miami headquarters. By tapping the ingrained local knowledge that community foundations uniquely possess about their regions and leveraging that knowledge to produce innovative community information solutions, Knight convinced a whole network of donors to see themselves as proactive problem solvers and effectively gave them an opportunity to take the lead in finding solutions for an important local issue. This is significant because traditionally, most community foundations have played a more passive role and have left the innovation and change making to their grantees.

This is a classic trait of catalytic philanthropy leaders (and their high-impact nonprofit counterparts): to advance the cause, Knight *worked with and through its peers.* Instead of consolidating authority and attempting to tackle the local news crisis alone—which Knight could have easily decided to do given its $2 billion asset base and robust staff—it enlisted an army of foot soldiers and inspired them to adopt the cause. The foundation's network of partners could then advance a ground game that played to the strengths that only place-based funders like community foundations possess. And this approach inured community foundations to the cause—effectively locking them into the fight to restore information and news in their towns. Like Warren Buffett, who concluded that his friend Bill Gates could do a much better job of giving away Buffet's fortune than Buffet himself could, Ibargüen saw that community foundations were much better positioned to help tackle the news crisis in their towns than his national foundation was.

Trabian Shorters, Knight Foundation vice president, explains: "The grants were a small piece of strategy. The program was really about getting these 700+ organizations to recognize that information is a core community need. And the best people to sell that idea [at the local level] are heads of community foundations. That nut cracks from the inside."[26]

The move is symbolic of how Knight conceives of itself as a philanthropic institution. The foundation does not define itself simply as a grantmaker writing checks to worthy nonprofits selected from its many eager applicants. Knight's vision is broader. The goal is to create transformative change. In the case of the Community Information Challenge, Knight saw an opportunity to catalyze a whole segment of philanthropic funders to tackle the information gap in their home communities. It capitalized on an often overlooked part of the philanthropy world that could become a critical part of a solution.

From Check Writing to Circuit Riders and Boot Camps

This knack for sparking others to take ownership of a cause is a theme that imbues much of the Knight Foundation's giving. What makes Knight's work with the Community Information Challenge truly catalytic is that the spark comes from more than just a motivational speech by the CEO or the announcement of a new grant competition. For Knight has intentionally developed *strategies that go beyond grantmaking* to create the sense of ownership of the local news and information challenge among its community foundation partners.

For example, the Knight Foundation dispatches digital technology *circuit riders* to serve as coaches to its competition applicants and grantees, and it hosts *boot camp* trainings for new grantees on subjects such as overcoming technology hurdles and evaluating impact in a digital context. Knight introduced these technical assistance tools because it recognized that most community foundation leaders were novices in new media technology and that the problem of the disappearance of local news and information was still crystallizing for them.

Knight goes beyond grantmaking in other ways too. It requires that community foundation leaders attending its now annual Media Learning Seminars always bring at least one board member. This condition creates a higher level of engagement, as community foundation board members who attend the seminars are able to more effectively represent to their fellow trustees the importance of dealing with their local community's information needs. Knight also has invested the time and energy to identify leaders in the community foundation field who have earned respect from their peers, and it gives these leaders additional resources to support them as champions for the cause. Knight knows that the most direct way to build a field and galvanize a movement is to invest in leaders.

With these fundamentals in place, Knight can more effectively build the network of community foundation leaders around its cause. Knight does this by providing coaching and evaluation resources that afford "shared learning" opportunities, so that Knight grantees can communicate and share best practices on a peer-to-peer basis. The result is that grantees learn from each other as well as from Knight's technical assistance programs, rather than operate in their own silos. In Practice 6, Learn in Order to Change, we explore further this notion of how donors increase their impact by creating fieldwide learning systems. And in the next chapter, which addresses empowering the people, we'll also see how Knight deploys a place-based strategy in which individual community residents take on the challenge of restoring local news and other important information to their communities.

Whether dealing directly with individuals or with a network of intermediaries like community foundations, the Knight Foundation's secret weapon is to employ catalytic strategies that surrender a degree of control in the short term in order to gain greater impact in the long term.

THE RELEVANCE OF NETWORK THEORY

With the dawn of the Internet age, network theory has come to dominate much of management thinking. The proliferation of user-driven social networking sites like Facebook, LinkedIn, and Twitter, along with the unexpectedly superior performance achieved by some open-source platforms such as Linux and Mozilla, have redefined success for the profit seekers. Bill Gates has said, "I live in a world where all of my partners are potential competitors and all of my competitors are potential partners," recalls Knight Foundation president Ibargüen.[27]

As for-profit companies enter this brave new world, they learn through experience that industry relationships are now cast in shades of grey, rather than black versus white. Capitalists have thus come to learn what social change leaders have long known: when you want to get results, the most direct route is not always the most effective one. When you want to exert the greatest level of force against a problem, releasing power and distributing it widely can yield better results rather than trying to consolidate authority and centrally control decisions. It's a counterintuitive concept. It requires leaders to cross formerly forbidden boundaries and adopt a nuanced understanding of their firm's relationship with others. It also calls for redefining success and recasting the timeline against which progress is measured.

Network theories about how the virtual world operates have parallels in the natural world. Complexity science and systems dynamics thinking have produced useful tools for understanding how actors operate in biological settings—where phenomena occur organically and events transpire according to principles that are less predictable than those that govern linear, mechanistic models in the human-made world. The authors of *Getting to Maybe*, whom we also cited in Chapter One for their relevant insights, point out that complexity science can shed light on the process of social change, commenting that "we must move from seeing the world as simple, or even merely complicated. To understand social innovation, we must see the world in all its complexity." They explain how traditional methods of seeing the world compare its workings to a machine, whereas by looking at the natural world, complexity theorists see life as it is: "unpredictable, emergent, evolving, and adaptable—not the least bit mechanical."[28]

These authors further suggest that some challenges are simple, like baking a cake. If you follow the recipe, measure and mix the ingredients properly, and cook it at the right temperature for the instructed amount of time, chances are you will eat cake. Other challenges are highly complicated, like sending a rocket to the moon. Multiple types of experts are required, as well as a high degree of coordination among them. Formulas and the latest scientific evidence must be applied to predict the trajectory and path of the rocket. But if all the specifications are met, systems are tested, and everything is done in the right order, say the authors of *Getting to Maybe*, then there is a high degree of certainty that you can control the outcome.

But most social problems are not simple or even merely complicated. They are better described as complex. *Getting to Maybe* uses the analogy of raising a child. "Unlike baking a cake or sending a rocket to the moon, there are no clear rules to follow to guarantee success . . . . [E]very child evolves and changes in response to forces that parents do not control. The flour does not suddenly change its mind, and gravity can be counted on. Children, however, have minds of their own."[29] The child changes her mind, the parents adapt their approach, and the family members progress forward in a constant state of interdependency that is iterative and unpredictable, rather than merely linear.

Social problems are similarly emergent. But most donors—
and many nonprofits—still approach social change as if it were a
simple challenge like baking a cake or at times even a complicated
one like launching a space rocket. Philanthropy is mired in a
traditional mind-set, stuck in a mental model that says, "I pick
grantees, they solve the problem, and at the end of the year
they send me a final report and I feel good." Donors continue
to measure progress grantee by grantee, often oblivious to the
fact that one nonprofit's solution may create another nonprofit's
problem. And though they may work collaboratively through an
affinity group to track and even anticipate changes in their field,
they miss the bigger opportunity for change because they fail to
act in a unified way on the knowledge they've gained.

Catalytic donors see that their chosen field or cause—whether
reforming education, preserving the environment, protecting
democracy, or some other issue—is different from the sum of
its parts. These donors understand that it is the *interconnection
between parts* that makes progress possible. They've learned to see
the forest despite the trees. Rather than solely fund nonprofits, they expend considerable additional resources to ensure that
these organizations are working in concert to achieve a desired
outcome—in essence, they are funding the *relationships between
nonprofits*, the interconnective tissue that doesn't always come with
a 501(c)(3) tax-exempt status but nonetheless is what drives social
innovation. The most skillful donors accomplish change not by
imposing top-down solutions but by seeding collaborations and
nurturing peer networks so that the parts function together in
unison to solve the problem. To paraphrase Knight Foundation
vice president Trabian Shorters, they crack the nut from the
inside.

Conclusion

Strive's funders and Fundación AVINA, the Knight Foundation,
and the other organizations profiled here don't do anything
different from what is done by the high-impact nonprofits profiled
in *Forces for Good*. It's just that they do it from their position as
funders rather than as grantees. Whichever side of the funding
equation leaders are on, the most catalytic will forge peer networks

as their lever for changing the world. Indeed, the power of networks is the only thing that ever has.

Key Principles for Forging Nonprofit Peer Networks

1. **Focus on the relationships** *between* **nonprofits.** Fund opportunities for relationships to grow between your grantees and other allies in the field; support the development of the interconnective tissue between groups that constitutes a network.

2. **Create the conditions for collaboration.** Don't focus on what the solution itself might be but on the conditions necessary for grantees to develop a shared solution by themselves. Nonprofits and funders need physical space and time to build trust and work together. The founders of the Strive Partnership invested significant thought, time, and financial resources in creating a fair process for diverse groups to come together and act collectively; Strive leaders didn't set the five goals but they created the conditions so participants could come to *collective* agreement.

3. **Commit to constant communication and continued learning.** Networks are most powerful when all players involved meet on a regular basis and have a system that enables transparent sharing of knowledge and a commitment to learning. And networks are most successful when both funders and nonprofits contribute time, intellectual capital and other resources to the project. As AVINA staff have learned, don't make the mistake of defining your role simply as check writer and leave the problem solving solely to the grantees. At the same time, don't attempt to overly control the outcomes of the group; being an equal participant in the democratic process is key.

4. **Measure progress together using shared metrics.** Ensure that network members agree to evaluate and report on their progress using the same measures. Build their understanding of *collective* successes and challenges to encourage learning across the network, and revise strategies as needed. (We explore this further in Chapter Eight, which addresses learning systems.)

5. **When an issue is emergent, encourage the proliferation of networks**. Sometimes an alliance or coalition already exists and a funder can augment its impact by underwriting it and fostering a more coordinated collective approach. But when such alliances don't already exist because a problem is so new, funders can tip the field toward solutions by creating the conditions for networks to proliferate, as the Knight Foundation did in response to the challenge of disappearing community news.

6. **Cede control to the network**. Although funders often create the conditions for networks to develop and grow, they must also give up some control over how their funding is spent if they want to leverage the creativity, insights, and talents of the group.

CHAPTER SIX

PRACTICE 4
Empower the People

Catalytic donors don't treat individual community members as charity recipients. They instead view individuals as potent participants in the process of solving problems—for themselves.

The U.S. civil rights movement is one the most significant examples of successful wide-scale social change in modern American history. It culminated in the passage of Civil Rights Act of 1964, which banned discrimination based on race, color, religion, or national origin. It brought about the Voting Rights Act of 1965, which restored and protected rights for African Americans who had long been excluded from voting by blatant racism and subtler forms of discrimination. Among other things, the movement also produced a new immigration policy, which further opened the door to voting for people of non-European descent.

The civil rights movement transformed the fabric of American life. It changed where millions of people were able to live, where they could work, and where their children attended school. It altered big things, such as empowering an often excluded race to fully participate in democracy. And it changed small things, such as taking away prohibitions dictating from which water fountain a person could take a sip.

If you were to be asked who the most significant funder of the civil rights movement was, you might name the Ford Foundation. If prompted to list others, you might point to the

National Association for the Advancement of Colored People (NAACP). But you would be mistaken. The donor that made the most significant difference in the civil rights movement cannot be defined as a single philanthropic or nonprofit institution. The most significant funder was actually, taken altogether, the countless people who gave their individual dollars, their time, their freedom, and in some tragic cases, their lives.

They were people who stood up, like Rosa Parks. They were the Little Rock Nine—children who braved jeers, rocks, and insults on their way to school. They were the Freedom Riders on the buses and the lunch-counter sitters; they were the people who marched on Washington and those who rioted in the face of police brutality. They were migrant farmworkers fighting for fairer treatment by employers. And they were the multiple organizers who collectively orchestrated the movement's many streams—including those operating from the center, like the Reverend Martin Luther King Jr. and the Southern Christian Leadership Conference, the Leadership Conference on Civil Rights, and the NAACP—as well as others on the edges, like Stokely Carmichael and the Student Nonviolent Coordinating Committee, the Black Panthers, and Malcolm X.

PHILANTHROPY'S BROADER PICTURE

If you define philanthropy as a function of elite institutions, such as foundations with endowments or other permanent revenue sources—as we've mostly done until this point in this book—then you frame a certain picture of philanthropy. But enlarge the frame, as foundation executive and African American history scholar Emmett Carson advises, and a larger picture emerges.[1] And it is in this larger picture—one that frames philanthropy in broader terms and includes a wide range of types of contributions—that you see most clearly how major social change happens.

Part of what makes some people see philanthropy through a narrow lens has to do with terminology. What a white American might call *philanthropy*, a black American might call *self-help*. While a white American might say she *volunteers*, a black American might say she is *helping out the church*—and a Latina might say the most important *service* she can perform is to fill out her Census form so her people can be counted. While mainstream (white) America talks about civic engagement, people of color talk about community participation and grassroots organizing. And so while white Americans today may be bowling alone, Americans of other hues are busy giving back through their churches, supporting each other through fraternal societies and membership organizations, and engaging in all kinds of mutual aid.[2]

The difference cuts deeper than semantics. The conflicting terminology reveals a fundamental discrepancy in the meaning of *making a difference*. African Americans call this self-help because they have been engaged in a struggle to do just that—help lift each other out of their disadvantaged position in society and gain access to opportunities historically denied them. Hence the line between giver and receiver is blurred; the difference between volunteer and aid recipient becomes moot. Unlike some members of the more advantaged segments of society, who may extend a hand out of a sense of noblesse oblige, disenfranchised blacks, Hispanics, Asians, and their fellow civil rights proponents have worked together, hand in hand, to bootstrap themselves into a better life.

Here is why the distinction is so important: donors who want to make the biggest difference—those who want to catalyze big change in world—have figured out that they must embrace and empower people at the individual or community level to advance the cause. The people most directly affected by a problem aren't always affiliated with a formal nonprofit organization or association. So it can be challenging for funders to communicate—let alone collaborate—with individual community members. But the people closest to the problem are critical to its successful resolution—both in generating ideas for solutions and in implementing the chosen solutions in ways that actually work.

Empowering people at the individual level is an extremely complicated thing to do. It can be uncomfortable, as it requires donors to cross lines of class, race, and geography, which may mean entering into the unfamiliar. And the process can unleash forces that extend far beyond the control of any single philanthropic institution or even of a network of nonprofit peers of the kind we described in the previous chapter. Yet sparking individuals to take part in the change that a funder seeks to create is perhaps the most powerful lever available—whether the donor's goal is to revitalize a few city blocks, foster a national movement, or advance a cause that touches communities across the globe. It's also a lever that has become increasingly relevant in this digital age, when the possibilities of engaging multitudes are expanding at exponential rates given the Internet's many-to-many communication capabilities. In this chapter we'll see what some of the most forward-thinking catalytic donors do—using both new media and older means—to empower people to change the world.

HEAR THE PEOPLE SPEAK

The 2008 annual meeting of the Consumer Health Foundation wasn't a typical philanthropic convening. Although the offices of this private health foundation are housed in a prime location near Dupont Circle in Washington, D.C., the meeting was not held in the foundation's carpeted conference room. And the attendees were not just the predictable mix of trustees, financial advisors, and legal counselors.

One of the first to arrive was Ms. Lady, a dark-faced, hunched figure wrapped in a dirty blanket, who shuffled as she muttered about health care and experts who purport to know so much. "I'm an expert too—a Ph.D.," she said, "**P**oor, **H**omeless, and **D**isabled."[3] Soon came Mr. Herbie Segura, a young disabled veteran of the Iraq War, who had come to the United States as an undocumented child immigrant from El Salvador. He spoke about his decision to join the Army to repay his debt to America, and about the prejudices he encountered getting both medical and mental health care after his honorable discharge. "I've shown that I'm willing to fight for this country," he said, "but I don't want it to fight me back." And then there was Mrs. Levine, a seventy-eight-year-old Jewish widow whose husband had lost his health care benefits while being treated for a heart attack, only to die soon thereafter of a second heart attack. Mrs. Levine is still paying her husband's medical bills five years later and avoids all medical care herself.

While these weren't actual people—they were composite characters played by performance artist Sarah Jones—their message rang true. They symbolized the concerns of thousands of low-income D.C. and regional residents who lack access to affordable health care. Consumer Health Foundation (CHF) president and CEO Margaret O'Bryon had invited Jones, a Tony Award–winning playwright, to perform her one-woman play *A Right to Care* at the foundation's thirteenth annual meeting. The setting was Washington, D.C.'s Woolly Mammoth Theatre, and filling the hall to capacity were community members, leaders of CHF nonprofit grantee organizations, and CHF board members. They had gathered to learn about health care problems facing the city and to discuss what the foundation could do about fixing them.

Following the performance, houselights flooded the hall and Jones took questions. The room was a sea of color, with African Americans, Latinos, Asians, and Caucasians in attendance. Issues of race, class, "skin privilege," and social injustice emerged. The event at times created noticeable discomfort for the audience. O'Bryon describes a moment when Jones talked about "shaking your family tree" to discover your personal connection to systemic public health care failures—"'Shake it out! Shake it harder!! Who's really in your family tree?' ... It was intense."[4]

The foundation's annual meetings aren't always this raw. The two prior gatherings had featured a more academic, data-centered approach, with panel presentations by local and national experts who spoke about the impact that social and economic factors have on overall health. But whether the meeting is artsy or analytical, CHF makes a point of convening individual members of the community to both share important information with them and to hear their ideas about how best to go about solving their problems. This approach has led CHF to operate in unorthodox ways.

O'Bryon took the leadership of CHF at its inception, when this health conversion foundation was required to be formed after the nonprofit Group Health Association was sold to for-profit Humana. From the outset the foundation has positioned itself as a "catalyst for social change, open to new ideas, and willing to take risks." It's not the biggest funder in the D.C. area—its $2 million in annual grantmaking is dwarfed by larger players in the region like the Morris & Gwendolyn Cafritz and the Eugene and Agnes E. Meyer Foundations in Washington, D.C., and the Annie E. Casey Foundation in nearby Baltimore. But it has made an outsized difference relative to its level of financial assets. CHF *punches above its weight*.

One major reason for its success is that CHF is solely focused on health for low-income communities—it is committed to a cause. Another important reason is that the foundation defines its role as much more than grantmaker. Although CHF donates to advocacy and direct-service groups in the region, it invests heavily in working directly itself with D.C. area residents. For instance, CHF has organized Speak Outs in local community centers to solicit residents' ideas about how to solve their health care access problems. The foundation recorded and compiled the residents' testimonies, and after reading and analyzing hours worth of ideas, boiled them all down into six key recommendations, which then formed the basis for policy change proposals. For instance, CHF promoted the establishment of a place for one-stop information sharing and dissemination, where residents could obtain the information they needed to better navigate the health care system. The foundation calls this the Ngozi Project, naming it after Ngozi Hall, the resident who offered the solution.

After starting at ground zero by learning directly from individuals, CHF worked through locally based coalitions and alliances of other funders and nonprofits as well as through networks of business and policy leaders in the region. One such alliance was the first-ever health working group in the region, which O'Bryon helped to catalyze through the Washington Regional Association of Grantmakers. O'Bryon also helped to coalesce the Regional Primary Care Coalition, an alliance to get primary care providers across Virginia, Maryland, and Washington, D.C., to coordinate a collective regional response. As these examples, show, engaging individuals and forging nonprofit networks (as described in the previous chapter) go hand in hand.

As a result of CHF's collaborative and at times unconventional efforts, D.C. residents have enjoyed major improvements in their ability to access health care. For instance, D.C. has adopted Medical Homes D.C.—a major capital and quality improvement initiative that will add 140,000 visits and 130,000 square feet of space to the city's primary care health system. To date, six clinic expansions have been completed and six more are in planning and construction phases. Medical Homes D.C. has also assisted six clinics in migrating from paper to electronic health records and has created a regional health information organization (RHIO) that allows clinics and hospitals to share critical patient information. When the initiative work is completed, the city will have a network of patient-centered medical homes—a model for health care delivery promoted in the national health reform legislation. And since CHF has been actively advocating in alliance with other leaders for increased access to better health care for local residents, D.C. now has the *second lowest* rate of uninsured residents (6.2 percent) in the United States[5]—only Massachusetts, which has universal coverage, has a lower rate. However, CHF would not claim sole credit for that success. "I attribute this to a conscious effort," explains O'Bryon. "It's not just one organization that is pivotal. Health care providers, primary care associations, advocates, government, foundations and residents must come together if you're going to improve our community's health."[6]

Consumer Health Foundation engages individuals because that gives CHF better results in its work. And it is not alone in this approach; it's a common strategy employed by catalytic donors who see the power in engaging individuals to speak about and be part of solving their own problems. Although it is difficult to do, and requires intensive time and effort on the part of the donors, the benefits can outstrip the costs when it is done right. And the donors who do it have demonstrated that they take an uncommon view of the role of the individual in their work. They have a *different mind-set*.

THE ROLE OF INDIVIDUALS IN CATALYTIC PHILANTHROPY

Figure 5.2 (in Chapter Five) showed the differences between the views of common (or traditional) and catalytic donors around the role of peer networks. Table 6.1 offers a look at common and catalytic donors' different views of the role of individuals.

Traditionalists embrace a mental model that plays out something like this: nonprofits are scripted into the role of *service providers* or *advocates*. Individual community members are cast as *service recipients* or *beneficiaries*. And the donor plays the role of *check writer*.

TABLE 6.1. COMMON VERSUS CATALYTIC DONOR VIEWS ON INDIVIDUALS.

Common	Catalytic
Recipients of charity	People responsible for and capable of self-help
Clients to be handled directly by grantees (nonprofits)	Partners in the practice of philanthropy
"Subjects" to be studied; a "problem" to be solved	Sources of solutions, knowledge, and new ideas
End-target of the donor's strategic objectives	Shapers of the donor's strategic objectives

Catalytic donors take an opposite view—and they demonstrate it on all kinds of causes, representing both sides of the political aisle. We described the civil rights movement earlier, a central cause of liberal funders, but conservatives are similarly adept at leveraging the power of individuals. In *Forces for Good*, the authors profiled The Heritage Foundation, a preeminent conservative policy think tank that is credited by leaders on both the left and the right with seeding a host of conservative policy wins; when President Reagan took office, he got through Congress most of the policy changes that Heritage proposed. But if you're not a member of The Heritage Foundation, then you likely aren't aware that it actually *has* members—nearly a half million. As an organizational type The Heritage Foundation looks more like the Sierra Club than the Brookings Institution or the Urban Institute. Whether on the left or the right side politically, when donors make this shift in mind-set, they open themselves up to nontraditional ways of advancing their causes.

Specifically, engaging and empowering individuals helps funders to

- Generate new and better solutions to pressing problems.
- Build collective will to solve problems on a wider scale.
- Bridge divides of class, race, and place.

Next, we examine how three funders of three different types empower individual community members to actively participate in solving the problems that affect them. These funders are the Jacobs Family Foundation (the private foundation in San Diego, California, described in Chapter Two), Foundations for a Better Oregon (a statewide network of mostly private foundations), and The Boston Foundation (a community foundation in Massachusetts). Each of these funders' community engagement work has not been easy, and they have made mistakes along the way. But their efforts to empower individuals have paid off in terms of better outcomes for these individuals' communities—because the communities themselves were part of the change.

GENERATE NEW AND BETTER SOLUTIONS

People living in underinvested communities face tough problems like a lack of quality health care, low-paying jobs, and under-performing schools. And although they didn't necessarily create these problems, they are at the center of them, and catalytic donors believe that these individuals should be a primary source of ideas to generate solutions. All too often foundations rely on academic research and third-party experts to provide solutions. Catalytic donors also go directly to the source.

Resident meetings and resident *working teams* are two ways the Jacobs Family Foundation and the Jacobs Center for Neighborhood Innovation ("the Jacobs foundations") effectively engaged individuals living in the Diamond Neighborhoods of southeastern San Diego to create the remarkable Market Creek Plaza site, a project introduced in Chapter Two.[7] The plaza and other initiatives have attracted millions of dollars in additional investment to the neighborhood, have created hundreds of jobs, are expected to spawn dozens of new, locally housed businesses over the next ten years, and in general have transformed this urban community from one of blight and neglect to one of hope and involvement.

The Jacobs foundations began work on the plaza site not by moving dirt but by sending a local resident, Roque Barros, into the living rooms of this community to listen to what residents needed. Barros, who is director of community building for the Jacobs Center for Neighborhood Innovation (JCNI), encouraged several residents to invite ten of their neighbors to attend meetings in their homes. (JCNI paid them $100 to cover the cost of refreshments and of "renting out" their homes for the evening.) In these informal settings, residents discussed with Barros and each other such topics as what they liked about the neighborhood and what they would change.

Barros then invited some of the resident meeting participants and hosts to form an *outreach team*, which eventually surveyed 600 residents and 200 business leaders to receive broader input on what the community needed. These are some of the things they heard local people say they wanted:

- A major chain grocery store
- A bank
- A sit-down restaurant and a coffee shop
- Living-wage jobs close to home
- A place to go with their families for cultural entertainment

JCNI then used that input to form resident-led working teams focused on arts and design, construction, business and leasing, and other areas, which local people joined according to their skills or interests. These teams became an important source for ideas for solutions, and in many cases team members were part of the solution implementation.

For example, as described in Chapter Two, a dry creek bed runs through the middle of the property the Jacobs Family Foundation (JFF) sought to develop. Although water hardly ever flows through it, when there is rain, says JFF executive director Jennifer Vanica, "it comes through with a vengeance." For this reason, commercial developers and other outside firms had declared the site undevelopable. The JFF board members weren't about to let the dry creek stop them, although the agencies and departments with whom they had to consult made formidable opponents. They battled with institutions ranging from the Army Corps of Engineers and the California Department of Fish and Game to the various California zoning agencies and jurisdictions that had authority over the creek because it was part of a protected wetlands network.

They were close to giving in, when finally at one resident team meeting a local person asked, "What *can* you put in a waterway?" Other residents—some of them with architectural and building knowledge—responded: "a barge," "a dock," "a boat." That naive sounding question sparked an innovative, unconventional idea that traditional architects or developers had not considered. What if you built a structure in such a way that it floats when it rains?

And that's what Market Creek Plaza residents did. One of the things residents had said they wanted was an entertainment venue. So they designed an amphitheater with a stage that extends *over* the creek bed and uses the grassy banks of the creek as a naturally sloping seating area. This remarkable structure serves as both a physical and a symbolic reminder of the value of engaging individual community members in solving problems for themselves.

This process yielded two important results. First, by taking the time to reach out and listen to residents, the Jacobs foundations found out what people in the neighborhood really *needed*. Residents didn't ask for more services or aid. They wanted what other, more affluent communities enjoyed: a place to deposit their paychecks; a family restaurant; a grocery store that sold fresh fruit, vegetables, and meat and not just salty chips and sugary sodas. And second, residents were able to devise solutions to problems that so-called experts, such as commercial developers who lived outside of the community, couldn't see. They invented homegrown solutions that were both innovative and appropriate to their unique geophysical situation.

BUILD COLLECTIVE WILL

Engaging residents in solving their own problems produces another important effect. The process of devising homegrown solutions transforms them from passive "victims" of dysfunctional systems into proactive problem solvers with a collective power to advance their own interests. It effectively weds them to the cause. In *Forces for Good*, authors Crutchfield and McLeod Grant described the process of "inspiring evangelists"—the means by which high-impact nonprofits engage individuals in meaningful experiences that transform them into passionate advocates for the cause.[8] Catalytic donors tap into this same principle to spark big change on statewide and broader regional levels.

Take the Chalkboard Project based in Portland, Oregon.[9] In 2003, five of Oregon's most influential funders teamed up to take on an ambitious goal: transform Oregon's K–12 school system and bring it to such a high level of success that it moves from the middle of the pack up into the nation's top ten systems. Like the nonprofits in Cincinnati's Strive Partnership (profiled in Chapter Five), Oregon's leading funders had been spending millions on education reform by fighting individual battles with isolated results. In 2004, frustrated by the slow pace of change and the failure to improve the system statewide, they combined their efforts by establishing Foundations for a Better Oregon, an independent, nonpartisan, charitable organization. Then Foundations for a Better Oregon created Chalkboard as a separate 501(c)(3) organization (see the sidebar "Chalkboard's Funders"). Sue Hildick, a respected leader with strong public policy credentials, was hired to lead the effort. The cornerstone of Chalkboard's strategy? Involving the community in designing solutions and advocating for statewide change.

Chalkboard's Funders

Most of Chalkboard's support comes from the members of its sponsoring organization, Foundations for a Better Oregon:

The Collins Foundation

The Ford Family Foundation

JELD-WEN Foundation

Meyer Memorial Trust

The James F. and Marion L. Miller Foundation

The Oregon Community Foundation

First, Chalkboard commissioned the states' largest public opinion poll in history. Then the initiative kicked off with a *listening tour* of focus groups held in each of Oregon's thirty-six counties. This approach was similar to Roque Barros's method of holding meetings in residents' living rooms in San Diego, as described earlier, but executed on a much broader scale across the state. Later came regional meetings with community leaders, in the form of *sojourn theater performances* (regional discussions), community-based discussion groups, Web-site visits, and an interactive online survey.

After combing through the results of their initial focus groups and polls, and then considering their findings in light of evidence-based research on best educational practices, Chalkboard leaders narrowed the multitude of ideas into a core set of priorities, things that Oregonians believed needed to be changed about their schools. Then they used the data and opinions they had gathered to bolster these policy change proposals—the first of which was proposed in early 2007. Oregonians are able to partic-ipate in these reform initiatives by volunteering with Chalkboard through the Citizen Corps—a growing group of local leaders from throughout Oregon who support Chalkboard's long-term K–12 education reform efforts. These volunteers serve as ambassadors for Chalkboard in their communities and promote Chalkboard's broad set of school improvement proposals. Through this work with individuals, as well as active engagement with state legislators at the policy level, Chalkboard has mobilized stakeholders around several education reform initiatives in areas such as early learn-ing opportunities, support for teachers, and measures to enforce more school district financial accountability and efficiency. All told, in five years Chalkboard has engaged more than 100,000 Oregonians.

This mass mobilization effort is paying off. For example, in three school districts where a Chalkboard-driven teacher devel-opment initiative is under way, student achievement indicators are positive.[10] "And even more compelling," says Hildick, is that "teacher attitudes in these first three CLASS districts are dramatically different." As shown in our discussion of forging peer networks (Chapter Five), funders acting in lockstep—as has occurred in Cincinnati's Strive Partnership and is likewise occurring in Oregon—creates a powerful focusing mechanism. Chalkboard built that same mechanism and has augmented it with enormously widespread engagement and community input that infuses its policy change proposals with public will.

BRIDGE DIVIDES OF CLASS, RACE, AND PLACE

Community engagement applies not just to those who face problems like substandard health care or failing school systems. Effective civic engagement involves each economic stratum—the well-off, the middle class, and poor residents. And it reaches every corner of a region. Participants may live on the same block or in the same town, city, or greater metropolitan area. Regardless of members' relative proximity, each member of the wider community shares both the responsibility for social change and the benefits from it.

Take The Boston Foundation (TBF). This ninety-five-year-old institution is one of the oldest and largest community foundations in the country, encompassing some 900 separate funds and possessing assets of $740 million. Despite its impressive size, historically TBF was a quiet foundation that operated mostly behind the scenes. That changed when Paul Grogan joined as CEO in 2001. A veteran of the community development movement who had run a local initiatives support corporation (LISC) and what is now known as the Boston Department of Neighborhood Development, Grogan was a recognized expert in community revitalization—influencing the field as a practitioner and also through published works such as *Comeback Cities* (coauthored with Tony Proscio).[11]

One of the innovative things Grogan did when he joined The Boston Foundation was to involve the foundation in public policy change work, which at TBF is called *civic leadership*. But Grogan's approach to policy change involved more than work with statehouse legislators and other key policymakers. "I wanted to have more of a grassroots connection," explains Grogan. "We had already moved into public policy, but our focus was with the elite players who were well known. There is a whole other world out there that isn't part of any 501(c)(3) organizations—and they are people who really matter." Grogan wanted to reach beyond the state's formal nonprofit sector "and go straight to the storefronts, the street corners, housing projects." As he explains, "There are ladies who live in public housing who do so much—they influence people but they are not part of any formal organization."[12]

Grogan looked at his staff and realized that, to reach into the neighborhood, he was going to need someone with authentic, community-based credentials. He recruited an exceptional candidate—Robert Lewis Jr., a recognized local leader who had formerly served as executive director of City Year's Boston site and the Boston Centers for Youth and Families. Lewis had founded an innovative street-workers program in the 1990s, which employed ex-gang members, reformed addicts, and other community members and trained them to patrol the streets, promote peace, and discourage young men and women from life on the streets. "Violence is done by, and affects, a relative handful of individuals who are committing violent crimes, but they are creating a climate of fear in the whole neighborhood," says Lewis. The problem of violence and fear of violence was preventing kids from being active, forcing them to avoid playgrounds and not sign up for afterschool sports because their parents and caregivers wanted them inside after school, so they would know their kids were safe.[13]

At TBF, Lewis was able to update and relaunch that program, adding a service component designed to help kids move out of destructive habits; the program complemented the foundation's efforts to find new ways to help people help themselves.

Lewis also gives out *action grants*, which go out in small increments to organizations and local community leaders—such as the ladies in housing projects—who may not have an official business card or work for a community development corporation but who nonetheless know what needs fixing in their neighborhood. Through these action grants, TBF is funding microlevel projects—clearing an abandoned lot, fixing up a dilapidated shelter—recognizing that these local acts of positive change are powerful examples of individuals solving community problems—*for themselves.*

The Boston Foundation doesn't stop there. In addition to engaging residents living in the communities it also aims to serve, the foundation connects across class and geography as well. For the past two years, TBF has sponsored the Boston at Night Tour. These evening tours start after sundown, and participants who hail from tonier addresses like Beacon Hill and Cambridge can visit tough neighborhoods in places like Roxbury that middle- or upper-class residents are unlikely to be familiar with. Tour participants visit the street corners where drugs are sold, see playgrounds that have turned into battle zones, and get a firsthand look at the hospitals where kids wounded by street violence end up. It's a powerful experience—one that connects city with suburbs, haves with have-nots. It has become so widespread that it's now common for people in Boston to say, "Have you done *the tour*?" It also puts The Boston Foundation at the center of the action, while enabling outsiders to become insiders and raising their support for the cause.

THE BROADER RETURN—AND THE RISKS

So what do these cases tell us? Individually, they show how community and private foundations that invest the time and resources to directly engage individual community members reap a big return. Through this engagement they gain a deeper understanding of the problems their communities face and generate more creative solutions for those problems. A second benefit of community engagement is that the participants become excited about the cause and inspired to become evangelists for it on a broader scale. And finally, engagement introduces a way for otherwise disconnected segments of the community to come together around a cause—whether they were formerly separated by class, race, or geography or all three of these factors—catalytic donors bring them together to advance the larger cause.

Collectively, these cases show us how catalytic donors think about the role of individuals. Their approach is different from that taken by most foundations. Whether they do it consciously or not, catalytic donors approach individuals not just as service recipients or an audience to be marketed to but as an integral part of the social change process. They demonstrate a mind-set shift that is not common among other donors, and this failure to think differently about individuals prevents other donors' philanthropy from achieving greater levels of impact.

"Grantmaking initiatives often fail when the foundation remains isolated from its grantees and the communities they both serve," write Kathleen Enright and Courtney Bourns in the *Stanford Social Innovation Review*. Enright, who is CEO of

Grantmakers for Effective Organizations (GEO), and Bourns, who is GEO's vice president of programs, believe that it is critical for donors to become more engaged with individual community residents and other stakeholders who aren't usually part of a foundation's internal team. These authors say that philanthropic institutions historically have made grantmaking decisions "from inside their own walls, and then handed those decisions down, in many cases reflecting a charity orientation to their giving."[14] Even for those catalytic donors who *have* made the mind-set shift to engaging individuals in their work, carrying out this intention is rarely easy. But when done right, individual empowerment can lead to better outcomes, even though the process can be frustrating, demoralizing, and at times extremely uncomfortable.

"I cried after a negative article ran in a local community publication that contained blatantly untrue accusations," admits Jacobs Family Foundation board member Valerie Jacobs. As committed as the JFF board has been to engaging and listening to local residents in its efforts to revitalize the Diamond Neighborhoods—JFF even moved its offices into the neighborhood and hired local residents—not every community member trusts or understands what the Jacobs foundations have been trying to do. Their distrust is not unwarranted, explains Jacobs, because commercial developers and other outsiders have been coming to this community for years and promising big changes but rarely delivering. "It's hard. It's discouraging. It's frustrating. It's the negativity that we encounter because we are doing things in a new way, which is very difficult for some people."[15]

Receiving harsh criticism and getting yelled at aren't typical experiences for most foundation executives or wealthy individuals. These experiences are a far cry from the platitudes a donor receives when he or she is honored at a gala benefit or touted in some nonprofit newsletter. By positioning themselves within shouting distance of the community they seek to serve, catalytic donors receive a perspective on the process of social change that's wholly different from the view most funders get.

However, not every donor has to dive into the level of intense community engagement that Valerie Jacobs and the other donors profiled here have done. There are additional ways to involve individuals in a foundation's work, and these other approaches also enable donors to better understand the needs of local residents and adapt their giving strategies accordingly. Funders can start by simply opening up their foundation's board to include local community members, or they can invite residents to meetings and involve them in events. At the end of this chapter, we offer principles to follow for donors who want to take a step in this direction and also for more experienced donors who seek to deepen their practice. Additionally, the report *Do Nothing About Me Without Me: An Action Guide for Engaging Stakeholders*, published by GEO and Interaction Institute for Social Change, offers further information and useful case studies.[16]

WIKI-PHILANTHROPY

So far in this chapter we've focused primarily on how catalytic donors engage individuals *on the ground* to help develop new ideas and better solutions, build collective will, and connect traditionally divided communities. They use old-fashioned techniques that have proven highly effective, such as walking door to door and sitting down in living rooms to listen and really understand what people need. But these days, with the advent of the Internet and the proliferation of virtual technologies, individuals can also be engaged through a host of other means, making possible community organizing and idea sharing on a scale and in time frames previously unimaginable.

For instance, we described in the previous chapter the Knight Foundation's innovative attempt to forge a network among community foundations so that they would recognize and take on the challenge of restoring residents' access to local news and information. The Knight Foundation also works directly with individuals, engaging them in actively addressing their community's information gaps through open-sourced approaches and other opportunities to seed innovation.

With a grant from the Knight Foundation, the New Voices program of J-Lab (at the School of Communications at American University in Washington, D.C.) solicited and reviewed hundreds of proposals from individuals and local groups outlining their ideas for restoring news in their communities. One group of winners hailed from bucolic Deerfield, New Hampshire. Knight Foundation vice president Eric Newton sets the scene this way: "Imagine a town with green grass, white picket fences, picturesque mountains in the background—but no news." Deerfield had neither local reporters nor a newspaper, and its City Hall didn't even have a Web site. No one wanted to run for office, so some public seats remained vacant for multiple terms.[17]

What Deerfield did have was a library, and some active members of the local Friends of the Library formed a small group named The Forum and proposed to restore democracy to Deerfield. They received a total of $17,000 to build a Web site and cover emergent issues in town, sharing with residents what was happening in the public and community realms. After The Forum started publishing online in 2005, Deerfield soon found itself with rising voter turnout rates, fewer vacant public offices, and fewer uncontested elections, among other changes. Within a year, Deerfield voters had elected their first woman to the state legislature. The grant The Forum received was a small amount to pay for restoring democracy to an entire town.

And here is where it comes full circle. By engaging individuals directly through open forums and competitions facilitated by the Internet, as well as by working through networks of community foundations, Knight has found ways to spark innovation at the ground level. With the goal of helping individual citizens solve problems for themselves, Knight is building a bottom-up movement—not to bail out the publishing industry's traditional printed products, which may be forever lost as a profitable concern—but to save news and information itself.

THE BUSINESS OF ENGAGING INDIVIDUALS

The uncommon way catalytic donors engage members of the public in problem solving for themselves parallels a profound transformation sweeping the private sector. With the advent of new media technologies and the transformation of the United States and other developed nations to knowledge-based economies, the private sector's relationship with consumers is undergoing a fundamental paradigm shift. No longer simply passive purchasers of widgets, consumers in the new economy expect to shape and interact with the products and services they receive. They become what futurist Alvin Toffler calls *prosumers* rather than *consumers*.[18] Table 6.2 summarizes this paradigm shift.

TABLE 6.2. INDUSTRIAL VERSUS DIGITAL ERA VIEWS OF INDIVIDUALS.

Industrial Era	Digital Era
Consumers are "target market" for products.	Consumers are codevelopers of products.
Consumers are buyers.	Consumers are builders.
Business sells to many consumers (B to C).	Consumers sell to other consumers (viral marketing) (C to C).
Competition.	Co-opetition (cooperative competition).

This shift in the relationship between consumers and producers is made possible by the Internet's many-to-many communication. As we explored in the previous chapter on forging nonprofit peer networks, social networks exist because millions of individuals can independently post Web pages, create links to others in the network, and have others link to them—all without the facilitation of a central point of production or control. The company provides the enabling Web-based platform, but the individual "buyers"—through the very act of "consuming" the product—actually "produce" the end product. The web of networks they create through these countless, self-directed, one-to-one linkages become the product. Individuals are, so to speak, building the airplane as they fly it.

THE COMPLEXITY OF INDIVIDUAL EMPOWERMENT

Online networks are important not just because they offer a powerful new tool for businesses and nonprofits alike to actively engage individuals in social networking, collaboration, and other collective activities. Online networks are important because they provide a visible *analogy* for understanding how social movements work, for a network of individuals and organizations that is creating a social change movement shares many of the same properties found in online social networks; both can be thought of as *complex systems*.

In Chapter Five, we proposed that social innovation and complexity science are linked. "We must move from seeing the world as simple, or even merely complicated. To understand social innovation, we must see the world in all its complexity,'' write the authors of *Getting to Maybe*.[19] As a domain of study, complexity science has existed since the early 1900s, but the rise of digital networking technology has moved it to the forefront of research. Scientists who study complex systems focus on how relationships between parts give rise to the collective behaviors of a system, and how the system interacts with and forms relationships with its environment. Complex systems take all shapes and forms: the human brain, immune systems, even global markets made up of individual consumers and producers.[20]

Although much is known about the individual elements that make up these kinds of complex systems, scientists do not fully understand how the elements function together as a whole. How does an immune system fight disease? How does a group of cells organize itself to be an eye or a brain? Or perhaps most mysteriously, "how do phenomena we call 'intelligence' and 'consciousness' emerge from nonintelligent, nonconscious material substrates?" as Melanie Mitchell, author of *Complexity: A Guided Tour*, asks.[21]

The same questions can be asked of social change movements. Take the civil rights movement, or for that matter any major movement—the French Revolution, Gandhi's Salt March, or any issue-based campaign for the environment, labor, people with disabilities, or AIDS. Like the complex systems that arise in the natural world, movements are made up of disparate, loosely connected individuals who act in unison without direction from a single central controller. As Robert F. Kennedy told us in a speech back in 1966: "It is from the numberless diverse acts of courage ... [and] belief that human history is shaped. Each time a person stands up for an ideal, or acts to improve the lot of others, or strikes out against injustice, he sends forth a tiny ripple of hope, and crossing each other from a million different centers of energy and daring, those ripples build a current that can sweep down the mightiest walls of oppression and resistance."[22]

Although Kennedy didn't have the benefit of the World Wide Web and its complex network of nodes and links to illuminate his view of how change happens, he understood at a fundamental level how complex systems work. He recognized that an energy that was created from the combined result of an infinite series of individual acts could cause an effect that was greater than, and different than, the sum of its parts.

The challenge for philanthropy—and indeed for anyone who sees himself or herself as a force for social change—is to try to understand how complex systems work, and then apply that knowledge in the quest for change. Some of the most forward-thinking donors are tapping into the power of collective impact—working in partnership with, and reaching beyond, their nonprofit partners to interact directly with individuals at the community level, trying to harness the energy of these individuals and steer it toward advancing a common purpose or goal. To do this, donors must first change the way they view individuals—seeing them not as charity recipients but as partners in change.

This is difficult to do—and the results it may generate are even harder to measure. Today nearly every foundation gathering is dominated by discussions of measuring outcomes, not just outputs. Indeed, the very definition of modern philanthropy is rooted in Andrew Carnegie's "scientific" approach which hinged on "evidence" and tackling root causes, not just symptoms of problems. Yet when it comes to engaging individuals, it's not always clear what the outcome should—or could—be. Sometimes the best result a donor can hope for is that as a consequence of one small grant, a person switches from apathy to action—sending forth into the universe one more ripple of energy that didn't exist before. In this way, social movements challenge everything that is rational, scientific, and "known" about how things are supposed to work.

Movements are fuzzy. They operate in sometimes mysterious ways. They are Robert Kennedy's "numberless diverse acts of courage" that sometimes add up to amazing outcomes. Movements don't come with an IRS letter for 501(c)(3) tax-exempt status attached. They don't arrive in a donor's mailbox or e-mail inbox in response to a request for proposals. And yet movements exist. Just as a human brain exhibits intelligence and consciousness even though it is made up of nonintelligent, nonconscious substrates, social movements form. They are capable of producing results that are greater than, and different than, the simple sum of their parts. None of us can explain exactly how they exist or what makes them successful. We only know that they do exist, and they can change the world.

CONCLUSION

At the end of the day we are advocating that donors engage and mobilize individuals as a powerful lever for change. The effort can be frustrating, demoralizing, and difficult—so donors should consider carefully before attempting to adopt this practice. But for those who embrace this approach and are able to successfully engage individuals, the ends amply reward the means.

The Consumer Health Foundation profiled earlier in this chapter believes in engaging and empowering individuals. So do the five foundations that collectively launched Oregon's Chalkboard Project. The Knight Foundation and its networks of community foundations and local residents believe in it. Conservative funders who support The Heritage Foundation and other right-wing think tanks especially believe in it. And the collective contributions of the countless individuals and institutions that propelled the U.S. civil rights movement also believe in empowering individuals.

The question for readers of this book is, do you?

KEY PRINCIPLES FOR EMPOWERING THE PEOPLE

1. **Adopt an individual empowerment mind-set**. Instead of viewing individual community members as recipients of charity or keeping them at arm's length, consider engaging individuals in the change you seek to create in the world. Open up your board to include experts from nontraditional backgrounds, including people who live in the communities you aim to serve. Invite local residents to meetings and events. Look for other opportunities for foundation trustees and staff to explore alternative perspectives.

2. **Engage individuals and communities to advance change**. Solicit, support, and nurture the development of solutions and new ideas from individuals who may or may not be affiliated with a particular nonprofit. Donors can work directly with

individuals and also through their grantees to generate new and better solutions to pressing problems; build collective will to solve problems on a local or regional level; and bridge divides of class, race, and place. Start by

- Conducting resident meetings, listening tours, and any other activities that can be designed to directly solicit input from community members.
- Creating opportunities for local residents to participate in policy change and other campaigns—establish a volunteer corps, resident working teams, and issue-based working groups that facilitate participation.
- Designing ways for cities and suburbs and for low-income and wealthy communities to come together—host night tours, stage regional cultural events, engage residents in coming up with ideas to bridge traditional societal divides.

3. **Prepare for the conflict.** Empowering people at the individual level can be uncomfortable. It will often entail crossing lines of class, race, and place, and the process can unleash forces that are beyond your control. Conflict is often a result of distrust, so when disputes arise, focus on the ultimate outcome—improving lives—and understand that not every individual will appreciate, trust, or understand what you are trying to do.

4. **Work *wikily*.** Leverage the power of new technology to forge new connections and foster discussion across formerly disconnected populations; use social networking technology to spread messages and build awareness and also to do the work of the foundation. Look for ways to engage individuals in your work via virtual technologies as well as on the ground.

CHAPTER SEVEN

PRACTICE 5
Lead Adaptively

*To take advantage of Practices 1 through 4,
philanthropists must perceive and respond to
opportunities in their environment, orchestrate
activity among key players, and shape conditions so
that others can make progress toward the cause.*

The dinner wasn't going well for Paul Grogan. Three years into his tenure as the CEO of The Boston Foundation, Grogan had convened the chiefs of the major Boston area hospitals for an evening to discuss how businesses could improve the livelihoods of the working poor living within the region. His goal was to motivate Boston's private health care sector to help with creating a system that would enable low-income individuals to develop relevant skills for higher-paying jobs, leading to greater self-sufficiency for them and their families.[1] "It was a really lousy evening," remembers Grogan. "They were very guarded and it was difficult to generate conversation. In philanthropy we always have this attitude of 'let's work together,' but these guys were bitter competitors. Friendly . . . but they compete."

Exercising the numerous charms that had enabled him in his short time at the foundation to win over many of the city's wealthy donors and political elite, Grogan nonetheless found himself stymied in attempting to foster a collaborative approach among the players at the table. "The discussion was stunted and stilted," says Grogan. Finally, one of the executives at the table, the head of

Beth Israel Deaconess—one of the city's largest hospitals—said, "Paul, the reason this isn't working is because we compete. Why don't you play to that? Why don't you ask us to compete and be the best at what you want to see happen?"

"So that's what we did," said Grogan, "and it worked beautifully. We ended up getting unprecedented cooperation. It wasn't how we anticipated things happening but these executives saw it was in their enlightened self-interest to try something new and different and ultimately they made it happen."

PAUL GROGAN'S ADAPTIVE LEADERSHIP

The inability to move beyond minimum wage jobs undermines the efforts of millions of Americans to support themselves and their families. The results are bad for families who want to live a decent life, bad for businesses that need more skilled employees, and bad for local governments in search of a healthy tax base to pay for public services. Yet getting local communities to pay attention to the challenges and opportunities of matching low-skilled job seekers with the necessary training to get higher-paying jobs is nearly impossible. It's complicated math to bring low-income job seekers together with the type of training that leads to job opportunities that can pull families out of poverty. The system is so fragmented that rarely can anyone connect the dots.

Paul Grogan connected the dots. He could see the patterns of the workforce challenge in Boston. He could foresee a nasty downward economic spiral if the community didn't start helping more low-income individuals to improve their lot. But he needed to connect the dots in a way that would compel leaders in the community to do something about it, because he could never single-handedly take on the challenge through his foundation. Grogan didn't have the answers, but he had a sense of who needed to be involved and thoughts on how to engage them. So over a ten-year period beginning in 2001, Grogan and The Boston Foundation (TBF) found a way to put others to work to find solutions. Along the way, through multiple creative interventions, Grogan leveraged each of the four practices we've discussed already: advocating for change, blending profit with purpose, forging nonprofit peer networks, and empowering individuals.

He employed these practices by exercising *adaptive leadership*, a unique form of leadership that catalytic donors must adopt in order to bring about real change. Let's take a look at how he did it.

Reframing the Problem

As we've already suggested, Grogan's first task was to reframe the problem of helping poor workers get out of dead-end jobs, and he had to put it in a way that would motivate—rather than turn off—community stakeholders. He says, "I had ideas about the deficiencies of workforce [development]. In the '70s and '80s, all the job training programs I observed were federally funded. I had lengthy experience in how deficient they were—with a coloration of social service and assistance for needy individuals rather than helping business and the economy."

To increase the community's sense of urgency, Grogan converted the idea of workforce development from an issue that was typically viewed as welfare to an economic development issue that struck at the very heart of regional employers' unmet needs. In this reframing, he capitalized on data that were surfacing from TBF's Boston Indicators project, which tracks regional progress on shared civic goals in areas such as education, the economy, health, and the environment. Using these data, the foundation portrayed the brewing of a nasty "perfect storm": a rapidly aging workforce; a below-replacement birthrate in Massachusetts; growth in the unskilled immigrant population; and an outmigration of skilled young people, who were finding Boston's cost of living too high for raising a family. These factors added up to a damaging erosion of Boston's historical advantage in human capital.

When Grogan and TBF staff first highlighted these findings in 2001, they weren't greeted as saviors. It's difficult to shoot the messenger when the messenger is one of the community's largest foundations, nonetheless TBF's report was rejected by some as unpatriotic and excessively negative. The report did, however, says Grogan, "initiate conversation and became an important table setter for our later undertakings. The whole issue got elevated in a kind of worrisome way."

Keeping It Visible

TBF followed up its initial spotlight on Boston's evolving human capital challenges with more activity to keep the issue visible. It commissioned additional research to dig deeper into the challenge and then revealed what it was finding at local forums, where Grogan and TBF staff were able to engage face to face with a range of stakeholders from the community: nonprofits, government officials, neighborhood activists, and businesses. Grogan also enlisted key influential individuals in the region to advocate in the media in support of helping low-skilled workers. For example, in a media event on the eve of new governor Deval Patrick's inauguration, The Boston Foundation helped arrange a *Boston Globe* editorial written by two prominent local individuals, Robert Haynes and William Tinti, who represented labor and business interests respectively. The editorial presented the new governor with a roadmap for success in building the workforce, including continued statehouse support for Skillworks, the collaborative workforce initiative that TBF had assembled with several other local funders.

Getting Beyond the Usual Suspects

Visibility and communication weren't the only things that TBF needed to orchestrate among funding partners and various other players. Grogan felt that just working through the "usual suspects" of community-based organizations doing job training wasn't going to succeed at addressing workforce development quickly and at scale. "We needed to put employers, along with nonprofits, in the driver's seat," said Grogan. "This was to be a hugely different way for us to do business."

Step 1 for Grogan in engaging local business was mobilizing the members of Boston's health care sector to bring their weight to bear on the problem. Boston boasts one of the most vibrant local health care clusters in the country. Its world-class hospitals had been growth engines for the local Boston economy for decades, and local hospitals had significant need for new entry-level and above-entry-level workers. But the hospitals weren't set up effectively for finding and recruiting the entry-level workers they needed, job-seekers weren't aware of hospitals' needs, and local nonprofit job training programs weren't tailored to hospital requirements.

The confluence of these conditions led Grogan to orchestrate the hospital executive meeting you read about at the start of this chapter. Out of meetings like that one, The Boston Foundation and its collaborating partner funders created new types of *workforce partnerships*. These partnerships focused on specific industry sectors, bringing together employers, nonprofit agencies, educational institutions, labor unions, and government.

For example, in response to TBF's call to action, the construction industry formed a partnership called the Building Services Career Path. To create career advancement opportunities for low-skilled building custodians, this partnership combined efforts from the nonprofit arm of Service Employees International Union Local 615, six local building management companies, Harvard and MIT Universities, the janitors union, a number of community-based organizations, and the Massachusetts Worker Education Roundtable. Notably, this partnership came together on the heels of a 2003 strike that had pitted the union representing the men and women who clean Boston's office buildings against the companies that manage services to many of those buildings. The initiative channeled the energy that arose through this labor-management conflict and enabled previous foes to become partners at the same table, working for shared outcomes.

Government, too, was engaged in novel ways as Grogan approached the mayor to solicit the City of Boston's involvement up front. The mayor turned over scarce, flexible dollars to the collaborative, which served not only to increase funding but also lent influential endorsement to the initiative's innovative approach. This endorsement proved particularly helpful in enabling The Boston Foundation to influence passage of important state workforce legislation.

THE PAYOFF

Results from Grogan's and The Boston Foundation's first five years of effort in workforce development have been impressive, particularly as they come in an arena where achieving substantial impact has been so hard. From 2003 to 2008, the initiative helped over 3,000 people to start on a career path toward jobs with family-sustaining wages. Over 500 community residents found new employment; over 250 people were promoted. Additionally TBF and its partners in the workforce collaborative have had a major influence in crafting favorable public policy, as their efforts led to passage of a significant 2008 law increasing funding for workforce development in Massachusetts.

Perhaps most impressive has been the change in behavior of a number of area employers. In the initiative's first five years, forty-two employers participated in this work, with the deepest engagement coming from the health care sector. Grogan took advantage of the fact that hospital heads did indeed want to compete. As hospitals have tried to one-up each other in building out new human resource operations focused on developing low-skilled workers, the beneficiaries have been threefold: the hospitals themselves, low-income families, and all others in the region who benefit from successful economic development.

A BROADER LOOK AT ADAPTIVE LEADERSHIP

An African proverb says, "If you want to go quickly, go alone. If you want to go far, go together." Most of today's troubling social problems have been with us for decades and aren't going to resolve themselves anytime soon if the approach taken by most donors is to address them alone. Our most difficult societal problems cannot be effectively solved by one individual or one organization.

Yet the time we have to reverse and eradicate problems like climate change, failing public schools, or poverty in both developed and developing countries is running out. To conflate the proverb, we need to "go far, quickly."[2] Going far quickly will require effective leadership, a good portion of which must come from catalytic donors who care about and fund these issues.

Capitalizing on Practices 1 through 4 requires a particularly nuanced and intentional type of leadership by donors—a form of leadership and influence that Paul Grogan and The Boston Foundation demonstrated in their work on workforce development. The leadership Grogan displayed was not the traditional sort in which the leader is responsible for defining the vision, creating an agenda, identifying solutions to the problem, and achieving success by pulling people along through force of personality.

Making progress in the social arena requires a subtle and dynamic view of leadership in which the people and institutions that lead are not expected to know the answer and bear the full responsibility of problem solving. Instead, they must work to create and sustain the conditions through which stakeholders take responsibility for tackling tough problems and generating answers adapted to the politics, culture, and history of their own unique situation. This approach was first defined as *adaptive leadership* by Ronald Heifetz at Harvard's Kennedy School of Government.[3] In place of the classic donor dilemma between passive and proactive giving, it offers a powerful, catalytic model for social change.

Even though more donors, such as The Boston Foundation, are now leading adaptively, their current numbers are still quite small because leading in this fashion challenges many traditional donor practices and assumptions. Perhaps most significantly, traditionally minded donors often believe that leading adaptively is an overassertion of donors' authority and potentially an abuse of the privileged position donors have as "the ones with the money."

But is that really the case?

ASSERTING LEADERSHIP, NOT JUST AUTHORITY

Leadership and *authority* are not the same thing. Individuals with authority, such as a military commander or the CEO of a company, have the power through their formal position to tell people what to do. And they can impose consequences if their subordinates don't perform as asked. By contrast, leadership should be viewed as an activity rather than a formal position or personal characteristic, and it may or may not be accompanied by authority.

Donors' authority typically extends over their grantees—the people who accept their money and therefore also their conditions. Beyond that, donors can use their stature, wealth, knowledge, and access to the corridors of power to exert leadership over a much larger arena. They can't tell society what to do, or penalize it for noncompliance, but they can influence society's thinking and behavior. Like Paul Grogan, they can set in motion chains of events that substantially influence mayors, states, local boards, media, and businesses. This kind of leadership is much more powerful than having authority, though often less comfortable for many donors to practice.

Keep in mind that it's not just donors who often lack the authority to impose solutions on a problem they care about; frequently there is no single entity anywhere with sufficient authority to solve it. Even if a donor were to discover *the* solution to an intricate social problem, no single grantee would be in a position to implement it. In reforming U.S. city school systems, for example, many stakeholders can lay claim to some authority over the schools, from school boards to the mayor to the taxpayer to the superintendant. Yet no one individual or entity controls the schools completely.

Paul Grogan and The Boston Foundation exercised both authority and leadership in their workforce development efforts, but it was Grogan's *leadership* that produced results. His authority was limited to the grantees who received TBF's funding. But making progress required *influencing* a much broader set of stakeholders.

FOCUSING ON ADAPTIVE VERSUS TECHNICAL PROBLEMS AND SOLUTIONS

Complex social challenges, such as mobilizing a community to assist low-income individuals in getting trained and connected to better-paying jobs, are adaptive problems, which are very different from technical problems. Effectively exercising leadership in the nonprofit sector depends on understanding this distinction, which we summarize in Table 7.1.

Technical problems are well defined. Their solutions are known, and people or groups with adequate expertise and organizational capacity can solve them. When a donor addresses a technical problem, the donor has a good idea of whom to fund, how much it will cost, and what the outcome will be. Examples of technical problems facing society are increasing access to higher education (by funding scholarships), increasing capacity for treating patients (by building a new hospital), increasing the efficiency

TABLE 7.1. TECHNICAL VERSUS ADAPTIVE PROBLEMS.

Technical Problems	*Adaptive Problems*
Characteristics	Characteristics
<ul><li>Problem is well defined.</li><li>Answer is known.</li><li>Implementation is clear.</li><li>Solution can be imposed by a single organization.</li></ul>	<ul><li>Challenge is complex.</li><li>Answers are not known.</li><li>Implementation requires learning.</li><li>No single entity has authority to impose solution on other stakeholders.</li></ul>
Examples	Examples
<ul><li>Funding scholarships.</li><li>Building hospitals.</li><li>Installing inventory controls for a food bank.</li><li>Developing a malaria vaccine.</li></ul>	<ul><li>Reforming public education.</li><li>Providing affordable health care.</li><li>Increasing organizational effectiveness.</li><li>Achieving 80 percent vaccination rates.</li></ul>

of a food bank (by installing better inventory controls), and finding a cure for malaria (by underwriting vaccines). In each case, the problem is clear, the solution depends on well-established practices, and given enough money, a single organization can implement the solution.

In contrast, adaptive problems are not so well defined, the answers are not known in advance, and many different stakeholders are involved, all with their own perspectives. Adaptive problems require innovation and learning among the interested parties, and even when a solution is discovered, no single entity has the authority to impose it on others. The stakeholders themselves must create and put the solution into effect because the problem is rooted in *their* attitudes, priorities, or behavior. And until the stakeholders change their outlook, a solution cannot emerge.

Many social problems that donors seek to address—from reforming education to ending hunger and homelessness—are adaptive. But in contrast to technical problems, merely throwing money at an adaptive problem never works. Indeed, *the tendency to address adaptive problems with technical approaches may be the single greatest barrier to donors' effectiveness, and the reason that many multimillion-dollar donor initiatives fail to create lasting social change.* Approaches that depend on a known answer and the authority and organizational capacity to impose a solution are not likely to be effective in solving adaptive problems that require multiple stakeholders to clarify their values, choose among painful trade-offs, develop previously unknown solutions, and implement them.

For donors to become catalytic, they must learn how to lead adaptively and thus become more effective at meeting complex social challenges. Catalytic donors who address adaptive problems must also be willing to accept what may become far more controversial public profiles.

Shaping Conditions with Stakeholders

It's no secret. Change is hard. People don't like to change even when their circumstances are difficult. And getting *groups* of people to change within or across organizational boundaries is even more challenging. But it's not impossible. Sometimes what it takes is a push to get things going. As authors Chip Heath and Dan Heath suggest in their book *Switch: How to Change Things When Change Is Hard*, even a small change can get people to see their situation in a new way.[4] And this can lead to bigger changes. The key is to get people unstuck from their current ways and into new ways that hold greater promise.

Grantees get stuck. So do whole communities. Catalytic donors know that part of their job, if they want to see improvements in the causes they care about, is to get people who are involved in the issue unstuck.

William "Bill" Graustein and David Nee, board chair and CEO respectively of the William C. Graustein Memorial Fund (GMF) in New Haven, Connecticut, are two individuals who spend a lot of time focused on getting people unstuck from their ways in preparing kids for success in school and life.[5] GMF was established in 1946 by Bill Graustein's father, but it wasn't until the mid-1990s that GMF received a large infusion of funds causing the board members to get serious about their focus. Bill Graustein set out to improve early childhood outcomes for kids in Connecticut by helping communities design and implement better educational, social, and environmental supports for kids, from their first year through age eight. Graustein and Nee developed a two-pronged strategy for the foundation: advocacy for early childhood support at the state level and work at the community level through tapping collaboratives that would work with and represent parents and children's interests.

There was already a lot of policy advocacy going on around early childhood in Connecticut, and GMF was puzzled as to why the childhood education groups couldn't get any wins. "The perception was, the field doesn't have its act together and can't get traction," explains Nee. So GMF commissioned one of the state's foremost authorities to conduct a differential analysis of GMF's major grantees, based on their distinct organizational capacities, and to look for opportunities for collaboration. It turned out that the two biggest nonprofits in GMF's portfolio possessed great but different strengths: one emerged as a leading research and development tank and the other as the leading mobilizer of parents and local community members. But when it came to fieldwide campaigns like policy advocacy and raising awareness, these two rivals collided. They effectively reached a stalemate, locked in separate advocacy campaigns and neither winning.

GMF proposed a solution: "We asked, what would it take for you guys to get on [the same] page?" said Bill Graustein. And then GMF offered to keep bringing the groups together to hammer out a unified agenda for reform. GMF contributed the funds, the meeting space, and staff sweat equity. Soon the Connecticut Early Childhood Alliance was born. With substantial effort by its nonprofit members and other key stakeholders, formation of the Alliance led to the organizations finally working in alignment. The group members collectively became a major influence in establishing the Connecticut state legislature's priorities for early childhood development.

Solving adaptive challenges requires work that can be done only by those who are involved directly with the issue. Change typically calls for a switch in behavior, beliefs, or values on the part of those with an interest in the problem, and this type of change can't be imposed by parties outside the issue. Catalytic donors committed to achieving adaptive change need to provoke debate, encourage new thinking, and advance learning by and among key stakeholders. They need to mobilize the parties to work *toward* a solution, rather than imposing one. It's all about creating the conditions for change to happen.

The authors of *Switch* refer to this process as "shaping the path." One way to shape the path is to tweak the environment for people. See if you can "make the journey easier. Create a steep downhill slope and give them a push. Remove some friction from the trail."[6] Graustein and Nee understood this as they engaged local collaborative efforts in Connecticut. Part of GMF's message to communities was to do the opposite of what people making plans for new resources typically do. Says David Nee, "We suggested to people that they *not* try to come up with big ideas that would cost big money. But instead look for low-cost ways to improve early childhood outcomes. This way they'd develop programs that could actually get implemented. We didn't suggest *how* they should do that, but we wanted them to think about it."

The city of New Britain was one of the Connecticut communities GMF began working with. Taking GMF's advice, New Britain came up with an innovative solution GMF never could have figured out for them. The solution came from an unusual source—someone who had never before been invited to the early childhood dialogue—the head of pediatrics at New Britain's largest hospital. This physician proposed that pediatricians in the community begin doing developmental assessments of children from newborns to age three to help determine children's individual needs. The kicker in the idea was that these developmental assessments would be reimbursed by insurance. Excited by the power of the idea, the pediatrics head became a champion among his colleagues for performing developmental assessments across the community—leading to improved, quality attention to early childhood outcomes at no additional cost to the city of New Britain.

GRABBING ATTENTION

Getting people to pay attention to tough issues is at the heart of adaptive leadership. This is an especially potent tactic for donors, as they are often in an unusually strong position to direct attention to specific issues through communications campaigns or merely by announcing their grantmaking intentions. Money talks, and that gives donors, particularly when acting collectively, a powerful voice.

As mentioned earlier, donors can use their authority to hold the attention of their grantees, but they can also be highly effective at directing attention well beyond the scope of their authority. Take Joshua Reichert, managing director of environmental programs at The Pew Charitable Trusts. Reichert has successfully focused national attention on targeted issues, even though his organization has no formal authority over the constituencies it seeks to influence. For example, Reichert's work played a significant role in the 1998 passage of President Clinton's Roadless Rule, which protected 58.5 million acres of national forest from infringement. As reported in the *New York Times*, the Pew Environment Group's Heritage Forests Campaign "was the force behind the effort that generated more than a million public comments for the rule." These comments provided critical backing for the U.S. Forest Service during its rule-making process.[7]

This type of leadership is one that many with actual power would envy. In fact, in the face of Pew's campaign some authorities felt much less powerful than the public charity. "Pew's environmental group is the 800-pound gorilla on environmental issues," said Doug Crandall, staff director of the Republican-controlled House Subcommittee on Forests and Forest Health at the time of the legislation's passing.[8]

Sometimes businesses, in their capacity as donors, may be even better positioned than private and community foundations to grab the attention of stakeholders around a given social problem. The General Electric Company, mentioned earlier in this book for its effective efforts in improving health care conditions in developing countries, has been a standout leader in grabbing community attention and helping to transform schools in local U.S. communities where many GE employees live. In 1989, GE began a program called College Bound. The effort was focused on

raising the college matriculation rate in selected schools; in most
of them the rate was below 30 percent. By using its bully pulpit
as a major local employer to grab the attention of city officials
and school administrators, GE began to raise the community's
expectations for attaining college degrees. Through mobilizing
community stakeholders and supporting their efforts with GE
funding and employee sweat equity, the company was able to help
increase college matriculation rates in most selected schools from
less than 30 percent in 1989 to over 70 percent in 2003.[9]

PACING PROGRESS

As we noted previously, simple technical problems tend to resolve
themselves quickly with the application of money and expertise.
Adaptive problems, in contrast, play out very differently over
time. A step forward may be followed by a step back, and the
level of distress experienced by participants will fluctuate over
time. Harnessing this sense of disequilibrium—and making sure
it stays productive—is a critical task of adaptive leadership. The
idea is to regulate this tension so that it stimulates but does not
overwhelm people engaged in adaptive work. Stress should not
be eliminated altogether—that would remove the impetus for
adaptive work—but rather maintained at a level that motivates
change.

Ron Heifetz likens the process of creating productive tension
to that of using a pressure cooker. Think about what happens with
a real pressure cooker. The cook regulates the pressure by turning
the heat up or down, while the relief valve lets off steam to keep
the pressure within a safe limit. If the pressure goes beyond the
carrying capacity of the vessel, the pressure cooker can blow up.
Conversely, with no heat nothing cooks. In their book *Leadership
on the Line, Staying Alive Through the Dangers of Leading*, Ron Heifetz
and Marty Linsky point out that when you generate this type of
heat there is always the chance that you may simply end up in hot
water, with no forward progress to show for your effort. Donors
who want to be catalytic will need to take this risk, however, or
deprive themselves and their cause of the possibility of making
headway.

Pressure Cooking with Donors

A donor's ability to create productive tension varies depending on the issue and also on the donor's skill and creativity as a leader. Paul Grogan showed great skill in being the pressure cooker for workforce development in Boston over a lengthy period of time. First, by raising the specter of declining regional competitiveness (through data gleaned from the Boston Indicators study), Grogan created a sense of urgency to "turn things around before it was too late."

Second, by soliciting outside funding for the initiative, Grogan introduced into the work heat from *another* set of funders: the National Fund for Workforce Solutions (NFWS), which includes national funders such as the Annie E. Casey Foundation, the Ford Foundation, Microsoft, Walmart, and the U.S. Department of Labor. With this funding came the establishment of a planning time frame required by NFWS, which served to pressure the workforce partnerships to complete their work in a prescribed amount of time. In an effort that required new ways of working and therefore ran the risk of happening very slowly, the national funding created a needed sense of urgency to get the work done.

Third, Grogan kept the issue of workforce development active in the media by capitalizing on key events, such as the election of a new governor, to reintroduce the need for urgency. And finally, Grogan leveraged the competitive instincts of local business executives to orchestrate a competition to be the best at creating entry-level positions and upward mobility for low-income workers.

Bill Graustein and David Nee at the Graustein Memorial Fund likewise employed effective tactics for creating productive tension in their early childhood partner communities. Like Grogan, GMF was able to use heat from another donor—in this case the State of Connecticut—to generate productive tension. Planning grants awarded in 2005 by GMF would be most valuable to those communities that completed plans in time for the state's legislative session in 2007, when it was expected that new state funds would be awarded to those communities that could demonstrate a comprehensive blueprint for "school readiness." This placed a limited time frame on communities to plan their early childhood work.

Additionally, GMF paid for consultants to work with local communities—not to give them the answers but to help keep them on track when there was risk of the communities getting derailed. This served to provide communities not only with needed technical support but also with a gentle, consistent reminder that there was work to be done and solutions to be reached.

Finally, GMF's approach to its 2010 grantmaking illustrated a remarkably creative way to maintain productive tension and "shape the path," as the Heath brothers would say. GMF has tiered funding levels to the communities with which it is working—rewarding those furthest along with the most support, while still keeping slower-moving grantee communities in the stable by providing graduated support appropriate to their circumstances. Through this strategy GMF has kept fifty-three of its initial fifty-four selected communities engaged in improving conditions for their youngest children.

Creating the conditions for change, as Paul Grogan and GMF have done, takes time and patience. This may be challenging for many donor boards and staffs to swallow. In one very important respect, however, donors are much better positioned to do this type of work than their nonprofit peers—they are typically removed from the day-to-day battles and deadlines of getting the actual work done in communities and at state and federal legislatures. This ability to step away from the work can be critical. Heifetz and Linsky write that adaptive leaders must learn to engage both "on the balcony" where they can see all the action, and occasionally "down on the dance floor," where they get the real-time experience with the issues. In their role as intermediaries, as opposed to implementers of social change, catalytic donors must learn to do as Heifetz and Linsky suggest and move back and forth between both vantage points in the dance of change.[10]

Ripening Fruit with Donors

Catalytic donors must be able to identify when an issue is ripe for public attention and corrective action. Whether it is ripe enough hinges on whether it is generating a widespread feeling of urgency. Has the issue fastened itself in people's minds? Legislators and the public are more likely to pay attention to proposed solutions to a problem they are already concerned about.

Timing is everything. In 1997, only two years into GMF's initial early childhood development work, representatives from the state legislature asked GMF staff to testify regarding the state of early childhood care in Connecticut. Rather than take the easy route here, and call on several research organizations to prep staff with early childhood facts, figures, statistics, and benchmarks, GMF decided to reach back out to communities. With only two weeks to prepare, GMF staff mobilized outreach efforts to residents in communities hard-pressed to provide early childhood care in order to obtain the "voice of the people." Two weeks later, as executive director David Nee completed his testimony to the state legislature and was thanked by grateful representatives for his compelling research, he was able to reply, "It isn't our research, it's the community's."[11]

COURTING CONFLICT

By its nature, adaptive work does not often fall within established organizational and social structures. A wide variety of interest groups, organizations, and communities may hold pieces of information about a problem. Moreover the solution may require adjustments in the attitudes and behaviors of many people across political, ethnic, religious, and socioeconomic boundaries. If stakeholders are excluded from defining and solving the problem, the result may be an incomplete or unworkable solution.

Adaptive leadership, therefore, plays a critical role in both generating and easing conflict among various stakeholders in ways that lead to positive change. This is often a messy process. Donors who lead adaptively must ensure that all voices—not just the loudest or most powerful—are heard. At the same time, they must regulate the conflict they have unleashed so that it doesn't get out of hand. What's required is leadership that views controversy and conflict as allies rather than as obstacles in achieving reform.

Although Paul Grogan didn't initially seek to create competition with hospital heads in pursuit of his workforce development strategy, he was game to use executives' competitive juices as a lever for change. Grogan carries this attitude into other areas of The Boston Foundation's work. In its efforts to lift charter school caps in the city of Boston, the foundation generated a lot of heat at City Hall. "We mostly have a good relationship with the mayor, but we got him mad over charter caps," mentions Grogan.

The pressure worked: Once the mayor of Boston endorsed an increase in charter schools, the state of Massachusetts followed along, becoming one of a number of states that have recently lifted charter caps.

Catalytic donors who lead adaptively learn that conflict can become their best friend. Says Paul Grogan, "It's uncomfortable to have the mayor mad at you but sometimes that's what's needed to get the job done."

TAKING THE HEAT

Most donors have long tended to adopt a low profile and shy away from controversy. But when they are leading adaptively, they must learn to influence those beyond their control, such as legislators, voters, or other funders. In so doing, they often need to take on a much higher profile and engagement with media. As a result, catalytic donor staff and boards will need the fortitude to withstand the sometimes intense public pressures associated with controversial and complicated situations. The Pew Charitable Trusts, for example, is not only one of the most important participants in framing the national debate in its environmental areas of interest, it is also one of the most controversial. As Reichert notes, "If you ride the ridges, you get shot at more often than if you stay in the valleys."[12]

Maintaining an environment of tension in which adaptive work can be conducted also departs in several ways from the norm for most donors. First, this work requires a time commitment that is much longer than the typical grant cycle—often requiring years of sustained effort before any conclusive results are known.

Second, donors, by their very charitable nature, are inclined to reduce rather than heighten distress. Well-meaning donors often bail out a financially troubled nonprofit or try to ameliorate an immediate crisis. But such short-term assistance may release the pressure that was needed for adaptive work, paradoxically enabling grantees to avoid the hard learning required to become more sustainable.

Finally, leading adaptively requires focus—commitment to the cause. Most donors cannot effectively shine the spotlight of attention or shape conditions on more than one or two major issues at a time. They must invest sufficient time and attention to fully understand the players and the interpersonal and organizational dynamics of their chosen issue so that they can orchestrate change in a productive way.

TO BE OR NOT TO BE AN ADAPTIVE LEADER

It's a fair question to ask: Is this type of leadership approach right for you? Leading adaptively is not for the timid. But neither is it for those who are power hungry. For catalytic donors, leading adaptively is about finding ways to encourage *others* to solve problems for themselves. It entails learning the critical skills required to work effectively with and through each of society's sectors—government, business, nonprofit, and individual.

Different types of donors may encounter varying advantages and disadvantages inherent to the kinds of foundations they operate when it comes to leading adaptively. For example, corporations are typically more skilled in communications than private and community foundations are. As evidenced with GE's success in its College Bound initiative, companies can often sound a compelling message when framing an issue to the community, given the visibility of their brands and facilities. However, some corporate donors may be disinclined to create productive tension in the nonprofit sector, for fear of damaging those same brands. Running their business based on quarterly earnings, corporations may also be less culturally comfortable with investing resources over long time periods for the uncertain outcomes inherent in leading adaptively. And because philanthropy is important to how corporations relate to society yet it is not their central reason for being, companies may feel they cannot devote sufficient resources to take a central role in leading an adaptive social change process.

Institutional and family foundation donors typically face less risk in putting themselves out in public by leading adaptively. They are also under the least pressure to manage within a limited time frame. David Nee of GMF cites these dimensions as key freedoms that enable his organization to lead with a long view. However, compared to businesses, these donors often possess less sophisticated professional skills in communicating, framing issues for action, and orchestrating adaptive processes that achieve progress. Family donors with little or no staff may feel, as corporations do, that they don't have sufficient human resources to lead adaptively.

Community foundations, as central go-betweens for wealthy donors and influential community leaders, are well positioned to leverage their relationships to shape conditions and influence action. However, community foundation boards and staff often feel a need to be perceived as neutral so as not to offend some donors, and may therefore elect to avoid the occasional controversy that comes with exercising adaptive leadership. Paul Grogan of The Boston Foundation would be the first to admit that the flexibility he has to be proactive in influencing conditions for change is not so easily granted by many community foundation boards to their CEOs and senior staff.

CONCLUSION

Regardless of the strengths and weaknesses different donor segments face in leading adaptively, the central need to "go far, quickly," with the nation's most serious social problems means that *all* types of donors will be called upon to participate more actively in the leadership process. The good news for donors who aspire to be more catalytic but who may feel discomfort with this more active and challenging leadership role is this: you need not—indeed should not—lead alone.

As we've shown in earlier chapters, large-scale progress on complex issues will be made only by sharing the leadership spotlight with other key influencers. To be successful you must broaden the leadership mantle. Both Paul Grogan at TBF and Bill Graustein and David Nee at GMF benefited greatly by establishing a set of funders, nonprofits, businesses, and government officials who not only collaborated in doing the work but also participated in *leading* the work.

For catalytic donors to make progress against the problems they have committed to solving, success in "going far together" must include not only leveraging other forces for change but also sharing leadership with those forces.

KEY PRINCIPLES FOR LEADING ADAPTIVELY

Leading adaptively is critical for donors who want to adopt Practices 1 through 4. Such leadership isn't easy, and most donors will need to master new techniques if they are to be successful. Getting started in leading adaptively with your cause means honing a skill set that for some donors is instinctual. For others, however, beefing up their adaptive leadership skill set will require new and intentional learning—perhaps in the classroom but also in learning by doing. A number of organizations (including Ron Heifetz's consulting firm, Cambridge Leadership Associates, and FSG) provide instruction in the art and science of leading adaptively.

Whether you pursue adaptive leadership training or learn on the job by applying the practices discussed in this book in real time, you can start developing your skill set by following these four principles, which are critical to leading adaptive change:

1. **Identify the adaptive challenge**. Separating adaptive challenges from technical ones is the first task in adaptive leadership. Once the adaptive challenges are defined, it's important to discern which stakeholders should be involved and what their stakes are. Paul Grogan knew that nontraditional workforce development players, such as businesses and the mayor's office, were important players to engage in developing new, innovative approaches. He considered what the political stakes would be for these parties as well as for the community-based organizations that traditionally led workforce development.

2. **Frame the issues to focus attention**. Getting the right leaders to focus on a cause requires knowing how to get their attention. The Boston Foundation focused local attention on workforce development by identifying and highlighting a nasty "perfect storm" brewing as the region's competitiveness declined. Issues must be framed in a way that can encourage participation by all stakeholders—even those who may hold different or even competing motivations. In another example, The Pew Charitable Trusts united traditionally liberal conservationists with conservative Republican anglers to fight commercial fishing in sensitive marine areas by directing both groups' attention to the upside of creating healthy marine biosystems.

3. **Orchestrate the process so stakeholders take responsibility**. Instead of telling stakeholders the answer, catalytic donors can assist stakeholders in solving their own problems by providing knowledge, tools and access to authority figures. Graustein Memorial Trust provided consultants to assist local communities with their work, shared early childhood best practices from across the country with participating community leaders, and connected community-level participants with key state level officials.

4. **Generate and maintain productive distress**. Adaptive problems often take a long time to resolve, with progress coming sporadically. The erratic pace often distresses stakeholders. The job of adaptive leadership is to not eliminate this stress—and thus reduce the motivation for various players to devise adaptive solutions—but to harness it, maintaining it at a level that motivates without overwhelming participants. The Boston Foundation maintained tension by getting local businesses to compete to be the best at creating opportunities for low-income individuals to advance into and from entry-level positions.

CHAPTER EIGHT

PRACTICE 6
Learn in Order to Change

Catalytic donors don't conduct evaluations *in the conventional sense of the term. They build* learning organizations *in order to look forward rather than backward when assessing whether their grants are an effective means of advancing their objectives.*

In 2000, the Bill & Melinda Gates Foundation launched a new program, Sound Families, with $40 million.[1] The ambitious goal was to triple the supply of transitional housing for homeless families around Puget Sound (where the foundation is headquartered in Washington State) and support them in ways that would help them escape from the cycle of homelessness. Over the next eight years, the foundation funded the development of nearly 1,500 housing units, supplemented by case management services, to help residents succeed as they transitioned to more permanent homes.

Final reports on the housing program showed impressive results. Families who lived in Sound Families supportive housing for six to eighteen months were less likely to depend on public funds (such as Temporary Assistance for Needy Families) afterward, and children's school attendance and stability jumped noticeably when their caregivers had secured a stable place to live. Nearly 70 percent of families in the program eventually moved on to permanent housing, although many remained dependent on housing subsidies to pay the rent. Nine in ten of those families remained stably housed one year later. State legislators were so impressed by the program's track record that they helped with creating the Washington Families Fund, a public-private partnership to sustain and expand the supportive housing work after the Gates Foundation's initial investment ended. Thus the program even catalyzed long-term public funding—the holy grail for large private foundations that dedicate themselves to piloting innovative programs.

"So, are we done?" asked Melinda Gates and the foundation's CEO, Patty Stonesifer, in a 2007 meeting with foundation staff. In spite of all of the progress, Pacific Northwest Initiative deputy director David Wertheimer and his team answered with a definitive no.[2] Even though Sound Families had helped an important segment of Washington's population transition out of homelessness, the state's overall family homelessness rate had actually *grown* over the life of the initiative. The program had done much of what it was designed to accomplish, but at the same time, the larger problem it had been intended to solve had grown worse.

So the Gates Foundation regrouped. The foundation's Pacific Northwest program team took a step back, and examined the bigger picture of family homelessness. They learned that across the state, the system of multidimensional, interwoven public and nonprofit interventions designed to address homelessness was deeply flawed. As one senior government official told the planning team, "we have lots of services for homeless families, but these services are not organized into a functional system of care."[3] Although each program was providing shelter and services as best it knew how, their myriad approaches added up to an uncoordinated, incoherent system of support that fell short of achieving the ultimate goal of ending homelessness.

In this dysfunctional environment, for instance, some families on the brink of homelessness were told that assistance could not be provided until they had literally lost their housing and moved into a shelter. Other homeless families had trouble accessing government services because of the geographical location and distribution of the programs for which they were eligible. And many that did find services were plugged into one-size-fits-all programs that didn't address their most urgent concerns—domestic violence, mental illness, and substance abuse, among others.

Meanwhile, other families were receiving relatively expensive, intensive support that included an array of services the families themselves didn't necessarily need.

By the end of the reassessment process, the foundation had mapped out the players and programs that made up Washington State's $200 million system of public and private resources directed at family homelessness. Then foundation staff crafted a new strategy designed to address the systemic dysfunctions that were leading to the perpetuation and growth of the family homelessness problem. The foundation identified both government partners and nonprofit intermediaries who could help it build a network and create a platform for more collaborative, coordinated action between all the agencies. At the time of this writing, the foundation had secured formal buy-in and participation from stakeholders at all levels of government and across the philanthropic sector, and was working with the three largest counties in the Puget Sound region to implement the new strategy in the next phase of work, which the foundation hopes will promote a 50 percent reduction in family homelessness by 2019 in the targeted communities.

The Gates Foundation and its partners could have declared victory back in 2007 for piloting an innovative, effective supportive housing program. Had they merely evaluated the programs they had funded, that would have been their answer. The program team could have responded to Gates and Stonesifer's query with a decisive, "yes, we are done." For truly, the grants had "worked." But the team didn't claim success. Instead, it admitted that the program had largely failed to promote needed changes at the systemic level—and then doubled down the investment and shifted strategy in order to deal with the problem of homelessness on the larger, far more complicated scale.

"It took seven years, and by time we'd finished, our theory of change and action had evolved substantially from where we had started," explains David Wertheimer. "For our new strategy, we have a new theory of change, but I'm convinced it will change too—we need to be able to accept that and to work with partners that can move with us and flex with us as we continue to learn."

So this is a story of *emergent* success. Although homelessness is still a major problem in Washington State, and the Bill & Melinda

Gates Foundation is just setting out in its quest to achieve systems-level change, it is now on a route to real impact. At the end of the day, philanthropy is not about determining "what worked" and attributing successful outcomes to one particular program or another. Rather, as the Gates Foundation has seen, even the most promising individual programs can only be successful if an entire system is aligned to appropriately meet the needs of homeless families and individuals. Ultimately, the foundation's Sound Families team is highly adaptive, and through an ongoing process of piloting, implementing, regrouping, and trying again, team members are learning what it will take to create systems-level change.

Learning to Learn

You might see this story as an illustration of how one donor approaches developing its strategy or modifying its approach to evaluation. It is in fact both of these things. But at its core this story is really about how a catalytic donor approaches learning.

Like other catalytic funders, the Bill & Melinda Gates Foundation is climbing a steep learning curve in how it learns about and adapts to the systems in which its programs operate. The Sound Families program, for example, exhibits the traits of what strategist and systems-thinking pioneer Peter Senge calls a *learning organization*: a place "where people continually expand their capacity to create the results they truly desire, where new and expansive patterns of thinking are nurtured, where collective aspiration is set free, and where people are continually learning to see the whole together."[4]

Moving from Reporting to Learning

Ideally, all funders would aspire to a learning orientation in their work. In reality, many foundations and the vast majority of individual donors today operate with what we call a *reporting* rather than a *learning* mind-set. To understand whether the programs they fund are "working," many funders rely on reports—be they cursory self-reports by the grantee or detailed academic studies from professional evaluators. Of course few of us actually have time to read these reports, let alone act on them. Foundation reporting often reverts to an empty ritual in which grantees report to evaluators, evaluators report to program officers, and program officers report to the trustees, each going through the motions without using the information in any meaningful way. In the words of Ruth Brousseau, former director of evaluation and organizational learning at the California Wellness Foundation: "We're swimming in files and reports, but none of the information is useable. It's more the practice in the field to put the reports on a shelf and never look at them."[5]

But what is the alternative to a sea of reports—no reporting? Many donors—especially modest family foundations that employ few or no staff—go this route because they are overwhelmed by what should be evaluated, how it should be evaluated, and whether it will inform their grantmaking in the future. "Finding evaluation costly, confusing, and impractical, many foundations do not attempt any assessment of their grantmaking at all," says Valerie Lies, CEO of the Donors Forum of Chicago.[6] This is unfortunate, because these donors miss the chance to learn from their efforts and change what they do. They also miss the opportunity to influence the field as a whole or to enable grantees to learn from each other. Relying only on after-the-fact program evaluations misses the chance to engage in a more fluid, interactive learning process—a constant inflow and outflow of information that can be applied, in real time, to adjust strategies and change course.

Catalytic donors understand that learning is a never-ending process, rather than a limited project with an end-point. As the authors of *Getting to Maybe* write, "success is not a fixed address."[7]

Table 8.1 contrasts the reporting and learning mind-sets. The reporting mind-set focuses on describing the impact of individual grants, with each grantee reporting different data in different formats to different funders. This has, unfortunately but inevitably, created a costly and burdensome process of evaluation throughout the nonprofit world. Worse, measuring each nonprofit's work in different ways means that funders cannot compare the relative effectiveness of different nonprofits, and nonprofits cannot identify and learn from their peers' best work. The value of published evaluations is limited when they each measure different things. In

TABLE 8.1.   ADOPTING A LEARNING MIND-SET.

Reporting Mind-Set	Learning Mind-Set
Retrospective. Asks "Did our grant work?"	*Timely and forward looking*. Asks "What is happening today, and how can we improve tomorrow?"
Isolated. Asks about the specific impact of an individual grant.	*Integrated*. Asks about the interplay of many different factors that influence the issue.
Report-based. Requires a customized report to be delivered at a single point in time.	*Knowledge-based*. Uses multiple sources of data to provide a continuous flow of information about the issue.
Dyadic. Results are known only by the funder and grantee.	*Networked*. Information is infused throughout the system.
Seeks to demonstrate attribution. "Did our grant cause the outcome?"	*Looks for contribution*. "Did our efforts contribute to the perceived change?"

Note: The content of this table was informed by these writings: M. Q. Patton, "Developmental Evaluation," *Evaluation Practice*, 1994, *15*(3), pp. 311–319; R. T. Torres and H. Preskill, "Evaluation and Organizational Learning: Past, Present, and Future," *American Journal of Evaluation*, 2001, *22*, p. 387; C. Russon, "An Eastern Paradigm of Evaluation," *Journal of MultiDisciplinary Evaluation*, 2008, *5*(10), pp. 71–77; M. Kramer with R. Graves, J. Hirschhorn, and L. Fiske, *From Insight to Action: New Directions in Foundation Evaluation* (Boston: FSG, Apr. 2007); and M. Kramer, M. Parkhurst, L. Vaidyanathan, "Breakthroughs in Shared Measurement and Social Impact" (Executive Summary) (Boston: FSG, July 2009).

short, this approach to evaluation has created a system that churns out reports, but doesn't promote learning.

By contrast, funders who adopt a learning mind-set are focused less on receiving year-end reports and more on understanding whether and how an organization's programs have contributed to advancing the desired outcomes. As a result, rather than focusing on a specific grant and determining whether that funding "worked," these funders can shift the unit of analysis to programmatic and even organization-wide outcomes as they attempt to understand the role the grantee plays in advancing the cause.

And once donors move past the idea that evaluation must be restricted to data about a specific grant, many new and often inexpensive forms of information become the grist of learning: public Census data, surveys, academic research studies, interviews with many different parties engaged with the issue, and other kinds of data can contribute to deeper understanding.

Which Snowflake Breaks the Branch?

Perhaps the biggest difference between reporting and learning involves *attribution*. The reporting mind-set is caught up in whether the funder's particular grant caused the change that is being studied. It hopes to prove that a particular intervention "solved" the problem. But this approach works only for technical solutions. In adaptive situations, catalytic philanthropists are trying to tap into trends in the greater system that are affecting their selected issue and to focus the energy in those trends toward positive social outcomes. This means that in most cases, it's almost impossible to measure or point to a single source or cause of an overall effect.

This is a paradox of philanthropy. The catalytic donor can be defined as one who wants to *cause or accelerate a change*. The donor strives to influence the pace of progress, to support key players in achieving positive outcomes and harness them together to achieve a larger, systemwide impact. And yet no single donor can claim sole or even significant credit—any more than he or she can bear the full responsibility for the problem. Catalytic donors operate in a space where goal orientation and the best-laid strategic plans bump up against messy, problematic, and ultimately uncontrollable systems. Attempting to attribute change to a single intervention just doesn't make sense. As the authors of *Getting to Maybe* ask, "Which snowflake breaks the branch?"[8]

A Practice Based on Three Assumptions

To become effective catalytic agents of change, donors must transition toward forward-looking evaluation approaches that provide them and their grantees with *timely information* and *actionable insights* from which they can learn to improve their efforts. Catalytic donors establish learning systems—whether deliberately planned or more organically cultivated—to guide their efforts in creating change. In order to assess the performance of their grantees and programs and understand how those efforts are contributing to moving the needle on an issue, many catalytic donors engage in a series of practices based on three simple questions: How can we better plan our work? How can we improve implementation? and, How can we track progress toward our goals?

Step 1. Better Planning

Any donor hoping to move the needle on the achievement gap in an area of interest—whether homelessness, rainforest protection, early childhood education, or another issue—needs to plan how to bring about the change he or she seeks. As we have emphasized, social change is not a predictable linear process, and it is highly unlikely that events will actually go as planned. But solid research about the issue and careful thinking about the options will put donors in the best possible position to respond to events as they unfold. In the words of General Eisenhower, "Plans are useless, but planning is essential."

Perhaps the most important part of planning is getting smart on what it will take to make progress. The odds are high that other funders and nonprofits have tried to address the issue before—they have probably even undertaken evaluations of their past efforts. Consequently, a key first question in getting started with planning is to ask yourself, Have I learned from past experiences by interviewing others active in the field so that I can avoid repeating any mistakes they may have made?

As you do additional homework to get smart on your selected cause(s) there are other key questions to ask yourself:

- Do I really understand the issue in all its complexities?
- Do I have a baseline showing where things stand right now so that I can tell if matters are getting better or worse as I work on the issue?
- Do I have the information I need to establish realistic goals?

Catalytic donors not only ask these questions when planning their work, they also employ innovative learning techniques to answer these questions. For example, in Chapter Seven we explored how The Boston Foundation, through the Boston Indicators Project, created new sources of information to understand murky and sometimes underresearched community issues. It also developed a searchable, online database of information about the local economy, public education systems, and environmental stressors, among other indicators. Funders interested in support-ing any number of local issues can now visit the Boston Indicators Project Web site to understand the current state of problems and tailor their funding plans.

In another case of innovative planning, previously discussed in Chapter Six, we saw how the funders who cofounded Foundations for a Better Oregon and then the Chalkboard Project polled and engaged more than 100,000 Oregonians to understand which public education issues were ripest for attention.

The essence of a learning organization is that the data gath-ering and planning never stop. Whereas conventional donors give grants first and collect data afterward to make backward-looking assessments about what worked, catalytic donors start with research to make (and constantly revise) their plans.

Step 2. Implementation

Once a program or investment is under way, the need for good information doesn't stop. So a learning organization gathers real-time data to better inform ongoing decisions. The Bill & Melinda Gates Foundation's Sound Families program team sets up checkpoints to learn what has been working and what hasn't, and makes midcourse corrections. By interviewing residents in its housing developments and soliciting their feedback, it has gained important information that it could immediately apply to improve the effectiveness of the program. In particular, it noticed that families were being evicted when their children were too disruptive—often because the housing project had no place for children to play and let off steam. The housing projects with on-site day care and playgrounds had a higher success rate. So midway through the program, the foundation changed its criteria to require that all new projects include safe play spaces for children.

Step 3. Tracking Progress

In addition to providing a forward-looking roadmap and a compass for navigating complex and changing programs, catalytic donors seek to track longer-term progress. Many donors shy away from tracking progress, believing it's too hard or costly to do. Depending on their goals, they might be right not to focus too much attention on the short-term results, as it is enormously difficult and often beside the point to try to single out the effects of one particular grant. Still, donors should try to understand their ongoing role in creating change. They should try to reach a happy medium as they attempt to learn whether the activities they and their grantees are engaged in are really contributing to change amid complex societal problems.

CEO Tom Ross of The Z. Smith Reynolds Foundation of North Carolina provided a useful perspective on hitting this happy medium when he described the orientation of one of his foundation's program areas. "We have six grantees that are working on water quality—they established baseline data and set a goal of reducing sediment in [our] river by a certain percentage. We care about whether they have reached their goal, not whether they have reached their goal *because* of us. At a certain point, we have to take a leap of faith that our money is in fact helping move the needles. We will never be able to take credit for that movement, but we want to know if things are improving."[9]

The German foundation Stiftung Mercator has committed to tracking progress and holding itself accountable for outcomes by announcing bold impact targets: for example, by 2020, it aims to contribute to a 40 percent reduction in Germany's emissions of greenhouse gases measured against 1990 levels, and by 2025, it aims to reduce by 70 percent the inequality of school and university qualifications for marginalized populations. Tracking progress against these goals will inevitably require that the foundation look well beyond the performance of its particular grantees and examine developments across entire ecosystems and industries. Such studies will undoubtedly prompt the foundation to regroup, reassess its plans, alter its implementation approach, and modify its progress measurement indicators accordingly.[10]

Taken together, these three steps of learning are, as you would expect, inextricably linked and best regarded as a single, integrated cycle of continuous performance improvement.

LEARNING TO HELP OTHERS LEARN

The more learning that occurs throughout a problem-solving system, the greater the likelihood of progress. Actors—peer networks, businesses, government agencies, and individuals—make independent decisions, and no funder's influence reaches them all. Increasing these actors' general knowledge and fostering learning can, however, lead both them and others to make good changes by themselves. As Figure 8.1 illustrates, learning needs to happen throughout the system. Catalytic donors work to help others—and especially their grantees—become learning organizations too.

CREATING LEARNING GRANTEES

Nonprofits are often hard-pressed to cover the costs of their core operations. Their leaders' passionate dedication typically makes every available penny go into programs and services. As a result, most grantees do not regularly and reliably measure the impact of their work. This may seem acceptable to some grantees—after all, grantee staff work directly with the people they help every day, so they can see firsthand the impact they are having. But the complexity of social problems means that things are not always as they appear.

FIGURE 8.1. LEARNING OCCURS ON THREE LEVELS.

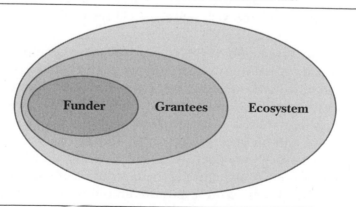

For example, as many individuals and organizations in the social sector are quickly learning, just knowing how many people a grantee's program has served—and tracking program recipients' immediate response to assistance—isn't enough. Grantees need to ensure that they move beyond tracking the *outputs* (direct products or results of program activities) of their work to understanding key *outcomes* (changes that occur for individuals, groups, families, organizations, systems, or communities during or after the program). Catalytic donors can facilitate this process of tracking outcomes and, along the way, inspire smarter work by those dedicated to the donors' selected causes.

Consider the case of the Latin American Youth Center (LAYC), a nonprofit serving Hispanic youth and families in Washington, D.C.'s leafy Columbia Heights neighborhood and the surrounding Maryland suburbs. As a nonprofit included in the first fund of Venture Philanthropy Partners (VPP), LAYC received hands-on support and multiyear funding totaling $1.8 million over three years.[11] LAYC began offering twelve-week parenting classes to its primarily low-income, immigrant clientele. Crammed together on metal folding chairs, Columbia Heights parents learned about effective discipline, communication with school officials, strategies for financial independence, and domestic violence prevention. Word of mouth and rising attendance rates suggested that the curriculum was helpful. Led by a committed teaching staff, the parenting classes were assumed to leave participants better equipped to handle the stresses they faced as new immigrants and low-income parents. At the very least, the classes couldn't be doing any harm.

On closer inspection, however, one well-meant component of the program turned out to be doing just that. Pre- and postclass surveys that focused on outcomes, funded by VPP, showed that parents who completed the domestic violence module came away more likely than they were before to believe hitting was an expression of love and an acceptable part of Latino culture. Women were also more likely to believe there was nothing they could do to stop their partners from battering them. In an unanticipated twist, the parenting classes *increased* positive attitudes toward domestic abuse.

Program staff scrambled to make sense of the data and immediately sought out domestic violence experts to advise them. They quickly eliminated the coeducational seminar model, extended time for discussion, and introduced a more serious tone to the module. These relatively minor tweaks turned results around. In evaluations after the next session, participants showed less positive attitudes toward domestic violence after the seminars. If LAYC had not had a real-time system for measuring the effectiveness of its programs, it might still be fueling a surge in domestic violence in a neighborhood already rife with abuse.

Before being funded by VPP, LAYC had tried to track progress across its programs—it offers more than fifty—but had stopped short of examining specific outcomes. LAYC had always measured activities and outputs, like class attendance and registration trends. Based on such bare-bones measures, the program would certainly have been deemed a success, given its growth and popularity. But when the simple client surveys that LAYC had been using were reworded, even though they were still a relatively basic tool, LAYC quickly understood the need to alter its parenting program. VPP's hands-on assistance and capital enabled LAYC to become a learning organization—in the nick of time.

Social change is a messy business and people are bound to blunder. An important antidote is to support grantees in becoming learning organizations too—and to give them the resources they need to track their outcomes. We don't mean simply donating a nifty, new software program. To effectively help grantees begin to measure outcomes and become more driven by results, donors must often work hand in hand with them—investing sweat in addition to funds. Victoria Vrana, VPP's vice president of communications and assessment, estimates the foundation spent about 10 percent of the capital in its first fund to help grantees create and deploy outcomes measurement systems. These resources enabled grantees to hire staff with expertise in evaluation, engage consultants to help them create theories of change and outcomes measurement frameworks, purchase or create systems for managing data, and train staff to be more knowledgeable in approaches to learning.[12]

It's important to understand that for many grantees, switching to outcomes measurement entails a *culture* shift. It's an adaptive rather than a technical challenge. As VPP founder and chairman Mario Morino writes: "The challenge of managing to outcomes has little to do with systems, processes, or technology. The real challenge is that organizations cannot hope to manage to outcomes unless they have in place ... a supportive performance culture."[13] That's what becoming a *learning organization* is all about.

CREATING LEARNING SYSTEMS

Gregory Dees, Duke University social entrepreneurship expert, notes that human-made social problems resemble the ecosystems of nature. Both involve complex webs of interrelated organisms that evolve together by random forces. "A flowering plant, for example, relies on certain birds and insects to spread its pollen. The birds and insects, in turn, receive nutrition from the plant ... and competing plants might rob the flowering plant of needed sunlight, water and nutrients," write Paul Bloom and Gregory Dees in "Cultivate Your Ecosystem." Likewise, functional and dysfunctional social systems are populated by all kinds of actors—"friends, foes, competitors, and even the innocent bystanders" within a larger environment of distinct laws, policies, social and religious norms, demographic trends, and cultural institutions.[14] What it takes to thrive in both kinds of systems is largely out of the control of any single player. Still, catalytic donors and the nonprofits they fund can find ways to infuse learning into the systems around them to foster the change they seek in the world.

In Chapter Five we noted that a major factor in the Strive Partnership's success to date is the way in which funders are working together so that more money flows toward achieving key outcomes and, conversely, less money is going to unrelated—even though also worthy—causes. Now let's look at the another major factor in Strive's early success: how its leaders fostered learning among hundreds of different organizations by riveting their attention on a single annual community *report card* of key indicators and, at the same time, enabling each organization to work together with a set of its peers to develop more specialized performance measures suited specifically to the activities group members performed. In this way, Strive facilitated a continuous learning loop that engaged all three hundred organizations in sharing knowledge and learning how to increase ongoing success—literally learning to change the system.

To understand how the Strive learning network works across each of the educational and social service systems that have an impact on the life of a young urban child, we must start by understanding the need for shared goals at two different levels: community-wide indicators of progress and organizational outcomes.

As we said in Chapter Five, through vigorous research Strive identified five critical transition points where interventions are most needed—starting kindergarten, starting middle school, entering high school, graduating from high school, and the first two years of college. It then identified a single goal for each of these points, supported by one or more *community-level progress indicators* that could be tracked in an annual report card to the community. Exhibit 8.1 lists Strive's five goals and ten indicators. The indicators galvanized a vast peer network and focused hundreds of nonprofit, educational, philanthropic, and corporate leaders on achieving the same set of goals. This kept all of them aware of the overall picture, rather than simply allowing them to focus on their own individual programs and grants. And it created an incentive for the entire network to work together in shared progress.

Exhibit 8.1. Strive's Goals and Community-Level Progress Indicators.

Goal 1. Every child is prepared for school.

- Indicator 1. Percentage of children assessed to be ready for school

Goal 2. Every child is supported in and out of school.

- Indicator 2. (At the time of this writing, Strive was in the process of updating its student support outcome indicator.)

Goal 3. Every student succeeds academically.

- Indicator 3. Percentage of students at or above proficiency in reading and math
- Indicator 4. Percentage of students that graduate from high school

Goal 4. Every student enrolls in college or career training.

- Indicator 5. Average score on the American College Test (ACT)
- Indicator 6. Percentage of graduates that enroll in college

Goal 5. Every child graduates and enters a career.

- Indicator 7. Percentage of college students prepared for college-level coursework
- Indicator 8. Percentage of students retained in college
- Indicator 9. Percentage of students graduating from college
- Indicator 10. Number of college degrees conferred

At the same time, Strive recognized that different organizations approached the issues in different ways and that there was a need for tracking individual organizational outcomes. To address this need, Strive grouped the three hundred organizations into fifteen action networks, referred to as *student success networks* (SSNs). Each network included ten to thirty local stakeholders working in similar ways, such as preschool programs, local tutoring organizations, or college retention programs. Representatives of each stakeholder in an SSN were expected to meet together for two hours every two weeks. To ensure the meetings were productive and resulted in well-defined outcome measures, Strive looked beyond the nonprofit sector and tapped big-business expertise.

Imagine systems engineers from Toyota, General Electric's Jet Engines Division, and Procter and Gamble gathered around a table, each highly trained in Six Sigma continuous improvement processes.[15] With sleeves rolled up and whiteboard markers flying, they translated the corporate processes they used to improve manufacturing into processes that nonprofits could use to improve school outcomes. With Strive staff's guidance, they reframed planning tools for identifying and meeting customer needs so that they could be used to identify and meet educational achievement goals. Together, Strive staff and the engineers arranged and rearranged each piece of the system until each SSN had a process to follow for identifying its members' own key success factors and learning together what worked best. In essence, Strive developed a modified Six Sigma workbook to facilitate the biweekly SSN meetings.

For example, the preschool SSN included dozens of non-profit education groups, Head Start centers, child care agencies, church-based nursery schools, and so forth. As we also described in Chapter Five, each had its own method of educating children, but the meeting process revealed that almost all children regress during the summer break before kindergarten. This impeded learning, especially for low-income students who enter kinder-garten underprepared and have difficulty catching up—a prob-lem that compounds over time. So the preschool SSN launched an innovative *summer bridge* session, a technique more often used in middle school. The result is that the average kindergarten readi-ness scores throughout the region have increased by 10 percent since 2005.

Strive created a systemwide learning network and, by engaging organizations in the process of developing shared performance measures, it focused their attention on opportunities to not only improve their own performance but also to work together more effectively. The biweekly SSN meetings provided the opportunity for learning, enabling disparate organizations to collectively gain better results.

The barriers to developing this kind of comprehensive, sys-temic, collaborative effort can look formidable. It requires a far-reaching vision across a strong network of leaders, millions of dollars in philanthropic and public investment, and years of intensive effort by large coalitions of interdependent organiza-tions. Despite this, catalytic donors are working hard to develop systemwide learning networks as a key tool for change and are actually seeing some rewarding results.

CONCLUSION

Catalytic philanthropists can show other donors how to boldly focus fieldwide with their money and effort. Catalytic donors do this because they see social and environmental problems for what they are—complex, emergent, often messy systems. They recog-nize that no single program or intervention can be accountable for solving such big and complex problems as Washington's rising homelessness or Cincinnati's failing public school and social service systems. Instead of picking up a measuring stick and trying to "prove" that their particular grants "worked," catalytic donors engage in an ongoing learning process that is more suited to helping them understand what contributions their grants and programs have made (if any) to advancing the larger cause. They embrace a learning mind-set that is forward looking, rather than focusing retrospectively on reports. Catalytic donors raise questions—for themselves, their grantees, and other organizations and individuals operating around an issue—that help all players raise their game in the race to create change.

KEY PRINCIPLES FOR LEARNING TO CHANGE

1. **Adopt a learning culture**. Build a continuous process of data gathering and feedback into your work as a donor. Don't wait for a retrospective study about the impact of a grant. Create the time and resources for staff and trustees to gather, reflect on, and use information from multiple sources. Even if you are an individual donor, being committed to the cause means carving out time for ongoing learning. Beyond asking for grant reports, select a number of key nonprofits and schedule a question and answer session with the CEO or senior program staff of each of them. Beyond asking for outcomes data, ask them to share stories of success and failure so that you can learn as they learn.

2. **Help your grantees to adopt a learning culture**. Nonprofits are often cash strapped and overburdened with client demands. Supporting a culture shift within grantees toward outcomes measurement and managing for results and away from tracking outputs and filing reports can be hard, expensive, and time consuming. Help eliminate the barriers by reducing those costs, and work with grantees to better evaluate progress in real time.

3. **Follow the three-step learning cycle—plan, implement, track progress**. Think of learning as an ongoing cycle. What information do you need to plan your strategy? What do you

need to know to make midcourse corrections? And above and beyond your individual grants, what progress is or is not being made on the problem you are trying to solve?

4. **Use knowledge systemwide as a tool for change**. Once you've mastered the learning cycle and helped grantees become learning organizations as well, shift the unit of analysis from progress at the individual grantee level to the larger system or field. This shift allows you to catalyze systemic change versus just advancing the work of one or several organizations; it enables you to leverage the best of all the actors influencing the problem.

CHAPTER NINE

TOWARD A MORE CATALYTIC FUTURE

Catalytic philanthropy may sound daunting, but as we said at the outset, it's not an all-or-nothing proposition. The basic idea is simple: if you want to increase the impact of your grants, you must do more than give. As a funder you have a unique role to play in catalyzing change. This doesn't mean you need to do the work of the nonprofits that you support, but you can complement their efforts by leveraging change in ways that can yield more powerful results than either of you can working alone.

The stories we have told in this book encompass a wide range of funders, from modest family and community foundations to the largest private foundations and public corporations in the world. They annually donate hundreds of thousands, millions, and even billions of dollars. Some have had a profound impact on local issues, and others have created changes with global repercussions. Some employ expert professional staff; others achieve impact primarily through the time of trustees. All of them have used some or all of the six practices we described in this book to change the world: practices that can be used by anyone who seeks to create social change.

In fact, even though our six practices are directed toward donors, they don't really require a large charitable giving budget at all. After all, most social entrepreneurs and nonprofit leaders don't start out with a personal fortune at their disposal. They use their time, talents, and passion as the human capital to create change, and they depend on donors to provide the financial capital that they also need.

At the other end of the spectrum, wealthy donors often lack the time, expertise, or single-minded focus needed to lead social change themselves, and so they depend on social entrepreneurs and nonprofits to turn their money into action. The difference in roles between grantor and grantee often blinds us to the fact that we can change the world only when both financial capital and human capital work together. Despite the differences in their external trappings and daily concerns, grantors and grantees are inextricably linked in a shared enterprise. There is a continuum of social change, with time and dedication at one end and financial resources at the other. Enough of one makes up for a lack of the other—and when you have both together, you are positioned to have the greatest impact of all.

As we suggested in the introductory chapter, "Catalytic Philanthropy," the traditional view of philanthropy is a linear model in which donors fund nonprofits to develop and implement programs that solve social problems. As this thinking goes, the grantee's job is to design effective programs and to execute them well, whereas the grantor's job is simply to select the best nonprofits. This approach may work for a small population with a specific issue—if your goal is to assist your local food bank to feed more people or your local art museum to grow its attendance—then good nonprofit management and well-structured grants will do the trick. But if your aim is more far-reaching, you need to adopt a different approach.

The traditional philanthropic worldview overlooks the complexity of large-scale social change. It treats the actions of grantors and grantees in isolation, as if they were the only actors necessary to solve social problems, without considering the many interdependent ways in which for-profit enterprises, governments, networks, and individuals influence social problems and each other—ways both predictable and unpredictable—to create or resist change.

The notion of catalytic philanthropy differs from traditional philanthropy in precisely this regard: catalytic donors grapple with the challenge of creating large-scale change in a complex and multifaceted world where all the different players that affect an issue must participate in creating the solution together, and where philanthropic dollars from even the wealthiest donors and nonprofit institutions cannot buy the change that is needed.

Nonprofits, government, businesses, and individuals all play an integral part, and those who wish to create change—whether donors or grantees—must find opportunities to engage all four of these sectors in the process of change.

We have earlier illustrated this interdependence among the different sectors as a series of interlocking gears, each of which turns the others, in contrast to the linear model in which donors simply fund nonprofits to implement the changes they seek. The metaphor still falls short—the interaction among sectors is not as mechanical as the interaction among gears—social and environmental problems are more unpredictable, like the motion of electrons around nuclei. Yet even the unpredictable electron conforms to certain patterns of behavior, and we believe the intricacies of social change do as well.

In short, we believe that social change can be achieved. Catalytic philanthropists help bring it about—and the many examples in this book reaffirm our conviction. We acknowledge that the process is complex and unpredictable, yet our research has led us to conclude that certain practices increase the odds of success, even though they cannot guarantee it.

For donors, the first essential step is to commit to your cause (and there is no parallel to this in the discussion of nonprofits in *Forces for Good*). This comes before the six practices because, unlike general purpose foundations, operating nonprofits are created to address particular issues. If you want to make change as a donor, you will be most successful if you make a significant commitment to one or a few causes, and take responsibility for advancing those issues by employing as many of the practices in this book as possible. You don't have to follow all of the steps under the six practices or all the recommendations at the end of each chapter. Any one of the next steps and recommendations that you pick can immediately increase the impact of your giving—whether you take proactive catalytic action or simply use these practices to inform your grantmaking in new ways.

In Appendix E, we offer a series of checklists for readers who want to begin implementing or to deepen their commitment to the practices described throughout this book. The checklists are organized by two levels of difficulty, beginner and experienced, so that readers at any level can start practicing them right away. And for those donors who have concluded that catalytic philanthropy might not be for them—they either can't invest the time or don't feel confident in their ability to master these steps—we also include in Appendix E some words of advice for how they can apply these concepts to more conventional grantmaking. This way, they can direct more of their funding toward systems-changing solutions even if they are not personally taking a catalytic role.

We believe that when you embrace these practices and become more catalytic in your approach, you will surely find the experience far more demanding than your usual philanthropy—but you will also find it far more exciting and rewarding. We cannot guarantee that you will advance your issue to the degree you hope to, but you will certainly bring your philanthropy a step closer to achieving impact.

There are a few examples in this book of *master donors*, individuals who artfully combine all elements of our six practices. But the majority of our stories involve donors who learned as they went, improvising in response to unexpected developments, seeking advice from experts but also following their intuition. Each donor was able to bring to bear her or his own talents and life experience to shape her or his philanthropic path. It is similarly the unique and highly personal combination of your own skills, networks, and values with the more general principles in this book that will give you the power to bring about change.

Beyond the six practices and the multiple recommendations at the end of each chapter are three basic, mutually reinforcing principles that can guide your efforts:

1. **Philanthropy is neither a solitary effort by the donor nor even a dialectical effort between the donor and the grantee**. Social change involves many different players from all sectors of society. It is through the engagement and alignment of these multiple players that catalytic donors achieve their impact. Grantmaking is a powerful tool for supporting nonprofits, but it has minimal direct influence on governments, businesses, and individuals, all of whom are equally necessary components of any large-scale change. It is through advocacy, harnessing the power of for-profit enterprise, forging peer networks, and

empowering individuals that you can influence each sector of society and enlist its support in your cause.

2. **Solving problems and creating change is not about knowing the answer**. This simple-sounding statement turns conventional philanthropy on its head because most charitable contributions are intended to fund programs that—rightly or wrongly—claim to solve social problems. The hope that writing a check will immediately somehow make things better is at the core of countless grant solicitations and motivations. We believe, however, that a more powerful and lasting process of social change comes from helping stakeholders discover and construct answers for themselves. Empowering individuals and leading adaptively are the rare but essential skills needed to work in this way.

   Adaptive leadership, in particular, sets a high bar. Of all the practices articulated in this book, it is one of the most complex and challenging arts to master and examples of its success are rare. The most important step, however, is simply knowing that you, the donor, do not—and should not—have the answers and yet you are still in a position to drive change forward. This perspective alone speaks to the most frequent objection to catalytic philanthropy: that donors should not drive change because the grantees know more than they do about the issues involved. This fear is founded on examples of well-intentioned donors who invented and funded solutions that proved ineffective and sometimes even caused more harm than good. Yet leaving social change only to the hard-working, underresourced, and fragmented nonprofit sector has so far not solved most social problems at scale either. The catalytic philanthropists featured as examples in this book did not impose heavy-handed solutions on unwilling grantees, yet they certainly created the conditions for change that would not have occurred without their active leadership.

3. **Catalytic philanthropy is not for the impatient**. Many of the success stories in this book occurred over a decade or more of persistent dedication to the same set of issues. It didn't take ten years to begin to see change: interim progress (as well as the occasional setback) was witnessed along the way. Yet all of our

examples refute the promise often made to donors that a problem can be solved in a one-year or even three-year grant cycle. Social problems arise from a confluence of forces, and the many actors who work hard to preserve the status quo may never cease their efforts to undo progress. Even a successful philanthropic initiative will be subject to the vagaries of a changing economy, a shifting political climate, or simply the evolving desires and passions of the individuals involved. None of the donors in our stories has ever been able to declare a complete victory and close the book on his or her initiative. Instead their efforts evolved over time in response to their increasing understanding and changes in external circumstances. Catalytic philanthropy is an ongoing process of learning and adaptation. To again quote from *Getting to Maybe*, "success is not a fixed address."

We fervently believe that the world would—and can—be a better place if more donors adopted the tools of catalytic philanthropy. We hope that you will take the first step by deepening your commitment to your cause, and that you will take to heart these basic ideas and begin to implement these practices in your philanthropic work. When you take these steps, you will be on your way to becoming more catalytic in your approach. In so doing, you will do more than give. You will be on your way to becoming a transformative force for change in the world.

RESEARCH METHODOLOGY

We wrote this book to understand and demonstrate how donors, broadly defined as foundation and corporate leaders and individual philanthropists, contribute to solving important social and environmental problems. Our research was grounded in the conceptual framework presented in *Forces for Good: The Six Practices of High-Impact Nonprofits*,[1] and in the principles articulated in the article "Catalytic Philanthropy," by FSG managing director Mark Kramer.[2]

The six practices of high-impact nonprofits framework in *Forces for Good* was developed by coauthors Leslie Crutchfield and Heather McLeod Grant, who engaged in four years of inductive, applied research on twelve high-impact nonprofits. Their goal was to understand how a select set of successful nonprofits achieved significant results in a relatively short time frame (each organization studied was less than four decades old). Their research was conducted in academic partnership with the Center for the Advancement of Social Entrepreneurship (C.A.S.E.) at Duke University's Fuqua School of Business, under the leadership of J. Gregory Dees. Alan Abramson of The Aspen Institute's Philanthropy and Social Innovation Program also provided academic and other support.

The research for this book, *Do More Than Give*, is based on the premise that the six practices of high-impact nonprofits can be applied by foundation and individual donors to create similarly high levels of societal change. Our assumption from the outset has been that even though foundations are tax-exempt, nonprofit organizations, they differ in important ways from the operating nonprofit groups that they fund. For instance, most foundations exist primarily to distribute funds and are not set up to directly deliver programs or services; so unless they hire full-time staff, their participation in catalyzing change is often limited to the efforts of trustees. Differences like these influence the ways in which foundations and individual donors employ the catalytic practices articulated in *Forces for Good*, and we were curious to understand more about how the six practices apply to the philanthropists' side of the funding equation. So we conducted a case-based inquiry into the ways that donors employ these practices to help solve important social and environmental problems. The results of our research form the content of the book you are now reading.

Some of the ideas and approaches to philanthropy that emerged as we wrote this book appeared to us to be new; other concepts discussed here have been employed for generations if not centuries. But in our experience, we have found that most funders do not take a catalytic approach to philanthropy—and we would like to see that change. Although we recognize that every donor may not have either the inclination or the ability to master each of these practice areas, we wrote this book to be as broadly applicable as possible because we believe these practices represent proven, high-impact ways of advancing the greater good. And we want to encourage philanthropists to consider adopting a more catalytic approach or deepening their existing practice of catalytic philanthropy if they are already inclined to it.

Our aim in undertaking this research is that, as a consequence of reading this book, donors will expand the way they think about and practice philanthropy. This book is aimed primarily at helping practitioners—foundation trustees and staff and also individual donors who give to nonprofits both directly and through private foundations, donor-advised funds, and community and corporate foundations. We present cases of donors who have achieved significant impact on social or environmental causes, with the goal of showing our readers how a diverse range of funders accomplished real results by using the catalytic practices articulated in *Forces for Good*.

Summary of the Research Process

Our research was conducted in three phases. These phases are summarized here and explained in greater detail later in this appendix.

Phase 1. We identified a diverse set of donors for further study, who met the following criteria:

a. They had achieved significant, measureable impact in a field or cause.
b. They were recognized by their peers or by the authors of this book as catalytic, which we defined as employing some or all of the six practices of high-impact nonprofits in their philanthropic pursuits.
c. They represented a diverse cross-section of philanthropy worldwide, as defined by geographical location and scope of activity, issue area(s) of interest, asset size and amount of annual giving, staff and board size and composition, leaders' demographics (age, race, ethnicity, gender), leadership characteristics, and type of foundation (private [or family], corporate, community, operating, and conversion foundations, among others).

Phase 2. We conducted background research on and interviewed dozens of leaders of a range of philanthropic organizations. We interviewed CEOs, program officers, and trustees of foundations representing each major category of giving vehicles, as well as contributors to donor-advised funds and intermediary organizations. We also interviewed leaders of nonprofit grantee organizations and other key stakeholders in select cases. Background research materials included publically available documents, internal documents provided by the donors, and research documents prepared by FSG during previous client work (in the select cases where FSG had prior knowledge of a particular foundation).

Phase 3. We analyzed and synthesized our research findings and then selected a subset of the cases we had studied to be featured in this book, choosing as final cases those that (a) best exemplified the "six practices of high impact nonprofits" articulated in *Forces for Good*, and (b) were sufficiently diverse according to the criteria we had established in Phase 1. During this third and final phase of the research, our understanding of the six practices deepened and broadened as we examined the ways in which foundations and individual donors employ them to catalyze change. As a result, new conceptual frameworks emerged from our research and are discussed in this book. Therefore the definitions and supporting frameworks for the six practices that are presented in *Do More Than Give* build on but also differ sometimes from the practices originally articulated in *Forces for Good*.

The findings that emerged from our early research excited and sometimes surprised us. For instance, we learned that before many of the donors we studied became highly engaged in any of the catalytic practices, they had to take an important initial step. They had to *commit to their cause*. This step has no parallel in *Forces for Good*, because the high-impact nonprofits studied there were already fully committed. But we have devoted all of Chapter Two in this book to this first step because, for many of the donors we interviewed, it was a critical precursor to fully embracing the six catalytic practices of high-impact philanthropy.

Although the research process behind *Do More Than Give* was intensive and rigorous, it was not designed to meet the standards of scientific or academic study. For instance, in writing this book, we did not set out to prove that catalytic philanthropy is the "most effective" or "best" way to practice philanthropy. Nor do we assert (or even mean to imply) that the foundations and individuals profiled here are the world's only exemplars of a catalytic approach. Rather, our aim was to select a robust set of case studies that met a threshold of demonstrated impact and showed evidence of employing some or all of the six practices in *Forces for Good* to catalyze change. We also strove to include a diverse cross-section of philanthropic institutions, so that cases would resonate with a wide range of practitioners—including individual donors and family, community, corporate, and private foundation stakeholders of institutions both large and small.

Detailed Description of the Research Process

Phase 1: Identification of a Diverse Set of Catalytic Philanthropists

To select the individual donors and foundations profiled in this book, we conducted a peer survey of more than 1,500 philanthropic leaders across the United States and Europe, and we examined our own networks of colleagues and clients for potential case studies.

The peer survey was distributed via e-mail in January and February 2010. Respondents accessed the survey via a Web-based hotlink embedded in an e-mail message. The e-mails were sent by an FSG staff member or by one of our partner organizations (these partners are described later in this appendix). The survey text is reproduced in Appendix B. Survey recipients included CEOs, senior executives, and trustees of private, corporate, and community foundations, as well as a selection of consultants and advisors with deep knowledge about the practice of philanthropy.

We distributed the survey with the generous help of the following partner organizations:

- Committee Encouraging Corporate Philanthropy
- Council on Foundations
- European Foundation Centre
- Grantmakers for Effective Organizations
- 21/64 (a division of the Andrea and Charles Bronfman Philanthropies)[3]

Additionally, in selecting cases for further study, we drew on the knowledge built through a decade of John Kania's and Mark Kramer's work with FSG in providing strategic guidance to hundreds of foundations and families. And we solicited feedback and suggestions from our research advisors, who included a diverse set of national and local philanthropy experts and a range of practitioners, including leaders of family, community, corporate, and large private foundations. A listing of these advisors can be found in Appendix C.

Using the peer survey results, our advisors' guidance, and our own knowledge and understanding of the foundations that surfaced for consideration, we chose a subset of cases to research more deeply. We attempted to explore examples from all major types of foundations, including private (or family), community, corporate, and operating foundations. And we aimed to include a diverse mix of foundations by asset size, geographical location, and scope.

Phase 2: Case Study Research

For the next phase of our research, we conducted extensive research on approximately two dozen foundations, following a rigorous process to gather data about each organization and to better understand the context in which each operated. We reviewed Web sites, annual reports, press coverage, budgets, and available evaluation materials for all the foundations in our sample. We conducted telephone or in-person interviews with CEOs, board members, and other senior leaders of these foundations; in addition, in select cases we interviewed nonprofit leaders who had formed partnerships with or received funding from the foundations. The interviews with leaders profiled in this book were conducted by at least one of its three authors and FSG consultant Amber Johnson. Background research was completed by the three authors, Amber Johnson and other FSG staff, and a team of students from the University of California-Berkeley, who also received ongoing support and supervision from Amber.

Phase 3: Analysis, Synthesis, Further Case Study Refinement, and Writing

After completing research on the initially selected set of individual and foundation cases, we wrote detailed summaries and analyzed and synthesized our findings based on our interviews and review of secondary materials. Then we stepped back and examined the collected data as a whole, looking for patterns in the ways donors practiced catalytic philanthropy and for new insights into the differences between the six practices when employed by donors and when employed by nonprofit leaders. We also consulted our advisory circle once again for guidance on which case studies to delve into even more deeply. We ultimately identified those examples that we believed best represented the practices we sought to illustrate and that also reflected the diverse nature of the philanthropic sector (reapplying the criteria that we had employed in Phase 1 to ensure diversity). We underscore again that the cases featured in this book are not meant to be a definitive list of "the best" donors—as one of our advisors, Tom Reis of the W. K. Kellogg Foundation put it, "we're not dispensing a 'Papal Blessing' on these foundations as all-perfect." Rather, we sought to establish a representative proxy of the foundations that employ catalytic practices in some of their programs.

PEER SURVEY QUESTIONS

The following survey text was distributed via a hotlink embedded in an e-mail.

EXHIBIT B.1. FSG AND *FORCES FOR GOOD* PHILANTHROPY SURVEY

Forces for Good co-author Leslie Crutchfield and FSG Social Impact Advisors are pleased to invite you to participate in this brief (five-question) online survey to solicit your nominations of exemplary donors for a forthcoming book on high-impact philanthropy. The driving idea behind our book is to highlight effective problem-solving philanthropy and to provide a roadmap for all donors who aspire to maximize the impact of their charitable resources. We hope this book will serve as a valuable resource for the field, and we greatly value your input at this early stage in the research process.

Specifically, we invite you to nominate a short list of peers whom you perceive to have achieved substantial, measurable impact on important social issues. We seek examples of individuals and institutions that have been "catalytic" in their approach to philanthropy, working across sectors to deliver exceptional results that greatly distinguish them from other funders with similar resources.

Here are some examples of the kinds of cross-sector activities that catalytic philanthropists engage in, often using some of the practices of high-impact nonprofits identified in *Forces for Good*. A catalytic funder will:

- Fund policy advocacy and even personally advocate for policy reform—as well as support direct service and research.

- Participate in collaborative initiatives and coalitions with the intention of advancing larger causes—rather than only directly funding organizations.

- Mobilize mass bases of individual support to mount campaigns and move larger causes—recognizing that a single intervention or worthy nonprofit is unlikely to alone succeed.

- Align their business interests with charitable activities through the corporate foundation—rather than separate their business activities from their charitable work.

The survey contains only a few questions that should require about five minutes of your time. You will be able to provide your responses anonymously, and all responses will be held in strict confidence and made available only for review by our book research team. (For a more in-depth discussion of catalytic philanthropy and the six practices of high-impact nonprofits, please see two attached *Stanford Social Innovation Review* articles, "Catalytic Philanthropy" and "Creating High-Impact Nonprofits.")

If you have any questions or technical difficulties with the survey, please contact Amber Johnson at amber.johnson@fsg-impact.org or (415) 397-8500 x205. For questions about the forthcoming book, please contact Leslie Crutchfield at lcrutchfield@forcesforgood.net or call her associate, Mary Pietrusko, at (617) 502-6122.

Catalytic philanthropist nomination

1. Based on our above description of catalytic philanthropy, please nominate up to 5 individual donors or foundations that you perceive to be catalytic and to practice some or all the activities outlined in *Forces for Good*. Feel free to nominate any type of foundation (e.g., family, corporate, private, community, operating.) We ask that you refrain from nominating yourself here, and we encourage you to share information about your work later in the survey.

2. If you have the time, please share with us why you listed the individuals or institutions above, providing brief, specific examples if possible. (You may refer to the description of catalytic philanthropy on the previous page by pressing the "back" arrow below if needed.)

3. Please share any information about how you or your organization is striving to be catalytic and implementing the practices detailed in *Forces for Good*. (If you elect to share information about your work here, please remember to include your organization's name. This identifying information will be kept separate from your nominations on the previous page, as we are committed to protecting the anonymity of survey respondents.)

Demographic information

4. My primary organizational affiliation is best described as (please check all that apply):

- Family foundation
- Private foundation
- Community foundation
- Funding intermediary
- For-profit company
- Social enterprise, B-corp, or other hybrid entity
- Donor advisor
- Other (please specify)

5. My organization operates or funds in the following geographies (please check all that apply):

- State, province, or area within a country (please specify)
- National (please specify country)
- Global (please specify countries or region)

Your responses have been received. Thank you for your participation. We truly hope that this book will advance philanthropic thinking and practice, and your contribution to this survey will help ensure that we capture and share the most innovative ideas and examples in the field.

Source: The FSG and *Forces for Good* Philanthropy Survey was created in January 2010 by author Leslie Crutchfield and FSG consultant Amber Johnson, and was distributed in February and March 2010.

RESEARCH ADVISORS

Large Private Foundation Research Advisors

- Kathy Calvin, chief executive officer, United Nations Foundation
- Paula Ellis, vice president/strategic initiatives, John S. and James L. Knight Foundation
- Peter Goldmark, program director, Environmental Defense Fund; former president, The Rockefeller Foundation
- Jacob Harold, program officer, The William and Flora Hewlett Foundation
- Darin McKeever, senior program officer, Bill & Melinda Gates Foundation
- Tom Reis, program director, W. K. Kellogg Foundation
- Edward Skloot, director, Center for Strategic Philanthropy and Civil Society, Duke University
- Diana Wells, president, Ashoka: Innovators for the Public

Community Foundation Research Advisors

- Brian Byrnes, president and CEO, Santa Fe Community Foundation
- Rebecca Graves, managing director, FSG Social Impact Advisors
- Jack Hopkins, consultant and former president and CEO, Kalamazoo Community Foundation
- Laura McKnight, president and CEO, Greater Kansas City Community Foundation

Family, Corporate, and Individual Donor Research Advisors

- Katherine Bradley, cofounder and president, CityBridge Foundation
- Courtney Clark Pastrick, executive director, Clark Charitable Foundation
- Kristin Ehrgood, president, Flamboyan Foundation
- Ann Friedman, philanthropist through a private donor-advised fund
- Susan Price, vice president, National Center for Family Philanthropy

REVIEW OF THE SIX PRACTICES
OF HIGH-IMPACT NONPROFITS
IN *FORCES FOR GOOD*

Do More Than Give is based on the framework articulated in *Forces for Good: The Six Practices of High-Impact Nonprofits*, by Leslie R. Crutchfield and Heather McLeod Grant.[1] As discussed in Appendix A, research for *Do More Than Give* began with the premise that the six practices of high-impact nonprofits in *Forces for Good* apply to, and can be applied by, donors to solve important social and environmental problems and to achieve systemic change.

For those who have not read *Forces for Good*, or who would like to refresh their understanding of the concepts in it, we include here a brief summary. (For a more complete overview of the key concepts in the book, readers may want to see the article "Creating High-Impact Nonprofits,"[2] or read the book itself.)

THE PREMISE BEHIND *FORCES FOR GOOD*

What makes great nonprofits great?

This was the driving question that compelled the authors of *Forces for Good* and their research partners to spend four years studying twelve successful U.S. nonprofits to uncover their secrets to success. This quest took them to well-known groups like Habitat for Humanity, to less well known nonprofits like Self-Help, and to unexpected organizations like The Exploratorium. Each group was chosen because it had achieved wide-scale impact in a matter of decades (a complete list of the twelve nonprofits appears at the end of this appendix). Their secret? Great nonprofits spend as much time working *outside their four walls* as they do managing internal operations.

The authors learned that being a high-impact nonprofit is not just about building a well-run organization and then expanding it to reach more people. Rather, high-impact nonprofits work with and through each sector to create more impact than they ever could have achieved alone. They build social movements and foster entire fields; they create change by leveraging government, business, other nonprofits, and countless individuals to achieve greater levels of impact than they could if they had just focused on building out their programs or launching more sites.

To derive the six practices of high-impact nonprofits, Crutchfield and McLeod Grant conducted a four-step research process from 2003 to 2007 that included surveying thousands of nonprofit CEOs for nominations of high-impact nonprofits; conducting hundreds of interviews with nonprofit leaders, board members, and other key stakeholders; and consulting with dozens of field experts. This approach was inspired by business management books such as *Good to Great* and *Built to Last*. By the end of this research, the authors found that six distinct patterns had crystallized to form the six practices that high-impact nonprofits use to achieve extraordinary impact. Here are brief descriptions of these practices.

1. **Advocate *and* serve**. High-impact nonprofits refuse to choose between providing direct services on the one hand and advocating for policy change on the other. Although most start out by primarily providing great programs on the ground, they eventually realize that they cannot achieve large-scale social change through service delivery alone. So they add policy advocacy to acquire government resources and to change legislation. Others reverse this learning process: they start out by doing advocacy and later add grassroots programs to supercharge their strategy. Ultimately, all high-impact organizations bridge the divide between service and advocacy. And the more they serve and advocate, the more impact they achieve.[3]

2. **Make markets work**. Successful nonprofits have learned that tapping into the power of free markets is far more effective than appealing to pure altruism alone. No longer content to rely on traditional notions of charity, or to see business as an enemy, great nonprofits find ways to work with markets and to help companies "do good while doing well." The authors found three specific ways successful nonprofits harness market forces to advance the greater good: they influence business practices, build corporate partnerships, and develop earned-income ventures to achieve social change on a grander scale than before.[4]

3. **Inspire evangelists**. High-impact nonprofits don't view their volunteers just as sources of free labor or their donors just as occasional check writers. They value volunteers, donors, and other external stakeholders not only for their time, money, and guidance but also for the contributions they can make as ambassadors and passionate evangelists for the cause. High-impact nonprofits build strong communities of supporters who help them achieve their larger goals. To inspire supporters' commitment, the nonprofits described in *Forces for Good* create emotional experiences that connect supporters to the group's mission and core values. These experiences convert outsiders to evangelists, who in turn recruit others in viral marketing at its finest. High-impact nonprofits then nurture and sustain these communities of supporters over time, recognizing that they are not just means but ends in themselves.[5]

4. **Nurture nonprofit networks**. *It's amazing what you can accomplish if you don't worry about who gets the credit*. This notion has been attributed to countless business and political leaders over the ages, and it applies as much to high-impact nonprofit leaders as to their successful corporate and government peers. Although most nonprofits pay lip service to collaboration, many of them really see other groups as competition for scarce resources. But high-impact groups succeed in part because they *help their peers succeed*. They build networks of nonprofit allies and devote remarkable time and energy to advancing their fields and larger causes. They freely share wealth, expertise, talent, and power with other nonprofits—not because they are saints but because it's in their self-interest to do so. They work in coalitions to influence

legislation or conduct grassroots advocacy campaigns, and they do this without worrying too much about which organization gets the credit. Great nonprofits recognize that they are more powerful together than alone.[6]

5. **Master the art of adaptation**. It's neither the strongest of the species nor the most intelligent that survives—it's the one that is the most adaptable to change. Charles Darwin's insight aptly describes the high-impact nonprofits in *Forces for Good*. They are exceptionally adaptive, modifying their tactics and plans as needed to improve and expand positive results. They are capable of change because they have built learning organizations that are highly attuned to shifts in the external environment and they have instilled internal processes that reward adaptive behavior. They have mastered the cycle of adaptation, which involves four critical steps. It starts with listening to feedback from their external environments and leads to modifying their plans and programs, interspersed with reflection and evaluation that add up to a continuous process of ongoing learning. It's a never-ending cycle that helps high-impact nonprofits increase and sustain their impact.[7]

6. **Share leadership**. The leaders of the twelve organizations in *Forces for Good* all exhibit charisma, but they don't have oversized egos. They share power and distribute authority across their management teams and work in partnership with their boards, empowering others to lead. High-impact leaders cultivate strong seconds in command, build enduring executive teams with long tenure, and develop large and powerful boards.[8]

The twelve high-impact nonprofits that the authors of *Forces for Good* studied use a majority of these six practices. But they don't use them in every situation, and they don't all employ them in the same ways. Some initially incorporated only a few practices and have added others gradually. Others focus more on pulling certain levers and apply them to different degrees. Yet they all converge on using more of these practices, not fewer. By working with and through their nonprofit peers and the other sectors of society, they have found powerful levers to increase their impact.

THE TWELVE NONPROFITS FEATURED IN *FORCES FOR GOOD*

- America's Second Harvest distributes donated food and grocery products to grassroots nonprofits to feed millions of hungry Americans; advocates for antihunger policy.
- The Center on Budget and Policy Priorities researches and analyzes state and federal budgets and fiscal policies; advocates on behalf of low-income and working-poor individuals and families.
- City Year builds democracy through citizen service, leadership, and social entrepreneurship in the United States and Africa; advocates for national service policy and helped catalyzed the national youth service movement in the United States.
- The Environmental Defense Fund addresses environmental problems with research, litigation, advocacy, market-based tools, and corporate partnerships; introduced the first public interest lawsuit on behalf of the environment.
- The Exploratorium operates a museum of science, art, and human perception that serves as a model for interactive museums around the world and has catalyzed a worldwide, hands-on science education movement.
- Habitat for Humanity seeks to eliminate poverty housing and homelessness by building homes, raising awareness, and advocating for change. Habitat homes have housed over a million poor people.
- The Heritage Foundation formulates and promotes conservative policy through research, general advocacy, and lobbying; considered to be America's most influential think tank.
- National Council of La Raza works to improve opportunities for all Latinos through national Hispanic civil rights advocacy and direct-service programs; has restored safety-net benefits to millions of immigrants and shapes legislation to protect them.
- Self-Help fosters economic development in low-income communities through lending, asset-building, research, and advocacy; fought the predatory lending industry to prevent it

from taking advantage of vulnerable low-income and minority
borrowers in more than half the U.S. states.

- Share Our Strength inspires and leads individuals and
businesses to end childhood hunger; has raised more than $200
million to fight hunger and helps nonprofits build
self-sustaining revenue streams through Community Wealth
Enterprises, a for-profit subsidiary.
- Teach for America is a national corps of college graduates who
commit two years to teach in urban and rural public schools
and bring long-term leadership to the broader education
reform movement. Teach for America brings thousands of
corps members into public schools annually, affecting the lives
of more than half a million U.S. students.
- YouthBuild has helped more than 60,000 low-income youth
learn job and leadership skills by building affordable
community housing while completing their high school
education or earning equivalency degrees; in the process it
produces tens of thousands of units of low-income housing.

APPENDIX E

GETTING STARTED WITH CATALYTIC PHILANTHROPY

We offer here a brief summary of each of the practices presented in *Do More Than Give,* and a series of checklists outlining next steps to help donors either start to apply these practices (for beginners) or strengthen their commitment (for more experienced donors). And for those donors who can't or don't want to personally adopt the catalytic practices described here but who desire to shift their giving to support nonprofits that pursue cross-sector, systems-changing strategies, we offer some suggestions about high-impact grantmaking opportunities and several ideas for how to outsource or partner with other foundations to get more bang for your dollars.

FIRST, COMMIT TO YOUR CAUSE

Donors who pick a strategic focus are able to achieve more than donors who scatter their funding and attention across many disparate causes. Once you've made a firm commitment to a cause, you can then act in catalytic ways and focus the majority of your efforts (although not always focus all of your funds) on advancing that cause. This is the essence of strategy: by getting clear on what they aim to achieve, donors are suddenly able to see what they need to *stop* doing. See Exhibit E.1 for two important factors in implementing this step. This step applies primarily to beginners, as experienced donors will already have narrowed their focus to one or a few causes.

EXHIBIT E.1. COMMIT TO YOUR CAUSE.

Adopt a portfolio approach

Donors can allocate their funds across the three categories of giving that motivate most funders, in order to "clear the air":

1. A sense of obligation to communities to which they belong

2. A commitment to honor personal and professional relationships

3. A desire to solve problems and make meaningful change in the world

Once they've developed a system to allot a percentage of funding for each of these three important categories, they then are free to focus the majority of their time, attention, and know-how on category 3—solve problems and make meaningful change in the world.

Choose a cause on which you can have real impact

To choose their cause, donors take stock of internal factors such as their personal values and any unique assets and capabilities they may bring to bear on an issue, and they assess external factors, such as the ripeness of the issue for change and the level of funding required to get traction.

PRACTICE 1: ADVOCATE FOR CHANGE

Advocacy is an uncomfortable concept for many donors. Traditional notions of charity are linked to giving aid or supporting direct-service programs, the results of which are appealingly tangible—it's heartening to know your gift helped to feed a hungry family or clean up a polluted stream. But systemwide change is rarely achieved without a range of advocacy and policy lobbying efforts. Donors who eschew advocacy miss important opportunities to advance their cause.

Exhibit e.2. Advocate for Change.

For beginners

- *Fund nonprofits that effectively combine service and advocacy;* high-impact organizations that do this well use information from their on-the-ground programs to inform their policy work and vice versa.

- *Remove restrictive language about advocacy* from grant award letters.

- *Give general operating support* rather than project-specific grants; nonprofits can then raise advocacy-specific funding more easily.

- *Build relationships with public officials* and make introductions for your grantees.

- *Commission research* to create or expand understanding of your issue.

- *Participate in coalitions and alliances* that advance your cause; launch, fund, and foster a cross-sector alliance if one doesn't yet exist.

- *Publish op-eds* defending or promoting your cause.

For more experienced donors

- *Hire a registered lobbyist* to advance your cause, or fund a coalition or nonprofit to hire one.

- *Register as a lobbyist* to represent your coalition or cause.

- *Establish a task force* to research and report to government on your issue.

- *Fund litigation* if protecting your cause warrants legal action.

- *Advocate to administrative agencies* to influence how laws are implemented and enforced once passed.

- *Withhold funding to government entities or other grantees* to enforce accountability to desired outcomes.

Practice 2: Blend Profit with Purpose

Until recently, large companies, private foundations, and wealthy individuals—many of whom also control foundations—typically avoided mixing business with charity. But donors are finding that by creating shared value, they can often achieve change more sustainably than by funding traditional nonprofits. Donors are also investing their endowments to yield market-rate returns while furthering their social objectives. And they are recognizing that some of the world's largest companies can do more good through their core business activities than through their philanthropy or corporate social responsibility programs. Across both the non-profit and for-profit sectors, catalytic philanthropists are learning to tap into the power of business as an engine for advancing the greater good.

Exhibit E.3. Blend Profit with Purpose

For beginners

- *Review your investment portfolio* to identify potential conflicts between your holdings and your values; rebalance your portfolio or vote your shareholder proxies accordingly.

- *Dedicate a portion of your investment portfolio to mission-related investments*, including program-related investments that can count toward the foundation's payout requirements.

- *Identify and enlist the support of businesses* through their foundations but also by leveraging their employees' skills, connections, clout, and other intangible assets.

- *Fund intermediaries or directly support nonprofit social enterprises* that generate revenue and achieve social or environmental objectives; intermediaries such as the Acumen Fund, Roberts Enterprise Development Fund, and Ashoka's Full Economic Citizenship portfolio offer screened opportunities.

For more experienced donors

- *File and campaign for shareholder resolutions* at public companies when that can advance your cause.

- *Build cross-sector alliances* that include businesses that affect your cause and involve them in advocating for solutions.

For corporations

- *Determine the expertise and resources* within your business that can contribute to advancing social and environmental causes; engage employees both within and outside the corporate giving department.

- *Deploy business skills, know-how, and other nonfinancial resources* to help nonprofits achieve greater impact.

- *Create shared value* by inventing and selling new products and services that address pressing social or environmental needs while generating a financial return.

- *Partner with nonprofits* to develop solutions to social problems or penetrate new markets.

- *Create social investment funds* to support social enterprises (both for-profits and nonprofits) that can improve economic prosperity in markets or geographical locations that are important to the company.

Practice 3: Forge Nonprofit Peer Networks

Instead of funding one individual nonprofit over another, catalytic donors see needs across entire fields—and then invest in building networks to foster true collaboration among all nonprofits that can advance the cause. It's popular today for funders to say they *partner* with their grantees and other donors, and almost every donor participates in some form of information-sharing and cooperative behavior. But what these congenial convenings lack is the force of mutual accountability that comes when funders and nonprofits alike hold themselves and each other responsible for the larger outcomes they seek to achieve, and funders *give power away* by sublimating their own ideas to the goals of the larger network.

EXHIBIT E.4. FORGE NONPROFIT NETWORKS.

For beginners

- *Join donor affinity groups that share knowledge and best practices;* leverage other grantmakers' know-how rather than recreate the wheel.

- *Screen grantees for effective participation in coalitions and alliances;* confirm that they add value by checking with nonprofit or foundation peers.

- *Fund coalitions and alliances* that advance larger causes rather than funding only individual nonprofits.

- *Participate in coalitions and alliances;* invest sweat equity and time of staff or trustees in collective campaigns to advance causes.

For more experienced donors

- *Develop a collective impact network* around your cause if one doesn't exist; provide funding so nonprofits can fully participate.

- *Design shared measurement systems* for nonprofits and funders that affect your cause; hold your grantees as well as foundation peers accountable to common goals and objectives.

- *Establish supporting infrastructure* to ensure that collaboration is sustained for the time period necessary to achieve desired results.

Practice 4: Empower the People

Catalytic donors don't treat individual community members just as recipients of charity. Instead, they view individuals as potent participants in the process of solving social and environmental problems—for themselves. Catalytic donors solicit individuals for ideas and involve them in campaigns to build political will to change policy and advocate more broadly for change; they build movements on the ground to create change at the block, neighborhood, regional, national, and even global level. Although catalytic donors are adept at leveraging elite institutions and influencing leaders at the grass tops of the government, business, and nonprofit sectors, they also engage individuals at the grassroots level—people who may not have any formal organizational affiliation but nonetheless are a powerful part of advancing most causes.

Exhibit E.5. Empower the People

For beginners

- *Include local residents or other community members* in board meetings and foundation events, reaching beyond the conventional issue "experts."

- *Ask individuals affected by an issue* what they see as the potential solutions, and act on those suggestions.

- *Fund nonprofits that empower individuals* and start by supporting those that engage you (the donor) as more than a check writer or occasional volunteer and those that work with their clients in creative ways.

For more experienced donors

- *Commission public opinion polls* and conduct other research to determine what a community needs.

- *Launch or join coalitions that include individual community members* as well as grass-tops leaders in order to collectively advance causes.

- *Subject your grantmaking decisions to community review*, allowing community members to influence the ways you prioritize what to fund.

Practice 5: Lead Adaptively

To work effectively across all sectors of society—government, business, nonprofit, and individuals—catalytic donors possess a rare, critical leadership trait: they are able to perceive changes and opportunities in their environments and respond accordingly as they foster the conditions for each player to advance the cause. The key to success is rooted neither in donor personalities nor in the fact that funders hold the purse strings. Catalytic donors are inordinately influential—not because they hold the formal authority afforded to leaders who hold a C-suite title at a corporation or a high military rank but because they are *adaptive* leaders. They see social and environmental problems for what they are—emergent, complex phenomena that require adaptive responses, rather than issues that can be resolved simply by making a grant to a nonprofit.

EXHIBIT E.6. LEAD ADAPTIVELY

For beginners

- *Adopt an adaptive leadership mind-set* rather than continue to approach complex problems as static issues that can be resolved by making a grant.

- *Hire staff with adaptive leadership skills* including proven ability to work across sectors, a commitment to creating systems-level change, and finesse at motivating leaders at the grass tops and individuals at the grassroots to act collectively to solve problems for themselves.

- *Identify other donors who lead adaptively* and partner with them through collaborative grantmaking and other joint ventures to learn the ropes.

- *Seek out and fund nonprofits with executives and board members who lead adaptively*.

For more experienced donors

- *Identify the adaptive challenge and frame the problem*, then engage both leaders at the grass tops from government, business, and nonprofits and individuals at the grassroots in the process of solving the problem.

- *Hold attention on ripe issues*, and prevent diversions from the work by remaining focused on solving problems over time and despite resistance.

- *Fund or create intermediaries* that can provide adaptive leadership on an issue when a leadership vacuum exists among existing players.

Practice 6: Learn in Order to Change

Catalytic donors are obsessed with measuring and evaluating their own effectiveness as well as the performance of the nonprofits they fund. This sets them apart from most donors, who rarely bother to invest in evaluations, let alone read the year-end reports their grantees submit. But catalytic donors don't conduct *evaluations* in the conventional sense of that term. They are less interested in receiving reports on past progress and more interested in engaging in processes that enable them and their grantees to learn about what's working and what needs to be fixed in order to advance a cause in the context of larger systems. As a result, they build *learning organizations*.

Exhibit e.7. Learn in Order to Change.

For beginners

- *Adopt a learning mind-set rather than a reporting mind-set* in order to focus on what can be learned from grantee progress to influence future directions, rather than relying on summative retrospective reports.

- *Invest in outcome-focused evaluations* rather than relying on reports that tally outputs such as number of people served or petitions signed.

- *Fund or provide technical assistance directly to nonprofits* to help them develop outcomes-based measurement systems; experienced evaluators can work directly with grantees if the funder lacks the expertise in-house.

- *Incorporate forward-looking checkpoints* in periodic reviews rather than waiting to read year-end reports.

For more experienced donors

- *Measure progress across the field or ecosystem* rather than focusing only on individual programs or organizations; find ways to determine how a field has collectively "moved the needle" on an issue.

- *Form or join networks and collaborate* to achieve commonly defined goals for the field; develop universal metrics and institute systems to collectively track progress.

- *Seek ways to confirm contribution rather than attribution*, and show how your efforts and funding have contributed to advancing the cause rather trying to "prove" that your grant worked or that you deserve primary credit for an achievement.

And finally, for those of you who may not yet be ready to dive headlong into these catalytic practices, there are still immediate steps you can take to increase the impact of your grantmaking.

EXHIBIT E.8. TIPS FOR GRANTMAKING WITH A CATALYTIC MIND-SET.

For donors who aren't ready to become catalytic but who seek greater impact

- *Outsource your strategy to foundations that are catalytic.* Donors who don't have the time or the ability to embrace catalytic practices can leverage the efforts of their peers. Identify catalytic foundations or individuals who are active in your issue area, and leverage their proven strategies. One example in *Do More Than Give* is e-Bay cofounder Jeff Skoll's partnership with Fundación AVINA; Skoll and AVINA agreed to match each other's funding, up to US$6 million, to fund nonprofit allies on the ground in Latin America to combat deforestation and preserve biodiversity in the Amazon rainforest. Skoll realized that without a footprint or strong connections in the countries that surround the Amazon, he could be more effective by levering the expertise of a seasoned local funder.

- *Fund intermediaries that support catalytic nonprofits.* Most foundations employ no or only a few staff members, so boards or individual donors that seek to spend minimal time while maximizing the impact of their gifts can fund experienced intermediaries that screen for catalytic approaches. Here are some specific examples of such intermediaries:

  Ashoka the oldest and largest venture fund supporting social entrepreneurs has provided fellowships and other supports to thousands of systems-changing social entrepreneurs in more than sixty countries. Ashoka employs a rigorous, time-tested screening methodology that ensures its grantees are pursuing systems-changing new ideas that hold the highest potential for wide-scale impact.

  Echoing Green, Draper Richards Foundation, and *Social Venture Partners* comprise a number of leading U.S.-based social entrepreneurship funds that support entrepreneurs at the start-up and early growth stages of development; *Skoll Foundation* and *New Profit* are leading funders of mezzanine-stage social entrepreneurs.

  Issue-specific funds include *New Schools Venture Fund*, which supports systems-changing education entrepreneurs, and *Acumen Fund*, which invests in revenue-generating social enterprises in developing regions of the world.

- *Directly fund nonprofits that employ catalytic practices.* The six practices presented in *Do More Than Give* correspond with and build upon the six practices of high-impact nonprofits presented in *Forces for Good*. The twelve high-impact nonprofits described in *Forces for Good* are excellent examples of groups employing cross-sector, systems-changing strategies. Use the practices in *Forces for Good* as a guide to your grantmaking; you can screen nonprofits to determine whether they employ some or all of these high-impact approaches. (For a review of the six practices of high-impact nonprofits, see Appendix D.)

Notes

Preface

1. M. Kramer, "Catalytic Philanthropy," *Stanford Social Innovation Review*, Fall 2009, pp. 30–35.
2. R. Heifetz, J. Kania, and M. Kramer, "Leading Boldly: Foundations Can Move Past Traditional Approaches to Create Social Change Through Imaginative—and Even Controversial—Leadership," *Stanford Social Innovation Review*, Winter 2004, pp. 20–31.

Chapter One

1. M. Bishop and M. Green, *Philanthrocapitalism: How the Rich Can Save the World* (London: Bloomsbury Press, 2008).
2. F. Westley, B. Zimmerman, and M. Patton, *Getting to Maybe: How the World Is Changed* (Toronto: Vintage Canada, 2007), Kindle location 209–214.
3. R. A. Heifetz, *Leadership Without Easy Answers* (Cambridge, Mass.: Harvard University Press/Belknap Press, 1994).
4. M. Nichols, "World's Mega-Rich Adding Wealth, Carlos Slim No. 1," *International Business Times*, Mar. 10, 2010, http://www.ibtimes.com/articles/10347/20100310/worlds-mega-rich-wealth-carlos-slim-no-1.htm, accessed Aug. 9, 2010; L. DiCarlo, "Billionaires," *Forbes*, 2000, http://www.forbes.com/finance/lists/10/2000/charts.jhtml?passListId=10&passYear=2000&passListType=Person, accessed Aug. 9, 2010.
5. Foundation Center's Statistical Information Service, *Number of Grantmaking Foundations, 1975 to 2007*, http://foundationcenter.org/findfunders/statistics/pdf/02_found_growth/2007/03_07.pdf, accessed May 30, 2010.
6. Bishop and Green, *Philanthrocapitalism*. These authors note that previous golden ages of philanthropy occurred prior to the creation of modern foundations in the United States, and many other societies

had invented philanthropic organizations well before Rockefeller and Carnegie established their American institutions.

7. P. Brest and H. Harvey, *Money Well Spent: A Strategic Plan for Smart Philanthropy* (New York: Bloomberg Press, 2008), pp. 6, 206.

8. W. Drayton, "What Is a Social Entrepreneur?" (Ashoka, 2007), http://www.ashoka.org.

9. L. R. Crutchfield and H. McLeod Grant, *Forces for Good: The Six Practices of High-Impact Nonprofits* (San Francisco: Jossey-Bass/Wiley, 2008), p. 25.

10. R. A. Heifetz, *Leadership Without Easy Answers* (Cambridge, Mass.: Harvard University Press/Belknap Press, 1994).

11. P. Senge, *The Fifth Discipline* (New York: Doubleday Business, 1994).

12. M. Bishop, "Building Boundary Conditions for Progress," panelist presentation at UBS Philanthropy Forum, Singapore, Apr. 29–30, 2010.

13. Interview, conducted by the authors, with Lance E. Lindblom, president and chief executive officer of the Nathan Cummings Foundation, Mar. 23, 2010.

14. P. Frumkin, *Strategic Giving: The Art and Science of Philanthropy* (Chicago: University of Chicago Press, 2006), p. 125.

Chapter Two

1. Jacobs Family Foundation, Web site, Aug. 2010, http://www.jacobs familyfoundation.org. Unless otherwise noted, this discussion about the Jacobs Family Foundation is based on official foundation materials or interviews conducted by the authors with either Jacobs Family Foundation board member Valerie Jacobs or executive director Jennifer Vanica.

2. V. Jacobs, "Place-Based Philanthropy: Investing in Community Change," *Family Giving News* (National Center for Family Philanthropy e-newsletter), Mar. 2010, http://www.ncfp.org/newsroom /family_giving_news, accessed Aug. 2010.

3. This type of portfolio approach was first discussed by M. R. Kramer in his article "Mixed Motives," *Benefactor*, Winter 1998. For further discussion of this approach, see M. E. Porter and M. R. Kramer, "Redefining Capitalism: The End of Zero Sum Game," *Harvard Business Review*, forthcoming.

4. T. Bryan, "Transforming Blight into a Community Asset," *Economic Development Journal*, Winter 2010, *9*(1), pp. 5–12, and interviews with Valerie Jacobs and Jennifer Vanica.

5. V. Jacobs, "Place-Based Philanthropy."

6. Interview conducted by the authors with Lew Feldstein, who was then president of the New Hampshire Charitable Foundation, Mar. 26, 2010.

Chapter Three

1. The facts about Emily J.'s treatment and the subsequent lawsuit are derived from *Emily J. v. Weicker* 3:93CV1944 (D. Conn., Oct. 25, 1993) and subsequent actions taken by attorney Martha Stone of the Center for Children's Advocacy at University of Connecticut School of Law on behalf of the plaintiffs. "Emily J." is not the real name of the lead plaintiff; because they were minors, the plaintiffs were referred to by pseudonyms.

2. Interview conducted by the authors with Robert Francis, executive director of the Regional Youth/Adult Social Action Partnership (RYASAP), Mar. 23, 2010.

3. "Suit Aims at Juvenile Detention: Children, Ages 8 to 16, Deprived of Basic Rights, CCLU Claims," *The Hartford Courant*: Sept 28, 1993, p. A1.

4. The discussion of the work of The Tow Foundation is based on official materials provided by the foundation and from an interview, conducted by the authors, with the foundation's executive director, Emily Tow Jackson.

5. Interview with Robert Francis.

6. Interview with Robert Francis.

7. These data are from Tow Foundation documents and were provided by Tow Foundation executive director Emily Tow Jackson in an e-mail exchange with the authors, Nov. 11, 2010.

8. E. Banwell, "One Foundation's Story: The New Hampshire Charitable Foundation Makes a Significant Impact with Public Policy," paper presented at the Aspen Institute Nonprofit Sector and Philanthropy Program, Washington, D.C., Apr. 2006.

9. Alliance for Justice, *Investing in Change: A Funder's Guide to Supporting Advocacy* (Washington, D.C.: Alliance for Justice, 2004).

10. FSG online peer survey results (see Appendixes A and B for discussion of the peer survey and the questions asked), and Alliance for Justice, *Investing in Change*.

11. Alliance for Justice, *Investing in Change*.

12. All the PNC data and quotations are from C. Marquis, V. Kasturi Rangan, and A. Comings, *PNC Financial: Grow Up Great*, Harvard Business School Case 409108 (Boston: Harvard Business School Publishing, Apr. 28, 2009).

13. K. Peterson and M. Pfitzer, "Lobbying for Good," *Stanford Social Innovation Review*, Winter 2009, pp. 44–48.

14. Peterson and Pfitzer, "Lobbying for Good."

15. Alliance for Justice, *Investing in Change*.

16. Interview, conducted by the authors, with Lew Feldstein, who was then president of the New Hampshire Charitable Foundation, Mar. 26, 2010.

17. E. Banwell, *One Foundation's Story*. The discussion of the New Hampshire Charitable Foundation's work is based on this case study, on materials provided by the foundation, and on the interview with Lew Feldstein.

18. Banwell, *One Foundation's Story*.

19. Banwell, *One Foundation's Story*.

20. Interview with Lew Feldstein.

21. Banwell, *One Foundation's Story*.

22. New Hampshire Charitable Foundation, "Civic Leadership," http://www.nhcf.org/page.aspx?pid=532, accessed June 2010.

23. Interview with Lew Feldstein.

24. Interview with Lew Feldstein.

25. Interview, conducted by the authors, with Rebecca Rimel, president and CEO of The Pew Charitable Trusts, Apr. 2, 2010.

Chapter Four

1. The before and after descriptions of the NICU and the discussion of the GE Foundation's work are based on an interview, conducted by the authors, with Bob Corcoran, vice president, corporate citizenship, of General Electric and president of the GE Foundation, Mar. 25, 2010, and on FSG internal case files.

2. Interview with Bob Corcoran.

3. Royal Dutch Shell plc established the Shell Foundation as a U.K. charity in June 2000. The discussion of the Shell Foundation's work is based on materials provided by the foundation and on an interview, conducted by the authors, with Chris West, director of the Shell Foundation, July 28, 2010.

4. West's use of terms such as *growth finance* rather than *missing middle* reflects the same kind of reasoning employed by social sector leaders such as Bill Drayton, founder of Ashoka; Drayton prefers to use the term *citizen organization* rather than the term *nonprofit organization*, which is popular in the United States, or *nongovernmental organization*, which is better known in Europe and beyond, as the first of the latter two terms emphasizes that charities are not profitable (in the eyes of Americans) and the second stresses that they are not part of

government (in the eyes of Europeans and people living in other regions of the world).

5. All the data in the discussion of Tom Siebel and the Meth Project are from M. Kramer, "Catalytic Philanthropy," *Stanford Social Innovation Review*, Fall 2009, pp. 30–35.

6. M. Porter and M. Kramer, "Strategy and Society: The Link Between Competitive Advantage and Corporate Social Responsibility," *Harvard Business Review*, Dec. 2006, pp. 79–92.

7. This discussion of GE is based on FSG internal case files.

8. This discussion of Unilever and ICICI is based on FSG internal case files and on information from the Unilever Web site, http://www.unilever.com/careers/insideunilever/oursuccessand challenges/shaktiprogrammeindia, and from the ICICI Web site, http://www.icicibank.com/rural, both accessed Aug. 2010.

9. The discussion of Waste Concern is based on a presentation by the company founders at the 2005 Schwab Foundation Social Entrepreneurship conference. Current data is also available on the Waste Concern Web site, http://www.wasteconcern.org.

10. This discussion of the Nathan Cummings Foundation is based on an interview, conducted by the authors, with Lance E. Lindblom, president and chief executive officer of the foundation, Mar. 23, 2010.

11. Data reported in the study of donor loans to nonprofits are taken from FSG internal case files.

12. The F. B. Heron Foundation's investing is discussed in S. Godeke and D. Bauer, *Philanthropy's New Passing Gear: Mission-Related Investing, A Policy and Implementation Guide for Foundation Trustees* (New York: Rockefeller Philanthropy Advisors, 2008).

13. The discussion of the Packard Foundation is based on FSG internal case files and on information from the foundation's Web site, http://www.packard.org, accessed Aug. 2010.

14. For further information about Kiva, see http://www.kiva.org.

15. M. Kramer, A. Mahmud, and S. Makka, *Maximizing Impact: An Integrated Strategy for Mission Investing and Grantmaking in Climate Change* (Boston: FSG Social Impact Advisors, May 2010), p. 19.

Chapter Five

1. David and Lucile Packard Foundation and Monitor Institute, *What Networks Do and Why They Matter Now*, Fall 2007, http://www.packard.org/assets/files/capacity%20building%20and %20phil/organizational%20effectiveness/phil%20networks %20exploration/what_do_networks_do.pdf, accessed May 2010.

2. The discussion of Strive is based on FSG internal case files and on interviews, conducted by the authors, with Chad Wick, CEO

of KnowledgeWorks Foundation, Mar. 23, 2010; Jeff Edmondson, executive director of Strive, Mar. 5, 2010, and Mar. 3, 2009; and Kathy Merchant, president and CEO of The Greater Cincinnati Foundation and chair of the board at Strive, Feb. 18, 2010, and Aug. 27, 2010. Information about Strive will also appear in J. Kania and M. Kramer, "Collective Impact," *Stanford Social Innovation Review*, forthcoming.

3. Interview with Chad Wick.

4. CityBeat, "News: Striving to Improve Children's Lives," May 14, 2008, http://citybeat.com/cincinnati/article-4239-news-striving-to-improve-childrens-lives.html, accessed Nov. 25, 2010.

5. FSG internal case files and the interview with Chad Wick.

6. From a draft of Kania and Kramer, "Collective Impact."

7. L. R. Crutchfield and H. McLeod Grant, *Forces for Good: The Six Practices of High-Impact Nonprofits* (San Francisco: Jossey-Bass/Wiley, 2008).

8. Interview with Kathy Merchant.

9. C. Lucas and R. Andrews, "Four Keys to Collaboration Success," n.d., http://www.fieldstonealliance.org/client/articles/Article-4_Key_Collab_Success.cfm, accessed Oct. 26, 2010. Carol Lukas is president of Fieldstone Alliance and former director of National Services for Amherst H. Wilder Foundation and Rebecca Andrews is an illustrator.

10. The "paradigm of isolated impact" is discussed by Kania and Kramer, "Collective Impact."

11. Ben & Jerry's phased out Rainforest Crunch when it was revealed that the local shelling cooperative that processed the Brazil nuts used in this specialty flavor could supply only about 5 percent of the nuts needed and that Ben & Jerry's was sourcing the other 95 percent from Brazilian agribusinesses. Ben & Jerry's has committed to go "fully Fair Trade" by the end of 2013. See also J. Glasser, "Dark Cloud: Ben & Jerry's Inaccurate in Rainforest Nut Pitch," *Boston Globe,* July 30, 1995.

12. The discussion of the state of the rainforest and the work of Fundación AVINA and its Amazon rainforest program is based on materials provided by AVINA.

13. Interview, conducted by the authors, with Federico Bellone, Amazon program manager for Fundación AVINA, Aug. 12, 2010.

14. A. Franzeres and C. Prizibisczki, *The Route of the Smoke*, http://www.trajetoriadafumaca.com.br, accessed Aug. 12–28, 2010. This Web site contains a series of virtual reports on forest fires in the Amazon basin.

15. Interview with Federico Bellone.

16. Interview with Federico Bellone.
17. Interview with Federico Bellone.
18. Interview with Federico Bellone.
19. Interview with Federico Bellone.
20. Lukas and Andrews, "Four Keys to Collaboration Success."
21. The discussion of the John S. and James L. Knight Foundation is based on FSG internal case files and on interviews conducted by the authors with the following officers of the foundations: Alberto Ibargüen, president and CEO, Apr. 2, 2010; Paula Ellis, vice president of operations, Apr. 9, 2010; Trabian Shorters, vice president for communities, Apr. 14, 2010; Eric Newton, vice president for journalism, Apr. 21, 2010, and Mayur Patel, director of strategic assessment and impact, Apr. 9, 2010.
22. Interview with Paula Ellis.
23. Interview with Alberto Ibargüen.
24. Senate Committee on Commerce, Science, and Transportation, Subcommittee on Communications, Technology, and the Internet, *Hearing on the Future of Journalism*, Testimony of Alberto Ibargüen, President, John S. and James L. Knight Foundation, Wednesday, May 6, 2009.
25. Interview with Alberto Ibargüen.
26. Interview with Trabian Shorters.
27. Interview with Alberto Ibargüen.
28. F. Westley, B. Zimmerman, and M. Patton, *Getting to Maybe: How the World Is Changed* (Toronto: Vintage Canada, 2007), Kindle location 209–214.
29. Westley, Zimmerman, and Patton, *Getting to Maybe*, Kindle location 270–274.

Chapter Six

1. Dr. Emmett D. Carson, CEO and president of the Silicon Valley Community Foundation, has written and lectured extensively on the topic of framing philanthropy in more inclusive ways. See, for example, E. D. Carson, "The Roles of Indigenous and Institutional Philanthropy in Advancing Social Justice," in C. Clotfelter and T. Ehrlich (eds.), *Philanthropy and the Nonprofit Sector in a Changing America* (pp. 248–274), (Bloomington: Indiana University Press, 1999).
2. R. D. Putnam, *Bowling Alone: The Collapse and Revival of American Community* (New York: Simon & Schuster, 2001).
3. The discussion of the Consumer Health Foundation (CHF) board meeting is based on an interview, conducted by the authors, with

Margaret O'Bryon, president and CEO of Consumer Health Foundation, Mar. 26, 2010, and on an article in a CHF publication: "Actress Sarah Jones Transports Annual Meeting to Congressional Hearing on Health Justice," *Connections*, 2008, *10*(2).

4. Interview with Margaret O'Bryon.

5. Interview with Margaret O'Bryon.

6. Interview with Margaret O'Bryon.

7. This discussion of the Jacobs foundations' project is based on materials provided by the foundation and on interviews, conducted by the authors, with foundation staff and board members.

8. L. R. Crutchfield and H. McLeod Grant, *Forces for Good: The Six Practices of High-Impact Nonprofits* (San Francisco: Jossey-Bass/Wiley, 2008), pp. 81–103.

9. The discussion of Chalkboard is based on materials provided by Chalkboard and on an interview, conducted by the authors, with Sue Hildick, president of Chalkboard, Mar. 22, 2010.

10. This teacher development initiative is called CLASS (Creative Leadership Achieves Student Success). Its purpose is to improve the quality of instruction and management as a means to increase student achievement. Work is taking place in pilot school districts to design and implement professional development, create a career ladder, design new teacher assessment practices, and develop alternative compensation models for both teachers and administrators.

11. P. Grogan and T. Proscio, *Comeback Cities: A Blueprint For Urban Neighborhood Revival* (Boulder, Colo.: Westview Press, 2000). The discussion of The Boston Foundation is based on this book and on an interview, conducted by the authors, with Paul Grogan, president and CEO of The Boston Foundation, Apr. 16, 2010.

12. Interview with Paul Grogan.

13. The comment by Lewis was supplied by Paul Grogan in an e-mail exchange following the authors' interview with Grogan.

14. K. P. Enright and C. Bourns, "The Case for Stakeholder Engagement," *Stanford Social Innovation Review*, Spring 2010, p. 40.

15. The quotations and information in this paragraph come from e-mail exchanges between the authors and Tracey Bryan, communications director, and Valerie Jacobs, board member, of the Jacobs Family Foundation, Sept. 5, 2010.

16. J. Courtney Bourns, *Do Nothing About Me Without Me: An Action Guide for Engaging Stakeholders* (Washington, D.C.: GEO and Interaction Institute for Social Change, 2010).

17. Interview, conducted by the authors, with Eric Newton, vice president, Journalism Program, The John S. and James L. Knight Foundation, Apr. 21, 2010.

18. A. Toffler, *Revolutionary Wealth* (New York: Knopf, 2006).
19. F. Westley, B. Zimmerman, and M. Patton, *Getting to Maybe: How the World Is Changed* (Toronto: Vintage Canada, 2007), Kindle locations 209–214.
20. M. Mitchell, *Complexity: A Guided Tour* (New York: Oxford University Press, 2009), Kindle locations 194–204, 248–254.
21. Mitchell, *Complexity*.
22. Robert F. Kennedy, speech given in 1966 at the University of Cape town, South Africa, available (with audio) at "Ripples—Every Day Inspiration at City Year," *City Year Blog*, http://cityyearblog.org/blog /2010/10/05/ripples, accessed Oct. 27, 2010.

Chapter Seven

1. The discussion of adaptive leadership at The Boston Foundation is based on materials provided by the foundation and an interview with Paul Grogan, president and CEO of The Boston Foundation, Apr. 16, 2010. Quotations from Grogan are from this interview.
2. Former vice president Al Gore has used both this proverb and the "go far, quickly" form of it in his presentations.
3. R. A. Heifetz, *Leadership Without Easy Answers* (Cambridge, Mass.: Harvard University Press/Belknap Press, 1994). Heifetz has studied, taught, and written about adaptive leadership for almost twenty years and has written three books on the subject: *Leadership Without Easy Answers*; *Leadership on the Line: Staying Alive Through the Dangers of Leading* (with Marty Linsky, Harvard Business Press, 2002); and *The Practice of Adaptive Leadership: Tools and Tactics for Changing Your Organization and the World* (with Alexander Grashow and Marty Linsky, Harvard Business Press, 2009). He is also the coauthor, with J. Kania and M. Kramer, of "Leading Boldly: How Foundations Can Move Past Traditional Approaches to Create Social Change Through Imaginative—And Even Controversial—Leadership," *Stanford Social Innovation Review*, Winter 2004, pp. 20–31. The discussion of adaptive leadership in this chapter references Heifetz's original works and also Kania and Kramer's application of this body of thinking to the specific challenges of problem-solving philanthropy.
4. C. Heath and D. Heath, *Switch: How to Change Things When Change Is Hard* (New York: Crown Business, 2010), p. 147.
5. This discussion of the work of the William C. Graustein Memorial Fund is based on materials produced by the fund and on an interview, conducted by the authors, with William Graustein, the board chair of the Graustein Memorial Fund, and David M. Nee, the executive director of the fund, Apr. 8, 2010.

6. Heath and Heath, *Switch,* p. 181.
7. D. Jehl, "Charity Is New Force in Environmental Fight," *New York Times,* June 28, 2001.
8. Interview, conducted by the authors, with Joshua Reichert, managing director of the Pew Environment Group, June 10, 2004.
9. *Expanding College Access, Strengthening Schools: Evaluation of the GE Fund College Bound Program,* report prepared for the GE Foundation (Waltham, Mass.: Center for Human Resources, Heller Graduate School, Brandeis University, 2000). Today, the Developing Futures™ in Education program (which now encompasses the GE College Bound program) strives to raise student achievement through improved math and science curricula and increased management capacity in the schools. The program has been expanded with a grant investment of nearly $200 million in six targeted U.S. school districts.
10. Heifetz and Linsky, *Leadership on the Line.*
11. Interview with William Graustein and David Nee.
12. Interview with Joshua Reichert.

Chapter Eight
1. The discussion of the Bill & Melinda Gates Foundation is based on official foundation materials; the interview, conducted by the authors, with David Wertheimer, deputy director of the Pacific Northwest Initiative of the Bill & Melinda Gates Foundation, Apr. 1, 2010; and subsequent e-mail exchanges between Wertheimer and the authors.
2. Interview with David Wertheimer.
3. Interview with David Wertheimer.
4. P. Senge, *The Fifth Discipline* (New York: Doubleday Business, 1994).
5. M. Kramer with R. Graves, J. Hirschhorn, and L. Fiske, *From Insight to Action: New Directions in Foundation Evaluation* (Boston: FSG Social Impact Advisors, Apr. 2007).
6. Kramer, *From Insight to Action.*
7. F. Westley, B. Zimmerman, and M. Patton, *Getting to Maybe: How the World Is Changed* (Toronto: Vintage Canada, 2007), Kindle locations 807–811.
8. Westley, Zimmerman, and Patton, *Getting to Maybe,* Kindle locations 807–811.
9. Kramer, *From Insight to Action.*
10. Stiftung Mercator Web site, http://www.stiftung-mercator.de, accessed November 16, 2010.

11. The discussion of the work of Venture Philanthropy Partners with LAYC is based on materials provided by VPP and interviews, conducted by the authors, with Victoria Vrana, vice president, communications and assessment, of VPP and Carol Thompson Cole, president and CEO of VPP, Apr. 16, 2010.

12. Interview with Victoria Vrana.

13. M. Morino, "Social Outcomes: A Revolution in the Making," *VPPnews*, May 2010, http://www.vppartners.org/learning/perspectives/corner/0510_social-outcomes-revolution.html, accessed May 7, 2010.

14. P. N. Bloom and J. G. Dees, "Cultivate Your Ecosystem," *Stanford Social Innovation Review*, Winter 2008, pp. 47–53.

15. Six Sigma originated as a methodology and management system intended to reduce manufacturing defects, and was formulated by Bill Smith at Motorola in 1986. Over time, it has evolved from its original roots in manufacturing processes, and the approach is now used more widely as a business improvement methodology by a number of companies. This history is discussed in Motorola University, "About Motorola University: The Inventors of Six Sigma," 2010, http://www.motorola.com/Business/US-EN/Motorola+University/About/Inventors+of+Six+Sigma, accessed Sept. 1, 2010.

Appendix A

1. L. R. Crutchfield and H. McLeod Grant, *Forces for Good: The Six Practices of High-Impact Nonprofits* (San Francisco: Jossey-Bass/Wiley, 2008).

2. M. Kramer, "Catalytic Philanthropy," *Stanford Social Innovation Review*, Fall 2009, pp. 30–35.

3. This nonprofit involves an intergenerational network of emerging and established foundation leaders and trustees; network members range in age from (approximately) twenty-one to sixty-four.

Appendix D

1. L. R. Crutchfield and H. McLeod Grant, *Forces for Good: The Six Practices of High-Impact Nonprofits* (San Francisco: Jossey-Bass/Wiley, 2008).

2. H. McLeod Grant and L. R. Crutchfield, "Creating High-Impact Nonprofits," *Stanford Social Innovation Review*, Fall 2007, pp. 32–41.

3. Adapted from McLeod Grant and Crutchfield, "Creating High-Impact Nonprofits," p. 35. See also B. Smucker, *The Nonprofit Lobbying Guide* (Washington, D.C.: Independent Sector, 1999).

4. Adapted from McLeod Grant and Crutchfield, "Creating High-Impact Nonprofits," pp. 35–37. See also S. Sagawa and E. Segal, *Common Interest, Common Good: Creating Value Through Business and Social Sector Partnerships* (Cambridge, Mass.: Harvard Business Press, 2000); J. G. Dees, "Enterprising Nonprofits," *Harvard Business Review*, Jan.–Feb. 1998; and J. E. Austin, *The Collaboration Challenge: How Nonprofits and Businesses Succeed Through Strategic Alliances* (San Francisco: Jossey-Bass/Wiley, 2000).

5. Adapted from McLeod Grant and Crutchfield, "Creating High-Impact Nonprofits," pp. 37–38.

6. Adapted from McLeod Grant and Crutchfield, "Creating High-Impact Nonprofits," p. 38.

7. Adapted from McLeod Grant and Crutchfield, "Creating High-Impact Nonprofits," p. 39. See also C. W. Letts, W. P. Ryan, and A. Grossman, *High-Performance Nonprofit Organizations* (Hoboken, N.J.: Wiley, 1999); and R. A. Heifetz, *Leadership Without Easy Answers* (Cambridge, Mass.: Harvard University Press/Belknap Press, 1994).

8. Adapted from McLeod Grant and Crutchfield, "Creating High-Impact Nonprofits," p. 39.

INDEX

Page references followed by *fig* indicate an illustrated figure; followed by *t* indicate a table; followed by *e* indicate an exhibit.

A

ACCION New Mexico, 20
Action grants, 133
Actionable insights, 171–172
Acumen Fund, 75–76
Adaptive leaders: asserting leadership and not just authority, 149–150; catalytic donors as, 5, 14; courting conflict, 159–160; focusing on adaptive vs. technical problems and solutions, 150–152; focusing attention on tough issues, 155–156; key principles for, 163–164; making the decision to be an, 161–162; paging progress, 156–159; shaping conditions with stakeholders, 152–154; taking the heat, 160–161
Adaptive leadership: description of, 14, 143–144, 149; getting beyond the usual suspects, 146–147; high bar set by, 189; keeping the issue visible, 146; key principles of, 163–164; payoff of, 147–148; reframing the problem as, 145; taking a broader look at, 148–161. *See also* Leadership
Adaptive problems: description of, 151; technical versus, 151*t*–152. *See also* Social problems
Advocacy: barriers to donor, 48–49; differences between lobbying and, 44–45*t*; key principles for donor, 60–61; learning to embrace, 43–44; multiple dimensions of, 46*fig*–47; shareholder, 76–78; summary of legal restrictions on, 52*t*–53*t*; The Tow Foundation activities of, 47–48;

understanding meaning of, 44–48. *See also* Corporate lobbying
Advocate for change practice: community foundations as emerging policy change force, 54–57; corporate lobbying as, 49–53*t*; description of the, 11–12; embracing the, 43–44; *Emily J.* lawsuit to, 38–39; Emily Tow Jackson's experience with, 37–39; examples of activities facilitating, 47–48; political history of private foundations as, 57–59; The Tow Foundation approach to, 12, 39–43, 47–48; understanding what advocacy is for, 44–48; understanding what holds donors back from, 48–49
Affinity groups, 94–95
Amazon rainforest protection: corporate and nonprofit support of, 99–100; description of the problem, 100–102; Fundación AVINA network solutions for, 98, 102–107; mapping project for, 102–103
Amazon Regional Alliance (ARA), 102–104
Amazonian Network of Socio-Environmental Geo-referenced Information (RAISG), 102–103
American University, 136
Andrews, Rebecca, 97
Annie E. Casey Foundation, 31, 123, 157
Aparecida de Queiroz, Nelci, 101, 103
Archimedes, 92
"Artist formerly known as Prince," 59
As You Sow Foundation, 78

Ashoka, social entrepreneurship focus of, 35
Aspen Institute, 55
Authority: definition of, 149; leadership versus, 149–150
AVINA. *See* Fundación AVINA

B

Babel (film), 71
Baird, Abigail, 41
Bangladesh garbage collection problem, 74–75
Barros, Roque, 127, 128, 130
Bellone, Federico, 103, 106
Ben & Jerry's Rainforest Crunch, 100
Bill & Melinda Gates Foundation: global health and public education focus of, 35, 58; impact investments made by, 83; learning curve maintained by, 168; private foundation category of, 57; social change created by, 14; Sound Families program of, 165–168, 173
Bishop, Matthew, 6
Black Panthers, 120
Blending profit/purpose practice: create shared value strategy for, 64*t*, 73–76; description of, 12; invest for impact strategy for, 64*t*, 76–82; key principles for, 83–85; tap corporate know-how strategy for, 64*t*, 65–73
Bloom, Paul, 178
Bofinger, Paul, 55
Boston at Night Tour, 133–134
Boston Centers for Youth and Families, 133
Boston Department of Neighborhood Development, 132
Boston Foundation. *See* TBF (The Boston Foundation)
Boston Globe editorial (Haynes and Tinti), 146
Boston Indicators Project (TBF), 157, 172–173
Bourns, Courtney, 134–135
Bradley Foundation, 43
Brest, Paul, 7
Bridgeport Juvenile Detention Center, 37–38
Bronze Lion Award, 71
Brookings Institution, 126

Brousseau, Ruth, 169
Buffett, Warren, 111
Building Services Career Path, 147
Bush, George H., 44
Bush, George W., 44

C

California Wellness Foundation, 169
Calouste Gulbenkian Foundation (Portugal), 57
Cambridge Leadership Associates, 163
Cannes International Advertising Festival, 71
Carmichael, Stokely, 120
Carnegie, Andrew, 6, 140
Carson, Emmett, 120
Catalytic donor key principles: for blending profit with purpose, 83–85; for donor advocacy, 60–61; for empowering the people, 141–142; for forging nonprofit peer networks, 116–117; for leading adaptively, 163–164; for learning to change, 182–183
Catalytic donors: commit to your cause strategy by, 11, 19–36; comparing mind-set of common versus, 8*fig*–10; defined as causing or accelerating a change, 9–10, 171; description and characteristics of, 3, 43–44; interconnection between parts concept understood by, 115; making a difference goal of, 120–122; motivations for giving by, 24*e*–27, 120–122; moving from theory to practice, 15; peer-network mind-set of, 97–99*fig*; as philanthropreneurs, 9; potential of today's, 6–7; six practices of, 10–15; two main premises on, 4; views on individuals by common versus, 125–126*t*; views of nonprofits by common versus, 98–99*fig*. *See also* Donors; Master donors
Catalytic donors practices: 1: advocate for change, 11–12, 37–61; 2: blend profit with purpose, 12, 63–85; 3: forge nonprofit peer networks, 12–13, 87–117; 4: empower the people, 13, 119–142; 5: lead adaptively, 5, 14, 143–164; 6: learn to create change, 14–15, 165–183

Catalytic philanthropy: as adaptive leadership, 5; checklists for commitment to, 187–188; comparing traditional and, 7–10, 186–187; complexity of change challenge of, 140–141, 186–187; current need for, 4–5; description of, 3; embracing the future of, 16–17, 185–190; role of individuals in, 125–134; two main premises of, 4. *See also* Nonprofits; Philanthropy

Catalytic philanthropy premise: donors have something valuable to contribute beyond their money, 4; we inhabit a complex and globally interdependent world, 4

Catalytic philanthropy principles: 1: philanthropy is not a solitary or dialectical effort, 188–189; 2: solving problems is not about knowing the answer, 189; 3: catalytic philanthropy is not for the impatient, 189–190

Center on Budget and Policy Priorities, 58

Center for Children's Advocacy (University of Connecticut), 38, 39, 40

Ceres, 78

Chalkboard Project (Oregon), 130–131, 173

Chicago Community Trust, 109

Chicago Sun-Times, 109

Chicago Tribune, 109

Choosing your cause: assessing external opportunities, 29–30; assessing internal capabilities, 28–29; illustrated diagram on process of, 27*fig*; Jacobs Family Foundation's process of, 30–33; tips for process of, 33–36

City Year, 133

Civic leadership, 132

Civil Rights Act (1964), 119

Civil rights movement, 119–120, 139

Clackamas County (Oregon), 81

Clinton, Bill, 155

Collaboration: adopting peer-network mind-set for, 97–99*fig*; among affinity groups, 94–95; challenge for nonprofits, 93–95; creating learning systems as part of, 178–181; defining, 97; as power force for change, 93–99;

spectrum of nonprofit, 95–97; workforce partnership, 147, 157

College Bound program (General Electric), 155–156, 161

Comeback Cities (Grogan and Proscio), 132

Commit to your cause strategy: choosing your cause, 27*fig*–33; description of the, 11; getting committed, 21–27; how you can choose your cause, 33–36; Jacobs Family Foundation approach to, 19–21, 30–33

Commitment: beginning process of choosing your own cause, 33–36; checklists for implementing, 187–188; choosing a cause for, 27*fig*–33; as essential first step, 187; portfolio approach to, 23–24, 42; problem of identifying your, 21–23; understanding your motivations for giving and, 24*e*–27

Communities: building collective will in, 129–131; Deerfield (New Hampshire), 136–137; empowering individual people in, 13, 119–142; fulfilling obligations to different, 25; GMS's adaptive leadership engaging, 158–159; Jacobs Foundation's commitment to Diamond Neighborhoods, 20–21, 31–33, 79, 127–129; Knight Foundation's engagement of, 70, 94, 98–99, 107–113; LAYC serving Hispanic Columbia Heights, 176–177; TBF action grants to leaders in the, 133

Community Foundation Serving Boulder County (CFSB), 110

Community foundations: description of, 54; emerging as policy change force, 54–57; New Hampshire Charitable Foundation (NHCF) as, 12, 34, 54–57

Community Information Challenge, 112–113

Community Reinvestment Fund, 79

Community report card, 178

Complex systems: energy created by, 139–140; philanthropy challenge of understanding, 140–141, 186–187; social innovation as, 138–141

Complexity: A Guided Tour (Mitchell), 139

Conflict: adaptive leadership ability to use, 159–160; adaptive leadership taking the heat of, 160–161; Paul Grogan's experience with hospital rivalry and, 143–144

Connecticut Early Childhood Alliance, 153

Connecticut Juvenile Justice Alliance, 40, 41

Connecticut Voices for Children, 40

Consumer Health Foundation (CHF): empowerment facilitated by, 123–125; Sarah Jones performance at conference of, 122–123

Consumer paradigm shift, 137–138t

Copenhagen Climate Conference, 103–104

Corcoran, Bob, 67

Corporate foundations: General Electric (GE) Foundation as, 65, 66–67, 72, 73–74; legal restrictions on advocacy by, 52t; Shell Foundation (UK), 2–3, 65, 67–70

Corporate know-how: blending profit and purpose through, 64t, 65; General Electric's approach to tapping, 65, 66–67; Shell Foundation's approach to tapping, 65, 67–70; Tom Siebel's approach to tapping, 65, 70–73, 84

Corporate lobbying: description of, 44–45; downside of, 51–53; PNC Financial Services Group approach to, 49–51. See also Policy advocacy (lobbying)

Council on Foundations, 94, 108

Crandall, Doug, 155

Creating shared value: blending profit and purpose by, 64t; GE's approach to, 73–74; Hindustan Unilever's approach to, 74, 76, 84; solving garbage problem of slums by, 74–76

Crutchfield, Leslie, 10, 57, 93, 129

"Cultivate Your Ecosystem" (Bloom and Dees), 178

Cummings Foundation, 78

D

David and Lucille Packard Foundation, 57, 80

Deerfield (New Hampshire), 136–137

Dees, Gregory, 178

Deforestation. See Amazon rainforest protection

Deutsche Bank, 81

Diamond Neighborhoods (San Diego): empowering individuals in the, 127–129; Jacobs Foundation's commitment to, 20–21, 31–33, 135; Market Creek Plaza built in, 21, 32, 79, 127, 128–129

Digital view of individuals, 137–138t

Do Nothing About Me Without Me: An Action Guide for Engaging Stakeholders, 136

Domestic violence classes, 176–177

Donor collaboration spectrum, 95–97

Donors: advocacy by, 11–12, 37–61; barriers to advocacy by, 48–49; check writer role of traditional, 125; comparing catalytic versus common mind-set of, 8fig–10; current situation facing today's, 5–7; examining how to become more proactive, 1–2; motivations for giving by, 24e–27; views on individuals by catalytic versus common, 125–126t; views of nonprofits by catalytic donors versus, 98–99fig. See also Catalytic donors

Donors Forum of Chicago, 169

Draper Richards Foundation, 35

Drucker, Peter, 1

Duke Energy, 92

E

E pluribus unum, 93

Economist (magazine), 6

Education reform: Chalkboard Project (Oregon) on, 130–131, 173; Community Foundation Serving Boulder County (CFSB) work for, 110; GE's College Bound program, 155–156; GMF's adaptive leadership for early childhood, 153–154, 157–159; SSNs (student success networks) used in, 180–181; Strive Partnership's achievements with, 88–89; Strive Partnership's network strategy for, 89–93; Strive Partnership's use of Six Sigma process for, 72, 90; summer bridge session launched for, 91, 181

Eisenhower, Dwight, 172

Ellis, Paula, 108
"Emily J." (*Emily J. v. Weicker*): background information of, 37–39; The Tow Foundation's advocacy of, 39–43
Empowering the people practice: broader return and risks related to, 134–136; Consumer Health Foundation (CHF) experience with, 123–125; description of, 13, 119–120; engaging individual philanthropy for, 136–141; hearing the people speak to drive, 122–125; key principles for, 141–142; making a difference through, 120–122; role of individuals in, 125–134. *See also* Individuals; Leadership
Enayetullah, Iftekhar, 74
Energy-saving investment, 81–82
Enright, Kathleen, 134–135
Environmental problems: energy conservation efforts, 81–82; Marine Fisheries program on sustainable fish, 80; pollution, 77–78; Roadless Rule protecting national forest, 155; Stiftung Mercator's commitment to solving, 174
Eugene and Agnes E. Meyer Foundation, 123
Every Child Succeeds, 90
External opportunities: choosing a cause by acting on, 29–30; questions to ask about, 29

F

Facebook, 87, 113
F.B. Heron Foundation, 31, 79–80
Feldstein, Lew, 34, 54–55, 56
FINCA, 20
501(c)(3) public charities: Chalkboard Project created as, 130; informal networks versus, 88; legal restrictions on advocacy by, 53*t*; what drives social innovation by, 115
501(c)(4) advocacy organizations, 53*t*
Focus groups, 130–131
Forces for Good (Crutchfield and McLeod Grant): on funding social policy change leaders, 57–58; The Heritage Foundation profile in, 126;

on high-impact nonprofit practices, 10, 115; on the networking phenomenon, 93; on process of "inspiring evangelists," 129
Forces for Good (FSG): leading adaptively instruction by, 163; on motivations for giving, 24*e*–27; survey (2007) on loans to nonprofits, 78
Ford Foundation, 16–17, 57, 58, 157
Forging networks. *See* Nonprofit peer networks
The Forum (Deerfield, New Hampshire), 137
Foundations for a Better Oregon, 127, 130, 173
"Four Keys to Collaboration Success" (Lukas and Andrews), 97
Freedom Riders, 120
Frumkin, Peter, 17
Fundación AVINA: choosing a cause approach by, 35; collective action protecting the rainforest by, 102–105; peer networks forged by, 98, 102, 105–107; social change facilitated by, 105–106

G

Garbage collection problem, 74–76
Gates, Bill, 2, 14, 16, 111, 113
Gates Foundation. *See* Bill & Melinda Gates Foundation
Gates, Melinda, 14, 166
General Electric (GE) Company: attention through College Bound program of, 155–156, 161; Jet Engines Division of, 180; Strive's education programs supported by, 91–92; tapping corporate know-how by, 65, 66–67
General Electric (GE) Foundation: corporate know-how tapped by, 65, 66–67; creating shared value, 73–74; Honduras NICU improved through Six Sigma by, 66–67, 72
Getting to Maybe (Zimmerman and Patton), 5, 114, 139, 169, 171, 190
Gill Foundation, 44
Gingrich, Newt, 44
Global Impact Investing Network, 83

GMF. *See* William C. Graustein Memorial Fund (GMF)
Google Earth engineers, 103
Google Forests, 103
Government philanthropic role, 6
Grameen Bank, 68
Grantmakers in Education, 95
Grantmakers for Effective Organizations (GEO), 135, 136
Graustein, William "Bill," 152–153, 154, 157
Greater Cincinnati Foundation, 90, 91, 92
Green Revolution, 16
Greenhouse gas emissions, 174
Greenpeace, 100
GroFin (Shell Foundation), 68–69
Grogan, Paul: ability to empower others, 132–133; adaptive leadership of, 143–148, 149–150, 157, 158, 159–160; collaborative leadership cultivated by, 162
Group Health Association, 123
Grow Up Great program (PNC), 34–35, 50
Growth finance sector, 69

H
Haile/US Bank Foundation, 91, 92
Hall, Ngozi, 124
Hartford Courant (newspaper), 38–39
Harvard University, 147, 149
Harvey, Hal, 7
Haynes, Robert, 146
Head Start, 50, 90, 91
Heath, Chip, 152
Heath, Dan, 152
Heifetz, Ronald, 149, 156, 163
Heritage Forests Campaign, 155
The Heritage Foundation, 44, 126
Heron Foundation, 31, 79–80
Hewlett Packard Corporation, 80
Hildick, Sue, 130, 131
Hindustan Unilever, 74, 76, 84
Homeless families: Sound Families program to help, 165–168, 173; Temporary Assistance for Needy Families funds to, 165; Washington Families Fund for, 166
Humana, 123

I
Ibargüen, Alberto, 107, 108–109, 111, 113
Iñárritu, Alejandro González, 71
An Inconvenient Truth (film), 105
Individuals: bridging divides between, 132–134; building collective will out of, 129–131; Chalkboard Project empowerment of, 127, 130–131, 173; common versus catalytic donor views on, 125–126*t*; industrial versus digital era views of, 137–138*t*; Jacobs Family Foundation approach to empowering, 127–129; TBF (The Boston Foundation) approach to empowering, 127, 132–134; transformed into "inspiring evangelists," 129. *See also* Empowering the people practice
Institute for Contemporary Studies, 19
Interaction Institute for Social Change, 136
Internal capabilities: choosing cause by assessing your, 28–29; description of, 28
Investing for impact strategy: description of, 64*t*, 76; microfinance loans, 68, 81; social stock exchanges proposal as, 83; using your cash for, 78–82; using your stock vote for, 76–78

J
J-Lab (American University), 136
Jackson, Emily Tow, 2, 28, 37, 39, 42–43
Jacobs Center for Neighborhood Innovation (JCNI), 127–128
Jacobs Engineering Group, 19
Jacobs Family Foundation (JFF): approach to empowering individuals by, 127–129; conflicting agendas and views within, 49; Diamond Neighborhoods commitment to, 20–21, 31–32, 33, 127–129, 135; entering the realm of catalytic philanthropy, 20–21; Market Creek Plaza built by, 21, 32, 79, 127, 128–129; microfinance as initial cause of, 20; origins of the, 19
Jacobs, Joseph, Jr., 19, 20, 30–31
Jacobs, Linda, 19, 31

Jacobs, Meg, 19
Jacobs, Valerie, 19, 20, 32, 135
Jacobs, Vi, 19
John S. and James L. Knight Foundation: community foundation networks tapped into by, 98–99; Community Information Challenge work by, 112–113; community role in education reform initiative of, 109–111; creating conditions for social change, 107–113; engaging community efforts by, 70; Knight Community Information Challenge initiative of, 109; Media Learning Seminar hosted by, 109; working directly with individuals, 136–137
Joint Affinity Group, 94
Jones, Sarah, 122–123
Juvenile detention problem: "Emily J." (*Emily J. v. Weicker*) focus on, 37–39; The Tow Foundation's advocacy of, 39–43

K

K–12 education reform. *See* Education reform
Kania, John, 93
Kennedy, Robert F., 139, 140
Key principles: for blending profit with purpose, 83–85; for donor advocacy, 60–61; for empowering the people, 141–142; for forging nonprofit peer networks, 116–117; for leading adaptively, 163–164; for learning to change, 182–183
King, Rev. Martin Luther, Jr., 120
Knight Foundation. *See* John S. and James L. Knight Foundation
Knight Ridder, 70
KnowledgeWorks Foundation, 88, 89, 91, 106
Kramer, Mark R., 93

L

Lamb, Tom, 50
Latin American Youth Center (LAYC), 176–177
Latino culture, 176–177

Leadership: authority versus, 149–150; civic, 132; transforming individuals into "inspiring evangelists," 129. *See also* Adaptive leadership; Empowering the people practice
Leadership Conference on Civil Rights, 120
Leadership on the Line, Staying Alive Through the Dangers of Leading (Heifetz and Linsky), 156
Learning culture: adoption of, 182; domestic violence classes outcomes and, 176–177; learning outcomes requiring shift in, 177–178
Learning grantees: creating, 175–178; description of, 176
Learning organizations: creating change by building, 14–15; definition of, 168; learning to learn practice of, 168–174
Learning in order to change practice: description of, 14–15, 165–166; key principles for, 182–183; LAYC domestic violence classes as example of, 176–178; learning to help others learn, 175*fig*–181; learning to learn, 168–174; reporting versus learning mind-sets, 170*t*; Sound Families example of, 165–168
Learning to help others learn: creating learning grantees, 175–178; creating learning systems, 178–181; three levels of learning, 175*fig*
Learning to learn: attribution element of, 171; moving from reporting to learning, 168–171; three assumptions of, 171–174; timely information and actionable insights for, 171–172
Learning to learn assumptions: 1: better planning, 172–173; 2: implementation, 173; 3: tracking progress, 173–174
Lewis, Robert, Jr., 133
Lies, Valerie, 169
Lima Feeds (Kenya), 69
Lindblom, Lance, 16, 77
Lindsay, John, 54
LinkedIn, 87, 113
Linsky, Marty, 156
Linux, 113
Lions Clubs International, 74
Listening tours, 130–131

Little Rock Nine, 120
Live, Learn & Thrive program (P&G), 92
Lobbying: corporate, 49–53; differences between advocacy and, 44–45t
Local initiatives support corporation (LISC), 132
Los Angeles riots (1992), 20, 30
Los Angeles Times, 30
Lukas, Carol, 97

M

MacArthur Foundation, 57
McClatchy Company, 70
McDonald's Corporation, 72
McLeod Grant, Heather, 10, 57–58, 93, 129
Making a difference, 120–122
Malcolm X, 120
Marine Fisheries program (Packard Foundation), 80
Market Creek Plaza (San Diego), 21, 32, 79, 127, 128–129
Massachusetts Worker Education Roundtable, 147
Master donors, 188. *See also* Catalytic donors
Media Learning Seminar, 109
Medical Homes D.C. initiative, 124–125
Merchant, Kathy, 90
Merchat, Kathy, 94
Meth Project, 71–73
Meyer Memorial Trust, 81–82
Microfinance loans, 68, 81
Microsoft, 157
Missing middle concept, 68, 69
MIT, 147
Mitchell, Melanie, 139
Money Well Spent (Brest and Harvey), 7
Moriah Fund, 44
Morino, Mario, 178
Morris & Gwendolyn Cafritz Foundation, 123
Motivations for giving: fulfilling obligations to community, 25; making a difference as, 120–122; making meaningful change in the world, 26–27; portfolio of, 24e–25e; reinforcing personal and professional relationships, 26

Mott Foundation, 57
Mozilla, 113

N

NAACP (National Association for the Advancement of Colored People), 120
Nathan Cummings Foundation, 16, 77–78
National City Corporation (Cleveland), 51
National Council of La Raza, 58
National Fund for Workforce Solutions (NFWS), 157
Nee, David, 152, 153, 154, 157, 159, 161, 162
Needmor Fund, 44
Neonatal intensive care unit (NICU) [Honduras]: appalling condition of, 66; General Electric's corporate know-how changing, 65, 66–67
Network theory, 113–115
New Hampshire Charitable Foundation (NHCF): as advocate for change, 12, 54–57, 58; choosing several selected causes, 34; focusing on the cause approach by, 56–57
New Profit Inc., 35
New Voices program (J-Lab), 136
New York Times, 155
NewSchools Venture Fund, 35
Newton, Eric, 136–137
Ngozi Project, 124
Ngugi, Charles Githuka, 69
Nonprofit peer networks: Amazon rainforest conservation solutions through, 100–107; collaborative challenge of, 93–99; common versus catalytic donor views of, 98–99*fig*; creating the conditions for change through, 107–115; creating learning systems as part of, 178–181; description of, 12–13, 87–88; Fundación AVINA's approach to building, 98, 102–107; key principles for forging, 116–117; peer-network mind-set of, 97–99*fig*; relevance of network theory to, 113–115; Strive Partnership's experience with forging, 13, 72, 88–93; workforce partnership form of, 147. *See also* Relationships

Nonprofits: collaboration among, 93–99*fig*; common versus catalytic donor views of, 98–99*fig*; creating change as learning organizations, 14–15; as grantee, 98; as learning organizations, 14–15, 168–174; proliferation of, 99–100. *See also* Catalytic philanthropy; Philanthropy
Novogratz, Jacqueline, 75

O

O'Bryon, Margaret, 123, 124, 125
Olin Foundation, 43

P

Pacific Northwest Initiative, 166
Packard, David, 80
Packard Foundation, 57, 80
Parks, Rosa, 120
Partnership for Quality Pre-Kindergarten, 50
Peer-network mind-set, 97–99*fig*
Pennsylvania Early Learning Investment Commission, 50
The Pew Charitable Trusts, 58–59, 155, 160
Pew Environment Group's Heritage Forests Campaign, 155
Philanthropy: comparing catalytic and traditional, 7–10, 186–187; defining the purpose of, 1; funds availability of, 5–6; linear model of traditional view of, 186; making a difference as broader picture of, 120–122; modern changes in today's, 5–7; the "second Golden Age" of, 6; understanding complex systems challenge of, 140–141, 186–187. *See also* Catalytic philanthropy; Nonprofits
Philanthropreneurs, 9
PNC Financial Services Group: as advocate for change, 58; corporate lobbying activities of, 49–51; Grow Up Great program of, 34–35, 50
Policy advocacy (lobbying), 44. *See also* Corporate lobbying

Portfolio approach: description of, 23–24; The Tow Foundation's use of, 42
Pottery Barn, 100
Pre-K Counts, 50
Private foundations: legal restrictions on advocacy by, 52*t*; political history of advocacy by, 57–59. *See also specific foundations*
Procter and Gamble, 92, 180
Program related investments: description of, 78; investing for impact through, 78–82
Proscio, Tony, 132
Prosumers, 137–138*t*

R

Rainforest Action Alliance, 100
RAISG networks, 102–103
Reagan, Ronald, 44, 126
Regional health information organization (RHIO), 125
Regional Primary Care Coalition, 124
Regional Youth/Adult Social Action Partnership (RYASAP), 40
Reichert, Joshua, 155, 160
Reifsnyder, Rob, 90
Relationships: giving to reinforce personal and professional, 26; nonprofit collaborative, 93–99*fig*, 147, 157, 178–181; social networking sites and, 87, 113. *See also* Nonprofit peer networks
Rendell, Edward, 50–51
"Republican revolution" (1994), 44
A Right to Care (Jones one-woman play), 123
Rimel, Rebecca, 58
Roadless Rule (1998), 155
Robert Bosch Stiftung (Germany), 57
Robert Wood Johnson Foundation, 58
Rockefeller Foundation, 16, 57, 75, 83
Rockefeller, John D., 6
Rockefeller Philanthropy Advisors, 78
Rohr, Jim, 34, 49–51
Ross, Tom, 174
The Route of the Smoke (online series), 101
Royal Dutch Shell plc, 3, 65, 67, 70
Ruta, Gwen, 10

S

Sara Lee Corporation, 77

Scaife Foundation, 43

Senge, Peter, 168

Service Employees International Union Local 615, 147

Sesame Street (PBS show), 50

Shareholder advocacy, 76–78

Shell Foundation (UK): corporate know-how tapped by, 65, 67–70; GroFin spin-off of, 68–69; origins and description of, 2–3

Shorters, Trabian, 111, 115

Siebel Systems, Inc., 70

Siebel, Tom: Meth Project campaign funded by, 71–73; as Siebel Systems, Inc. founder, 70; tapping corporate know-how approach of, 65, 70–73, 84

Sierra Club, 126

Sinha, Maqsood, 74

Six Sigma, 72, 90, 180–181

Skoll Foundation, 105

Skoll, Jeff, 105

Small and medium-sized enterprises (SMEs): GroFin's loans to, 68–69; growth finance created for, 69

Smithfield Foods, Inc., 77

Social change: adaptive leadership for, 5, 14, 143–164; adaptive leadership pacing progress of, 156–159; advocating for, 11–12, 37–61; by building learning organizations, 14–15; catalytic donors as causing or accelerating, 9–10, 171; collaboration as powerful force for, 93–99*fig*; common versus catalytic donor mind-set on, 8*fig*–10; empowering people for, 13; Fundación AVINA's approach to, 98, 102–107; interconnection between parts concept of, 115; learning to create, 14–15, 165–183; as motivation for giving, 26–27; nonprofit peer networks to create conditions for, 107–115; six practices of donors who help bring, 10–15; Six Sigma approach to, 72, 90, 180–181; tracking progress of, 173–174; traditional philanthropy overlooking the complexity of, 186; understanding the real possibility of, 16

Social innovation: adaptive leadership for, 5, 14, 143–164; complexity of individual empowerment and, 138–141; drivers of, 115

Social networking sites, 87, 113

Social problems: adaptive leadership approach to, 145–148; Amazon rainforest destruction, 100–107; catalytic donors as part of the solution, 9–10; as complex and globally interdependent, 4–5; domestic violence, 176–177; environmental, 77–78, 80–82, 155, 174; examples of role of foundations in solving, 16–17; grabbing attention to tough, 155–156; homeless families, 165–168, 173; juvenile detention problem, 37–43; Montana's meth abuse epidemic, 71–73; networked strategy for education reform, 72, 89–93; relevance of network theory to solving, 115; slum garbage collection, 74–76. *See also* Adaptive problems; Technical problems

Social stock exchanges, 83

Social Venture Partners, 35

Society for the Protection of New Hampshire Forests, 55

Sojourn theater performances, 131

Sound Families program (Gates Foundation), 165–168, 173

Southern Christian Leadership Conference, 120

Speak Outs, 124

SSNs (student success networks), 91–93, 180–181

Stakeholders: adaptive leader ability to grab attention of, 155–156; adaptive leadership facilitation of change with, 152–154; advocacy by, 76–78; empowering individual, 13, 119–142

Standard Social Innovation Review, 134

Starbucks, 99

Stiftung Mercator, 174

Stone, Martha, 38–40

Stonesifer, Patty, 166

Strategic Giving (Frumkin), 17

Strive Partnership: community-level progress indicators and goals of, 179*e*–180*e*; corporate know-how tapped by, 72; description of, 88;

forging nonprofit peer networks, 13, 88–93; learning system created by, 178–179; position on the collaboration spectrum by, 95–96; SSNs (student success networks) grouped by, 91–93, 180–181; summer bridge session launched by, 91, 181

Student Nonviolent Coordinating Committee, 120

Success by Six, 90

Summer bridge session (Strive Partnership), 91, 181

Sununu, John, 55

Switch: How to Change Things When Change Is Hard (Heath and Heath), 152, 154

T

Tapping corporate know-how: blending profit and purpose through, 64*t*, 65; General Electric's approach to, 65, 66–67; Shell Foundation's approach to, 65, 67–70; Tom Siebel's approach to tapping, 65, 70–73, 84

Tax issues: program related investments under Tax Code, 78; Tax Reform Act (1969), 58

TBF (The Boston Foundation): Boston Indicators Project of, 157, 172–173; empowering the people practice by, 127, 132–134; Paul Grogan's adaptive leadership of, 144–148, 150, 157, 158, 159–160, 162; workforce development achievements of, 147–148, 150; workforce partnerships created by, 147, 157

Technical problems: adaptive leadership focus on, 150–152; adaptive versus, 151*t*. *See also* Social problems

Temporary Assistance for Needy Families, 165

Timely information, 171–172

Tinti, William, 146

Toffler, Alvin, 137

Tow, Claire, 39

The Tow Foundation: advocacy activities of, 47–48; as advocate for change, 12, 39–43, 58; assessing internal capabilities process by, 28; "Emily J."

(*Emily J. v. Weicker*) cause taken up by, 37–43; origins and description of, 2

Tow, Leonard, 39

Toyota, 51, 180

Trickle Up, 20

Trust for New Hampshire Lands, 55

Twitter, 87, 113

U

Unilever, 74, 76, 84

United Nations Development Programme, 74, 75

United Way of Greater Cincinnati, 90, 91

University of Cincinnati, 89, 90

University of Connecticut School of Law, 38

Urban Institute, 126

U.S. Department of Labor, 157

U.S. Forest Service, 155

USAID (United States Agency for International Development), 30

V

Vanica, Jennifer, 30

Vassar College, 41

Venture Philanthropy Partners (VPP), 35, 176–178

Voting Rights Act (1965), 119

Vrana, Victoria, 177

W

Walmart, 157

Washington Families Fund, 166

Washington Regional Association of Grantmakers, 124

Waste Concern, 74–75

Wellcome Trust (UK), 57

Wertheimer, David, 166, 167

West, Chris, 67–68, 69

White Mountain National Forest, 55

Wick, Chad, 89, 92

Wiki-philanthropy: complexity of individual empowerment for, 138–141; engaging individuals in, 137–138*t*, 142; examples of successful, 136–137

William C. Graustein Memorial Fund
(GMF): adaptive leadership pacing
progress by, 157–159; early childhood
education work by, 153–154, 157–159;
origins of, 152–153
Workforce partnerships, 147, 157
World Bank, 81
World Economic Forum, 16
World Wildlife Fund, 100

Y

YouthBuild USA, 58
Yunus, Muhammad, 68, 81

Z

Z. Smith Reynolds Foundation, 174
Zimpher, Nancy, 89, 90